Replication Research in Applied Linguistics

THE CAMBRIDGE APPLIED LINGUISTICS SERIES

The authority on cutting-edge Applied Linguistics research

Series Editors   2007–present: Carol A. Chapelle and Susan Hunston
1988–2007: Michael H. Long and Jack C. Richards

For a complete list of titles please visit: www.cambridge.org/elt/cal

Recent titles in this series:

Replication Research in Applied Linguistics

Edited by

Graeme Porte

University of Granada, Spain

CAMBRIDGE
UNIVERSITY PRESS

CAMBRIDGE UNIVERSITY PRESS
Cambridge, New York, Melbourne, Madrid, Cape Town,
Singapore, São Paulo, Delhi, Mexico City

Cambridge University Press
The Edinburgh Building, Cambridge CB2 8RU, UK

Published in the United States of America by Cambridge University Press,
New York

www.cambridge.org
Information on this title: www.cambridge.org/9781107671522

First published 2012

Printed in the United Kingdom at the University Press, Cambridge

A catalogue record for this publication is available from the British Library

Library of Congress Cataloging-in-Publication Data

Replication research in applied linguistics / [edited by] Graeme Porte.
p. cm. – (The Cambridge applied linguistics series)
Includes bibliographical references and index.
ISBN 978-1-107-67152-2 (paper back) – ISBN 978-1-107-02165-5 (hard back)
1. Applied linguistics–Research.   2. Replication (Experimental design) I. Porte,
Graeme Keith.

P129.R47 2012
418.0072–dc23   2011047171

ISBN 978-1-107-67152-2 Paperback
ISBN 978-1-107-02165-5 Hardback

This book is dedicated to two colleagues in the field, Johannes Eckerth and Cathleen Petree, both of whom passed away before they were able to see this project finally brought to fruition.

Contents

List of contributors

Rebekha Abbuhl, *California State University, United States*
Rebekha Abbuhl's primary research interests focus on the acquisition of second language (L2) writing skills and the effect of input and interaction on the development of both the written and spoken L2. She is also interested in teacher training and second language acquisition (SLA) research methods.

James D. Brown, *University of Hawai'i at Manoa, United States*
James D. Brown's areas of specialization include language testing, curriculum design, program evaluation, and research methods. In addition to over 200 book chapters and articles in publications like *TESOL Quarterly, TESOL Newsletter, Language Learning, Language Testing, The Modern Language Journal, System, JALT Journal, The Language Teacher,* and *RELC Journal,* he has published a number of books: *Understanding Research in Second Language Learning: A Teacher's Guide to Statistics and Research Design* (Cambridge, 1988); *The Elements of Language Curriculum: A Systematic Approach to Program Development* (Heinle and Heinle, 1995); *Language Testing in Japan* (with Yamashita, JALT, 1995); *Testing in Language Programs* (Prentice-Hall, 1996); *New Ways of Classroom Assessment* (TESOL, 1998); and *Using Surveys in Language Programs* (Cambridge, 2001).

Johannes Eckerth, late of *King's College, University of London, England*
In particular, Johannes Eckerth conducted extensive research on psycholinguistic and sociocultural approaches to SLA, task-based language learning and teaching, the analysis of L2 classroom discourse, and language assessment. Further research and academic interests included English as a lingua franca, the triangulation of qualitative and quantitative research methods, the use of conversation analysis in language-learning research, autonomous and technology-enhanced language learning, and curriculum design / material development.

Tess Fitzpatrick, *Swansea University, Wales*
Tess Fitzpatrick teaches undergraduate and postgraduate courses in applied linguistics, and supervises PhD dissertations in vocabulary acquisition, storage, and retrieval. She has recently succeeded Paul Meara as Director of the Swansea University PhD Program in Applied Linguistics. There are three main strands to her current research activities: the investigation of lexical processes through word association behavior; the creation and evaluation of vocabulary knowledge assessment tools; and the design and application of innovative language-learning techniques. These interests drive the research projects in which Tess participates, and are reflected in her published work.

Alison Mackey, *Georgetown University, United States*
Alison Mackey's research interests and numerous publications focus on L2 learning. The process of acquiring a second language is a complex one, involving learner-internal cognitive abilities and propensities as well as certain intricacies of the social contexts in which learning takes place. As such, the study of SLA requires flexibility and openness to interdisciplinary insights; rigorous, detailed consideration of the interrelationships among a wide range of variables; and expertise in both quantitative and qualitative research methods. Much of Alison's empirical research has been carried out within a framework that encourages the exploration and integration of these factors: namely, the interaction approach.

Hossein Nassaji, *University of Victoria, Canada*
Hossein Nassaji's teaching and research interests include communicative focus on form, task-based language teaching and learning, and the application of the sociocultural approaches to L2 research and pedagogy. His current research focuses on the role of corrective feedback and form-focused interaction in classroom and laboratory settings, involving both experimental/quantitative and descriptive/qualitative research. He also maintains an active research program in the areas of L2 reading, L2 lexical inferencing and vocabulary learning, and classroom discourse. His work has been published in a variety of leading journals in the field such as *Applied Linguistics, Applied Psycholinguistics, Language Learning, The Modern Language Journal, TESOL Quarterly, Reading Research Quarterly, Canadian Modern Language Review, Annual Review of Applied Linguistics, Language Awareness, Language Teaching Research*, and *System*. In 2001, Hossein was awarded the twenty-first annual Kenneth W. Mildenberger Prize of the Modern Language Association of America for the article he co-authored with Gordon Wells of the University of California, Santa

Cruz, titled "What's the Use of Triadic Dialogue? An Investigation of Teacher–Student Interaction."

Luke Plonsky, *Northern Arizona University, United States*

Luke Plonsky is Assistant Professor of Applied Linguistics at Northern Arizona University. His research, published in journals such as *Annual Review of Applied Linguistics, Foreign Language Annals,* and *Language Learning,* focuses mainly on L2 strategies, interaction, and quantitative research methods, with a particular interest in meta-analysis and the construct of "study quality" in SLA.

Charlene Polio, *Michigan State University, United States*

Charlene Polio's main area of research is L2 writing. She is particularly interested in the various research methods and measures used in studying L2 writing as well as the interface between the fields of L2 writing and SLA. She has also published and done research in the areas of SLA, foreign language classroom discourse, and behavior differences in novice versus experienced teachers. She is the current editor of the *Annual Review of Applied Linguistics.*

Graeme Porte, *University of Granada, Spain*

Editor of the Cambridge University Press journal *Language Teaching,* Graeme organized the American Association for Applied Linguistics (AAAL) colloquium on replication research upon which many of the contributions in the book are based, and is currently one of the main protagonists behind the drive for more replication research in the field of applied linguistics. He researches L1 attrition and the way recent discoveries about human perception impact on SLA. He has published widely in international journals, and his book on research critique, *Appraising Research in Second Language Learning* (John Benjamins, 2010), is currently used on over 70 applied linguistics doctoral courses worldwide and received its second edition in 2010.

Susanne Rott, *University of Illinois at Chicago, United States*

Susanne Rott has published widely on SLA, and has co-edited (together with B. VanPatten, J. Williams, and M. Overstreet) *Form–Meaning Connections in Second Language Acquisition* (Lawrence Erlbaum Associates, 2004). Her main research focus is the encoding, storage, and retrieval of individual lexical items, phraseologisms, and lexico-grammatical constructions. Her studies are based on linguistic descriptions and cognitive processes outlined in cognitive linguistics. In particular, Susanne investigates how form–meaning mappings develop across interrelated continua that mark partial to complete, weak to robust, and non-target-like to target-like language use by L2 learners in an instructed learning setting. In her studies she assesses the effect of linguistic aspects, such as length and morphosyntactic complexity; cognitive aspects, such as attention and phonological working memory capacity; and instructional aspects, such as awareness raising, frequency, and the effect of intervention tasks.

Series editors' preface

Applied linguistics shares many of the issues and challenges facing research across the social sciences, one of which is understanding the extent to which research results are sufficiently robust to be used for drawing conclusions and making decisions. This book addresses this fundamental issue with a multifaceted examination of the use of replication research as a means of testing and strengthening research results in applied linguistics. The authors astutely interpret the problem that the book addresses as the failure of the profession to embrace replication research philosophically. They then set out to demonstrate the value to be obtained by recognizing the need for replications, the means for encouraging the next generation of applied linguists to conduct replications, and the technical practices entailed in replication research.

In his introduction to the volume, Porte sets out the issues and needs in addition to distinguishing among different types of replication research and placing replication within the broader scheme of knowledge development in the field. This introduction sets the scope of the topic appropriately broadly to suggest that the need for change goes beyond the technical research methodological domain.

Part I provides background for understanding the need for replication research in applied linguistics with a chapter explaining why replication is useful and identifying areas where, in SLA, replication studies may be particularly apt at present. A second chapter fills in the background with a discussion of the historical use of replication in applied linguistics. The following two chapters discuss the place of replication research in applied linguistics from the perspectives of the research methodological issues of statistical significance testing and meta-analytic research.

Part II takes on the question of how to infuse perspectives and practices of replication research into the field through teaching in graduate programs. The two chapters in this part make practical suggestions of how to teach replication in graduate-level research methods classes in applied linguistics, and offer some reflection and analysis of the results obtained from doing so in one applied linguistics program.

Part III provides two examples of replication studies, with an illuminating discussion of their contents in a separate chapter, which also provides substantial advice about writing up replication research. The final part, therefore, holds significant didactic potential for all applied linguists wishing to explore replication research.

This broad treatment of research methodology spearheads current trends in applied linguistics and elsewhere, which aim to educate the next generation of researchers to better create knowledge and to evaluate the basis for knowledge claims. It is therefore a most welcome addition to the Cambridge Applied Linguistics Series.

Carol A. Chapelle and Susan Hunston

Acknowledgments

Thanks

The editor would like to record his thanks for the invitation extended him by Dr Jeffrey T. Connor-Linton (Georgetown University, Washington, DC, United States) to organize a colloquium on replication research at the American Association of Applied Linguistics conference in March 2009, and which proved to be the initial impetus for a renewed interest in the subject as well as the subsequent production of this book.

The editor and the contributors to the volume would also like to thank Jane Walsh and Joanna Garbutt of the Cambridge University Press for their advice throughout, and the series editors, Professor Carol A. Chapelle (Iowa State University, Ames, IA, United States) and Susan Hunston (University of Birmingham, England, UK) for their invaluable help throughout the process, from writing to production, and to our reviewers for their very constructive and detailed comments on earlier versions of the text.

Permissions

We would like to thank Cambridge University Press and the Estate of Johannes Eckerth for permission to reproduce his paper, originally published in 2009 in the journal *Language Teaching* (vol. **42**, 1, pp. 109–30).

Extract from T. S. Eliot's Little Gidding, *The Four Quartets* on p. 1 © Estate of T. S. Eliot and reprinted by permission of Faber and Faber Ltd.

Introduction

Graeme Porte

We shall not cease from exploration
And the end of all our exploring
Will be to arrive where we started
And know the place for the first time.
                    T.S. Eliot, Little Gidding, *The Four Quartets*

In 2007, the Cambridge University Press journal *Language Teaching* published a call for papers exclusively directed at studies which adopted a replication approach in their methodology. Whereas replication studies had previously been mentioned alongside other research as acceptable submissions in one or two journals, this was the first time that a journal in our field had decided to dedicate a specific strand exclusively to such work. As a result of the interest this announcement aroused, I was asked by the then President of the American Association for Applied Linguistics, Jeff Connor-Linton, to organize and chair a colloquium at the annual conference taking place that year (2009) in Denver, Colorado, on the subject of encouraging more replication research studies. This book represents the outcomes of that colloquium in the form of an extended number of papers from that event (contributions written by Rebekha Abbuhl, Tess Fitzpatrick, Alison Mackey, Hossein Nassaji, and Graeme Porte) together with other specially invited contributions (from James D. Brown, Johannes Eckerth, Luke Plonsky, Charlene Polio, and Susanne Rott) which, together, seek to provide further insights not only into the significance and contribution of replication research to our field, but also into its methodology, practice, dissemination, and encouragement.

In a continually changing and increasingly diverse research environment, this volume aims to inform about what is argued to be a more scientific approach to the quantitative research process and, specifically, one which sees such research as a systematic process of extending, limiting, or simply reconsidering previous outcomes in the light of what we subsequently discover rather than the accumulation of uncorroborated conclusions based on the outcomes of "a self-contained, unalterable body of work" (*Nature*, Editorial, July 2006). In this way, replication can be said to provide essential, methodical support for theory and has been described as "a linchpin of the scientific process" (*Nature*, ibid.).

This book focuses on the quasi-experimental research process and brings together a number of experts in the area who argue for the fundamental role of replication research in quantitative research studies through a combination of theoretical argument, detailed examples, and practical, down-to-earth advice from the choice of suitable studies to replicate (see the chapters by Abbuhl, Mackey, and Polio), through to the setting up, execution, and writing up of such work ready for presentation to a journal (see the chapter by Brown). It is also our belief that greater dissemination of replication research in applied linguistics will itself inspire more research specifically comparing past and present findings from related studies. By dedicating a monographic work to this kind of research we hope also to show that researchers should be encouraged to see the critical address of previous studies as an essential element in the self-correcting, cumulative cycle of acquiring empirical knowledge. This volume focuses on experimental and quasi-experimental classroom research, but most of its contents should apply equally well to other types of quantitative research in applied linguistics.

1 The role of replication research in scientific thinking and practice

To understand the nature of replication, it might be best to begin with a definition of the word itself. Having its origins in the Latin word "replicare," literally meaning "to repeat" or "to bend back," it encourages us to return to and repeat a previous study and compare what we discover with what was found or observed originally. Those working in natural or physical sciences typically embrace a research paradigm wherein they are encouraged or even required to see their work scrutinized, repeated, and verified in some way. A firm foundation for progress in their respective disciplines is then constructed by ascertaining how far their findings are reproducible by others. This foundation is strong enough for scholars to have emphasized replication as a fundamental principle of competent research (Kassen, 1960) and a basic tenet of science (Campbell and Jackson, 1979), and to have claimed that replication should be "adequately evidenced for any professional field that claims to be grounded on scholarship" (Muma, 1993: 927).

Repetition is therefore at the heart of replication research. This, in turn, echoes one of the primary assumptions of science: Nature is assumed to behave according to rules. One way of revealing this

behavior and discovering such order is by repeating a particular procedure in an attempt to establish its stability in nature and eliminate
the possible influence of artifacts or chance findings (Radder, 1996).
As will become clearer below and in the remaining chapters of the
book, however, repetition of a study can be carried out in a number
of ways and does not necessarily mean an *exact* repetition of the
original study. Indeed, an exact repetition of an experiment is one
which is reproduced rather than repeated; it can be similar to the
original but will not be identical in all its features (see below). Argu-
ably, much of the confusion surrounding replication research stems
from a failure to differentiate a number of approaches to repeating a
previous study.

In the field of the physical sciences, replication is regarded as an
essential element in carrying out the everyday work of science. To
this end, those that undertake research are likewise consumers of that
research and observers of the same. Those researching in a particular
area follow the work of their fellow researchers and revisit that work
in an effort to verify the outcomes. It follows that replicating a study,
and perhaps raising legitimate concerns about previous methodology,
analysis, or conclusions, is regarded as a laudable line of inquiry and
not to be misconstrued as a covert assault on the original author's
integrity.

A replication study attempts to discover whether the same findings
are obtained by another researcher in another context, and whether
the outcome appears to reflect knowledge which can therefore be
separated from the context in which it was originally found. Similarly, these researchers may then be expected to identify outcomes
which they find impossible to reproduce themselves. Hence, for those
working in these sciences, the research process is one of flux, wherein
future studies are often suggested as a result of a present finding.
Implicit is the acceptance that the advancement of knowledge is not
a straightforward endeavor but rather one which is most likely to
proceed piecemeal as more and more information is acquired about a
particular effect or relationship – "a more incremental and, at times,
patience-testing pace toward cumulative knowledge" – as Plonsky
describes it in his chapter (p. 117). In this sense, a replication study will
form part of an ongoing communication with fellow researchers in the
area, providing "feedback to an original investigation to strengthen
the evidence of research findings, to correct limitations, and/or to pro-
tect the community against errors" (Kugler et al., 2006: 15).

In the social sciences, however, this step-by-step, interrelated acquisition of knowledge across research is conspicuous by its absence.
Researchers often see their work as part of a series of discrete, one-shot

studies and with little perceived need to integrate replication into the structure of scientific inquiry. In contrast to those working in the physical or natural sciences, there is a thirst for generating new knowledge through the accumulation of findings from many extension or follow-up studies (see below) rather than the painstaking re-searching in previous work. Research and replication have thus become discrete practices and, somehow in the process, undertaking replication studies has acquired negative connotations.

It is easy to see why. Much of our work is based on a much less firm foundation and one which is in constant change, namely human subjects. Behavior is observed but often unrepeatable. As a result, background factors and the variability of these have to be taken into consideration in any attempt to replicate studies and, indeed, in deciding upon whether replication is possible at all where only qualitative research procedures are used.

2 Replication in qualitative research

Whereas replication with qualitative research procedures is not the focus of this book, its problematic nature is discussed in passing in a number of contributions, and it would be wrong in a volume which aims to encourage more replication research in the field of applied linguistics not to address the question, albeit briefly, in this introduction.

Research which focuses on the interpretation of outcomes, rather than the pursuit of generalizable conclusions which are independent of aspects such as time and context, assumes that reality is a social construction by humans. Advancing our knowledge through research about a phenomenon is inevitably a subjective enterprise, as the researcher might reasonably be using his or her preconceived notions about the context or participants throughout the research process.

Nevertheless, since the aim is then not to make predictions about the likelihood of an observation or outcome occurring in the future, replicating a study might serve a different purpose. Rather than repeat a study in an attempt to gain increasing amounts of confidence in the veracity of the findings or accuracy in what has been observed, we might do so to obtain a gradually clearer and more detailed picture of the phenomenon itself. At the very least, of course, such detailed pictures of one well-documented situation may form a basis for understanding others. As Goetz and LeCompte (1984: 228) maintain, generalizability in qualitative studies can be obtained, or at least approximated, by providing comparability through information-rich description for "other researchers [to] use the results of the study as a basis for comparison." Indeed, the growth of storage capacity on the Web, and access to full data sets, audit trails, and so on, means that it is now possible to upload and retain huge data sets. This has the potential for helping us change the way we look at replication and replicability from a qualitative perspective. In a reassessment of the potential contribution of replication studies in a qualitative research paradigm, Richards has shown how such research might best be presented in order to establish the essential links between studies that will generate the sorts of cumulative insights and understandings suggested elsewhere in this volume (Porte and Richards, 2012; see also, Chapter 10, Concluding remarks, this volume).

As Mackey argues in Chapter 1 of this volume, however, it is debatable how far generalizability is actually needed in research whose principal goal is data interpretation. As a consequence, she also points out, the failure to see a need for replication of these studies has led to an accumulation of findings which are essentially left unquestioned and open to interpretation (see Polio, Chapter 2, this volume). Since much of our research is liable to include error in some form, both of a methodological and conceptual kind, we might suggest such unidentified and unchallenged error is particularly problematic in a field where we would expect research to be reliably informing public policy on L2 teaching.

3 Replication studies in applied linguistics

Perversely perhaps, as I now go on to focus on quantitative replication research in the field of applied linguistics, it might be more sensible to begin by describing what is *not* a replication study, as there appears to be confusion among many researchers as to what constitutes such a study. In a replication, it is fair to say that the focus is always on the original study being replicated, rather than on the present study itself. There are many papers I have seen in my work as Editor of *Language Teaching* which claim to be "replication studies" but which, in fact, often use the same methodology and procedures as the original study, only to apply these to a new context with the aim of reporting what happens in that context. The focus thereby shifts away from the original study and on to the new findings only. Any comparisons with the original study will be peripheral. What these studies do, equally laudably of course, is to attempt to extend or follow on from the original research, into new areas in order to gather more information about those contexts (see below).

Second language acquisition (SLA) is – in terms of scientific inquiry – still a relatively young field, with systematic research work beginning only in the early 1970s. It follows, perhaps, that much remains to be explored; however, still more remains to be discovered about our present knowledge. As in any scientific endeavor, therefore, our research should take us on a journey of continuous discovery. It is one upon which we should embark with the realization that our goal is not necessarily always to reach a new and as yet undiscovered destination or outcome, but rather – borrowing the poet T. S. Eliot's image in *Little Gidding* – to explore more closely around the point of departure (in our case, the original study) in such a way that we are ultimately able to consider *that* in a new, or more informed, light. In so doing, we are directly contributing to the scientific debate about the study in question by revisiting previous assumptions or conclusions, verifying or otherwise what has been produced or thought by others before us.

That quantitative research studies can be replicated to have their robustness and generalizability tested is a requirement of scientific inquiry, and the authors in this book would argue that such a condition also needs to become more prominent in establishing and confirming many of the research outcomes in our field (see, in particular, the chapters by Abbuhl and Nassaji). To facilitate such replication, researchers would typically be expected to report the methodology used in some detail. What can at first appear to be a minor feature hidden away in the "limitations" section of a paper might – after replicating the study a number of times and in a number of ways – turn out to be a key factor impacting the outcomes obtained (see the chapters by Brown and by Mackey).

Some of the confusion regarding what is and what is not a replication study may stem from the descriptive words themselves. Both "replication" and "replicate" have connotations in research terms of producing something which is the "same" in any subsequent study. In fact, this interpretation of sameness applies to only one of the three major kinds of replication one might undertake of a study and is one of the least encountered or undertaken of the three – namely "exact" replications (see below). A replication study is not necessarily an exact repetition of a previous study. Other variants can address the robustness or generalizability of a study by the introduction of further variables or contexts alongside those used originally and which might be thought to provide further knowledge about, for example, whether different approaches produce different results. The researcher would then need to think about the reason why this has happened. However, the initial purpose of replicating a study is not of necessity to obtain similar results, and the failure to do so in no sense reduces the worth or contribution of either study. If similar outcomes are not obtained, some doubt may be thrown on the original results, but there should at least be the positive effect of encouraging further investigation about why there was this apparent discrepancy. In other words, whatever the kind of replication approach undertaken, knowledge will inevitably be gained about the outcomes of the original study which will help the community move forward and contribute to what is the self-correcting nature of scientific inquiry. At the very least, therefore, replication provides us with an all-important "second opinion" on the methods, outcomes, and conclusions in the original study.

I do not wish to suggest, of course, that scientific inquiry in our field should consist only of infinite numbers of replications of previous work, nor would I advocate that each and every study merits replication. However, one finds few researchers making a specific call for replication of their work, and it will often be one's own reading of a study which encourages one to think about whether there is a perceived need to do so, particularly – but not only – if the results were thought surprising or unusual. It is in the nature of scientific inquiry that one should be skeptical about outcomes, and it is this inquisitive, critical approach to research practice which this book seeks to encourage through its pages.

4 Definitions used in this book

The replication of a study involves repeating or reproducing that study in a particular way as a means of gaining more knowledge about it. The aim may vary, but in most cases the researcher will be looking to verify that what has originally been observed is not an isolated incident or outcome but one which is robust and can be replicated. Mackey and Gass begin their discussion of the subject with a general definition of a replication approach thus: "Conducting a research study again, in a way that is either identical to the original procedure or with small changes (e.g., different participants), to test the original findings" (2005: 364).

There are two types of experiment replication: **internal** and **external replication**. The former might reasonably be carried out by the original researcher or team of researchers and involves reassessing the data obtained, typically through statistical re-sampling and cross-validation techniques. External replication is concerned with new data from new subjects and/or a new context. Nassaji's chapter discusses the uses of internal replication in considerable detail and describes three common methods for carrying out such a replication.

The principal concern of this book is with external replication. When hypotheses are being tested through empirical research, a study or experiment should be repeated in such a way that those who carry out the research (and those that read it) can be reasonably certain that

‿ ᴜutcomes of both studies can be compared and, therefore, that they have measured the same phenomenon. Replications might be placed along a continuum depending on the amount of "similarity" to the study in focus. Three main approaches in replication methodology were outlined at the Denver colloquium on replication research, and these are the ones which will be employed in the majority of the chapters in this volume:

An **exact** replication (also known as a literal replication) involves duplicating a previous methodologically sound study exactly in order to confirm the original findings. This would include, for example, having the same participants, the same tasks, and the same physical setting. As mentioned above, however, there is inevitably some difference between the two experiments in the social sciences due to the fact that no subject population can be exactly duplicated and because of the time lag between the original and replication studies.

A more common type of replication in the social sciences is the **approximate** replication (also known as partial or systematic replication). This type of study involves repeating the original study exactly in most respects, but changing nonmajor variables (in a way that allows for comparability between the original and replication studies). For example, researchers may investigate a different population (e.g., a different age or proficiency level of student), perhaps in a different setting (e.g., English as a second language [ESL] vs. English as a foreign language [EFL]), or perhaps using a different task (e.g., a written one instead of an oral one). The purpose of this kind of replication "with changes" is to see if the results of the original study are generalizable, for example, to a new population, setting, or modality.

Conceptual (also known as constructive) replications are used in the social sciences as well. Conceptual replications begin with a similar problem statement as the original study but employ a new research design to verify the original findings. For example, a conceptual replication might use different, but related data collection procedures, such as observation instead of self-report, or use qualitative methods in addition to the quantitative methods relied on in the original study. If successful, conceptual replications present stronger support for the original findings as they provide evidence that the outcomes were not just artifacts of the original methodology.

As Polio illustrates in her review chapter, however, other definitions and nomenclature abound in the social sciences and have, to a certain extent, clouded the picture as to what constitutes each type of replication. In her historical review of replication studies, she describes a separate set of definitions proposed by Kelly, Chase, and Tucker (1979) – who place replications along a continuum according to what has been changed – which results in a larger group of studies that can be classed as replications. However, even this classification is not without its imperfections since variables of context or subject / participant are not specifically accounted for.

5 Using replication studies

There are a number of reasons why we might take up any of these approaches to replication at a particular point. An "exact" replication might be undertaken when, for example, a key theory is supported only by a limited number of studies, and we might want to see how far the outcomes in the original study were due to chance. By obtaining similar results to the original, reliability[1] and generalizability claims are strengthened. Indeed, some researchers and research teams go about exact replications of their own work in order to demonstrate their confidence in outcomes and also to reduce the risk of accepting spurious results as accurate. Despite their usefulness, however, there are a number of disincentives to doing such work (see below), particularly since there may not be the same kind of perceived need on the part of journal editors to publish this kind of study as there is with others. Editors – pushed to find space in their journals – might consider a "mere" repetition of a previously published study one in which little "new" information is provided.

"Approximate" replications are more often seen in print – but still comparatively rarely undertaken. By their nature, as they modify some element(s) of the original research methodology to some particular end, such replications are perceived to "add" to our knowledge and perhaps for this reason are regarded as more publishable. Such replications help us generalize to other subjects or contexts. With every variation that is successfully introduced into the equation the confirmatory power of a replication increases, and what we observe is generalized to a wider application range. A further advantage of such replications is that we might usefully increase the statistical power[2] of the original results by adding more participants, making those participants more homogeneous, or standardizing procedures more.

Conceptual replications are also useful to assess the generalizability of a study or to test the reliability of previous operational definitions by, for example, using a different treatment variable or a different measurement. Like exact and approximate replications, conceptual replications can be designed to assess the robustness and generalizability of a study and its findings. The *Language Teaching* Review Panel (2008: 3) suggests this approach to replication also serves to address previous results in another way: "If the original researcher offered three explanations for his or her results, the researcher undertaking a conceptual replication can manipulate nonmajor variables, operationalizations or design features of the original study in order to evaluate (and possibly rule out one or more of) those explanations." Whatever the approach, of course, all these suggestions assume sufficient data to permit replication or analysis is presented in the original paper itself (see below and Concluding remarks, pp. 269–70).

Other approaches have been suggested and have the advantage of introducing a replication element into the original design of the study. In one option, the researcher can factor in a much larger sample of subjects and/or data and randomly divide them into two samples, one of which acts as "control" data for the other (see Nassaji, Chapter 3). Another approach is through meta-analysis, which might see the researcher treating results from previous related studies on a topic as samples from approximate replications. He or she then uses statistical analyses to discover variability in these outcomes and thereby suggest how generalizable outcomes really are and the extent to which this might depend on individual differences in study methodology and design. Plonsky expands in Chapter 4 on the relationship between replication and meta-analysis, suggesting that replications not only help inform future meta-analyses, but that meta-analyses can inform future replications. As Nassaji points out in Chapter 3, however, whereas meta-analyses can increase our confidence in the evidence provided by combining research results from similar multiple studies, undertaking a replication study is what enables us reliably to have more (or less) confidence in its external validity.

External validity, or generalizability, refers to whether the results of data measurement can be extrapolated to other settings, times, subjects, and so on. The extent to which threats to such validity are met affects our ability to credit the results with generalizable outcomes. We would consider the representativeness of the study sample in ascertaining external validity, for example. The existence of "successful" replications would support a study's external validity or generalizability. Internal validity refers to the extent to which any findings obtained are exclusively the result of the variables being studied, or are potentially affected by other factors that are not part of the original relationship studied. These factors may derive from any number of aspects related to the study, but mostly arise from the research design and/or the procedures used. In a well-controlled and designed study there are unlikely to be serious objections to internal validity: The researcher (and the reader) will be able to have reasonable confidence in the description of any outcomes obtained (see Polio, Chapter 2, this volume, for discussion of replicating studies with external or internal validity issues).

As I explained above, a distinction needs to be made between *extending* a previous study's methodology into another context and *replicating* the original study itself in some way. In essence, there has to be comparability between the original and the replication. In an extension from an original study the researcher will perhaps be interested in the results obtained using the previous methodology in the new context or with the new subjects. Whenever a replication approach is chosen, the objective will always be the same: to focus on the original study being replicated, whether exactly, approximately, or conceptually, rather than on the present study itself. This is because we are to assume that the researcher's objective was to review the findings in that original study in some way, rather than simply produce a new study in a different context and with different subjects and report on that. In general, the more variables one introduces into the new study, the more distant that study becomes from what was done originally; therefore, it becomes less comparable to the original and more an extension or follow-up *from* that study rather than an assessment of that original study's general robustness and external validity. Replication research seeks to address this connection between what we already know and what is new, and does so in an explicit and systematic way. In this volume, for example, Rott's interest (Chapter 9) initially centered on the significance of the Involvement Load Hypothesis and the apparently inconsistent findings in the original study (Hulstijn and Laufer, 2001). Her replication attempts firstly to confirm or disconfirm the original findings by identifying her concerns with the interpretation of the original results, seeking to shed more light on these through the addition of additional data analyses and a recall protocol. She then attempts to strengthen the generalizability of the original study by adding a further word measure assessment and subsequent analysis before comparing the final outcomes.

6 Disseminating replication research

Albert Valdman's (editor of *Studies in Second Language Acquisition*) comment that researchers are attracted to "original" research because of the "aura of glamour and the exhilaration of innovation" that surround it (Valdman, 1993: 505) still remains valid nearly twenty years later. One of the consequences, however, is that such a situation feeds into, or is fed by, a research culture that appears precisely to value the "groundbreaking" and the "original." We might of late add the word "impact" as a further ingredient into the mix. In response, researchers and, indeed, journal editors may feel their time and journal space respectively is best spent on practicing and promoting such work. Indeed, their own institutions may discourage replication work: As Van der Veer, van IJzendoorn, and Valsiner (1994) have shown, where so-called original research is encouraged, one might come across situations where faculty who are in line for tenure and whose research history contains replication studies are questioned by their colleagues and even considered to be uncreative. It is possible, therefore, that faculty may become reluctant to undertake replication research if they understand that it is unlikely to have as much weight in their tenure cases as "original" research.

Similarly, I note with some sadness that the latest UK university research evaluation procedure (known as the Research Excellence Framework, or REF) offers guidance to the reviewing panels that they should give the highest ("exceptional/four star" and "excellent/three star") awards to research with "ground-breaking or transformative impacts ... highly significant or innovative work" (www.hefce.ac.uk/research/ref/impact/ – *Guidance to the expert panels* document). It remains to be seen how far the exercise will reward replication research at such lofty heights.

Journal editors are often faculty and referees themselves, of course, and are not immune to the perceived opinions of their readers and contributors: If the outcomes of a replication study are the same as that of the replicated study, the results can be perceived by readers as inconsequential and of little contribution to the field. Even a failure to reproduce results in an exact replication might not be publishable "news" in this sense as it might demonstrate only that the original work was flawed, or that there was insufficient description of original research procedures.

In other words, journals, university departments, and higher education authorities may themselves be participating in maintaining the apparent scarcity of replication studies in our field and creating a seemingly vicious circle in which the lack of published replication work is interpreted as a lack of interest from the field in their publication, which in turn leads to a similar indifference to their being carried out (see Mackey, Chapter 1, this volume). After all, the argument would go, why spend time on research that reduces the chances of getting published or obtaining precious research grants? Inevitably, the head of a department will want to present the most "suitable" research for evaluation or accreditation. The editor of a journal will be charged with making the "best" use of the limited space available in each issue. Even when replications are accepted, there may be predictable restrictions imposed by the publishers on the amount of data that can be printed in the eventual publication. This will mean a further obstacle to those researchers intent on replicating such a study, as they will likely need to consult the author if they intend to undertake a replication of any kind.

Similarly, one might also be working against perceived differences of approach between researchers in the social sciences and those in the "pure" sciences. There is a commonly held belief that opportunities for the former to carry out most kinds of replication, but particularly exact ones, are very limited by the nature of the science. Many of the settings used and much of the methodology employed is difficult to repeat exactly, and if results do not reflect those found in a previous study, replications might do little to advance the field. Ironically, however, many studies do rely greatly on producing so-called statistically significant results by typically attempting to reject a null hypothesis. This pursuit of statistical impact is often driven by the received opinion that rejecting a null hypothesis is somehow more significant than not rejecting it and, indeed, that journals are more likely to publish studies that do than those that do not succeed in rejecting such a hypothesis. A further consequence of such perceived judgments about the chances of publication is that researchers may use inappropriate statistical procedures for the methodology precisely in an attempt to reject the null hypothesis in question (see Chapter 3 by Nassaji). Such practices lend support to a call for journal editors not only to publish more replication studies but also to promote the publication of papers which fail to replicate a previous result yet also are unable to reject a null hypothesis (a point I will take up in more detail in my conclusion to this book).

7 Author contributions

The first section of the book aims to demystify the area by giving a thorough chapter-by-chapter coverage, from the reasons for replicating research, how, why, and when it is best carried out, through to the uses to which replication can be put in the field – such as in meta-analyses or in generalizing through replication. Later chapters also discuss the roles replication plays across diverse fields in the social sciences and how replication research has been integrated into graduate programs. These aspects, and others, are then used as the basis for the more didactic focus in the final section of the book, where model replication studies are presented and commented upon, and readers are shown how to write up the final paper prior to submission to a journal.

In *Part I: The case for replication studies*, **Alison Mackey** looks at the background to undertaking replication research in applied linguistics and then provides detailed examples and helpful advice about how to choose suitable studies to replicate in specific areas of the field. Finally, she takes us through a number of studies in different areas, explaining how, and why, each would benefit from replication. She also briefly discusses the issue of replicating qualitative research, which is a very different undertaking from the quantitative research that is primarily the focus of this collection.

In her historical overview of replication, **Charlene Polio** discusses what has been said about replication in applied linguistics and how it has been defined. She then provides a summary and discussion of studies that claim to be some type of replication. Using the example of written error correction studies, she further discusses the problem of determining what counts as replication and assesses the relationship between replication (and replicability) and how this has added, or may in the future add, to what we know about written error correction.

For **Hossein Nassaji**, replication is the most appropriate and reliable way to determine generalizability of research results. He looks at significance testing and presents a review of the misconceptions and limitations of such tests, including those related to the generalizability of research results, and suggests ways of overcoming these limitations.

Generalizability is further discussed by **Luke Plonsky** in Chapter 4. He argues that, although the approaches of replication and meta-analysis differ, both techniques are inherently concerned with this same question: How generalizable are results? After a discussion of the individual and combined potential of these complementary methods to substantiate generalizability from previous studies, he examines the use of replication at the meta-analytic level, illustrating key points with examples from previously replicated meta-analyses. Finally, he proposes a preliminary set of standards for meta-analytic reporting practices designed to improve the quality and replicability of meta-analyses in applied linguistics.

Part II: Replication studies in graduate programs presents two chapters which describe how replication research components have been introduced on graduate courses. **Rebekha Abbuhl** shows how to integrate replication research into such programs, including dispelling common misunderstandings, developing the skills needed to conduct (and write up) replications, and giving students the chance to conduct this type of research. She suggests that by taking the time to address replication research in our classes and by providing students with the skills, opportunities, and incentives they need to produce replication studies, we are helping ensure that the next generation of researchers does not view replication research as in any way inferior to other approaches to research.

Tess Fitzpatrick writes on the process of selecting, designing, implementing, and interpreting replication studies from the perspective of the novice, or apprentice, researcher. Building on the observations and insights from students of a postgraduate research program that includes replication work as an integral component, she offers a set of advisory guidelines for the successful integration of replication work into a university course.

Part III: Replication studies in practice covers replication research production from the preparation of a study for submission to a journal through to two chapters reporting on a replication study.

James Dean Brown addresses the critical reading of replication research and also suitable ways of writing up such research. He firstly discusses what kinds of information from the original study need to be included in the replication report and suggests how this information differs depending on the procedures being used (quantitative, qualitative, or mixed-methods) and the kind of replication report (exact, approximate, or conceptual). These questions, together with the issues the author needs to be aware of when reporting the replication findings, are addressed in terms of replication studies in general, and then the same framework is applied in detail to an example replication report (Eckerth, 2009; reprinted in Chapter 8, this volume).

The book ends with two sample replication studies, by **Johannes Eckerth** and by **Susanne Rott**. The former study, reprinted from *Language Teaching*, reports on an approximate replication of Foster's (1998) study on the negotiation of meaning. Foster investigated the interactional adjustments produced by L2 English learners working on different types of language-learning tasks in a classroom setting. The replication study duplicates the methods of data collection and data analysis of the original study, but alters the target language (L2 German) and adds a stimulated-recall methodology. The second study is an approximate replication of Hulstijn and Laufer's (2001) investigation, in which the researcher sought to further explore the predictive power of the Involvement Load Index to classify and manipulate the effectiveness of vocabulary-learning tasks.

One of our principal objectives in this book is to show that replication research is currently a neglected area of investigation in applied linguistics but one which we can ignore only at considerable cost. In my *Concluding remarks: The way forward*, I review the key issues raised in this book and suggest a number of ways in which we might encourage the undertaking and disseminating of more replication research.

Given the importance of, and contribution envisaged by, replication research in this Introduction, one might expect to find a large body of literature on the subject which presented precise answers to questions, such as "What is a replication study?" or "How does one go about choosing a study in need of replication?". One would also expect to have seen at least one monograph on how to go about conducting such a study and perhaps also by this stage, collections of replicated studies which together begin to provide answers to some of the key questions on our research agendas. However, for a number of reasons mentioned here and by our contributors, this is not the case. Despite its perceived importance and the respect it commands in other fields, there is precious little in the applied linguistics literature that addresses such research beyond the occasional paper or editorial comment, and considerably less in book chapters or monographs, even those claiming to provide comprehensive overviews of research methods in applied linguistics. Moreover, where there *is* attention to replication in the literature, there is often confusion as to what constitutes a replication study in theory and in practice, and continued debate as to the contribution such research can bring to the field. It is against this backdrop that the present volume seeks to be a timely addition to the arena of key texts for the researcher in applied linguistics at various levels of study and expertise.

Notes

1   Reliability in data measurement may be judged informally as the extent to which we believe the data-gathering instrument might produce consistent results under similar conditions elsewhere. It is formally tested in a number of different ways (see Polio, and Brown, this volume). A thorough discussion of test reliability and validity is beyond the scope of the present volume, and readers are recommended to consult reference books such as Bachman (1990).
2   It is important to consider power in the design of a quasi-experimental or true experimental study. If the calculated power of an experiment is low, there is then a good chance that the experiment will be inconclusive or lead to an incorrect interpretation of a statistical test.

References

Bachman, L. (1990). *Fundamental Considerations in Language Testing*, Oxford: Oxford University Press.
Campbell, K. and Jackson, T. (1979). The role and need for replication research in social psychology, *Replications in Social Psychology*, **1**, 1, 3–14.

Eckerth, J. (2009). Negotiated interaction in the L2 classroom, *Language Teaching,* **42,** 109–30.

Editorial (2006). Let's replicate. *Nature, 442,* 330.

Eliot, T. S. (2001). *The Four Quartets,* London: Faber and Faber.

Foster, P. (1998). A classroom perspective on the negotiation of meaning, *Applied Linguistics,* **19,** 1–23.

Goetz, J. and LeCompte, M. (1984). *Ethnography and Qualitative Design in Educational Research,* New York: Academic Press.

Hulstijn, J. H. and Laufer, B. (2001). Some empirical evidence for the involvement load hypothesis in vocabulary acquisition, *Language Learning,* **51,** 539–58.

Kassen, W. (1960). Research design in the study of developmental problems, in Mussen, P. (ed.), *Handbook of Research Methods in Child Development,* New York: Wiley, pp. 36–70.

Kelly, C., Chase, L. and Tucker, R. (1979). Replication in experimental communication research: An analysis, *Human Communication Research,* **5,** 338–42.

Kugler, C., Fischer, S. and Russell, C. (2006). Preparing a replication study, *Progress in Transplantation,* **16,** 1, 15–16.

Language Teaching Review Panel (2008). Replication studies in language learning and teaching: Questions and answers, *Language Teaching,* **41,** 1–14.

Mackey, A. and Gass, S. M. (2005). *Second Language Research: Methodology and Design,* Mahwah, NJ: Lawrence Erlbaum Associates.

Muma, J. (1993). The need for replication, *Journal of Speech and Hearing Research,* **36,** 927–30.

Porte, G. and Richards, K. (2012). Replication in quantitative and qualitative research, *Journal of Second Language Writing,* **21,** 3.

Radder, H. (1996). *In and About the World: Philosophical Studies of Science and Technology,* Albany, NY: SUNY Press.

Valdman, A. (1993). Replication study (editorial introduction), *Studies in Second Language Acquisition,* **15,** 505.

Van der Veer, R., van IJzendoorn, M. H. and Valsiner, J. (eds.) (1994). *Reconstructing the Mind: Replicability in Research on Human Development,* Norwood, NJ: Ablex.

PART I

THE CASE FOR REPLICATION STUDIES

1 Why (or why not), when, and how to replicate research

Alison Mackey

The importance and prevalence of replication research varies greatly depending on the discipline and research area. In the so-called hard or pure sciences, for example, replication studies are common, and play an integral role in the process of testing and demonstrating the generalizability of crucial findings. Gross (1997) notes two issues that support the need for replication studies in scientific disciplines. First, replication studies check the probability of error in the testing of null hypotheses, or the likelihood of a Type I or Type II error having been made. For instance, the probability for error in rejecting or accepting null hypotheses might have been affected by unrepresentative sampling or low numbers of participants. Thus, testing additional samples of the target population with the same methods provides supporting or contradictory evidence regarding the existence of a phenomenon. Second, replication studies are necessary to more effectively control for extraneous variables that might have confounded the original findings. As a result, replication contributes to increasing the explanatory power and generalizability of previous findings in the "pure" sciences.

In social sciences, such as sociology, psychology, and economics, as well as linguistics, conducting replication research contributes to "the essence of the scientific method" involving "observations that can be repeated and verified by others" (American Psychological Association, 2010: 4). Within social science research, some scholars believe a study is not complete until it has been replicated (Muma, 1993: 927), yet results often prove difficult to reproduce. For example, according to Schneider, "a major problem in educational research is that investigators find it difficult or are unable to replicate their work or that of their peers" (2004: 1472). This scarcity of replication and re-analysis of previous findings undermines "the community's ability to accumulate knowledge" (ibid.: 1473). Although calls have been made for more replications in many areas of the social sciences, including areas related to applied linguistics, such as speech and hearing research (Muma, 1993), research into how second languages are learned has only recently begun to be incorporated in replication studies.

1 Replication in L2 research and other fields

1.1 The interdisciplinary nature of SLA research

Whereas the research area of SLA borrows certain methodologies and research principles from social sciences research, the role and, accordingly, the value of replication research in SLA has not been clearly defined to date for a number of reasons. To begin with, SLA is a relatively young field that has come into its own only in the past 40–50 years. It is clearly interdisciplinary in that it "draws from and impacts many other areas of study, among them linguistics, psychology, psycholinguistics, sociology, sociolinguistics, discourse analysis, conversational analysis, and education, to name a few" (Gass and Selinker, 2008: 2). With such a variety of contributing fields comes a corresponding variety of approaches to studying and analyzing aspects of SLA, some of which rely more heavily on replication than others. Research in linguistics, for example, is not traditionally based on replication, in contrast to research in psychology (Polio and Gass, 1997). L2 research, however, is informed by linguistics, psychology, education, and even sociology. This interdisciplinary nature of SLA research has made it difficult to emphasize the need for conducting replication studies over the need to keep up with other methodological trends from all the associated sub-areas and fields. However, although this status quo may have been acceptable in the earlier years of the establishment and development of the field of SLA, it is increasingly the case that there are sufficient studies present in SLA that need replication, and there is a growing understanding of the importance of replication research (Santos, 1989; Ortega, 2008; Porte, 2010).

1.2 Categorizing replication research

Replication research in the field of SLA has so far been categorized in accordance with the degree of its closeness to, or difference from, the original study. Polio and Gass (1997) outlined a "continuum of replication," which was recast as different replication types in a *Language Teaching* Review Panel article (2008) on replication (see this volume, Introduction).

Exact replication is almost nonexistent in the field of SLA due to the fact that it is usually impossible to get exactly the same type of subjects and exact stimuli as would be found in the original study (see Polio, Chapter 2 this volume). As noted earlier, exact replications are more common in other fields – in the field of bioelectromagnetics, for example, Krause et al. (2004) conducted an approximate replication of Krause et al. (2000) on the effects of electromagnetic fields emitted by cellular phones on varying EEG frequency bands in participants performing auditory memory tasks. Although this replication resulted in disconfirmatory findings, the same memory tasks, data analyses, and methodologies, as well as comparable subjects, were used as in the original study. It is also worth mentioning that since some of the authors were the same as for the original study, they were replicating their own work, and thus they would not have to " 'prove' that they did things the same way" (*Language Teaching* Review Panel, 2008: 6). However, even within the hard sciences, exact replication possibilities are affected by subject and condition variation, particularly in the environmental and ecological sciences. Exact replications in fields like the physical sciences are more common due to the potential for less experimental variation in physiological and psychological factors (see Nassaji's discussion of "Internal replications" in Chapter 3 this volume).

In some areas of the social sciences, such as sociology, it is possible to carry out exact replications; for example, the often-cited Kessler and Stipp study (1984), which replicated Phillips' (1982) study investigating the impact of fictional TV suicide stories on fatalities in the United States. Phillips' original findings suggested a causal link between fictional suicides on daytime television serials, or soap operas, and subsequent real-life suicides and fatal or nonfatal single-vehicle crashes. From the increasing trends of suicides and single-vehicle accidents, both fatal and nonfatal, after soap opera suicide stories, Phillips concluded that "soap opera suicide stories trigger some overt suicides and some covert suicides disguised as motor vehicle deaths" (1982: 1354). However, Kessler and Stipp's exact replication contradicted these results. They found that in using newspaper summaries as sources for the soap opera suicide stories, Phillips assigned an incorrect date range to eight out of 13 stories. Kessler and Stipp corrected this problem by investigating the exact date each story was aired and disaggregating the time series from weekly to daily information, allowing for a more precise before–after analysis. Their analysis also included important stories and controls that had not been included in the original study, and their findings found no substantial and statistically significant relationship between fictional and real-life suicides. Rather, they found "an average decrease of one-half of a suicide and a decrease of seven single vehicle motor fatalities" (Kessler and Stipp, 1984: 166).

Another widely known replication study from the field of psychology involves the investigation of the "bystander effect." Darley and Latané (1968) examined the murder of Kitty Genovese in 1964, which was supposedly witnessed by 38 people who did nothing to intervene. They (and colleagues) conducted a series of studies (Latané and Darely, 1968; Latané and Rodin, 1969; Latané and Darley, 1970; Latané and Nida, 1981) investigating how participants reacted to dangerous situations, with the overall finding that the presence of bystanders (i.e., other people in the situation) hinders a person's helping behavior. Further replications simulating dangerous emergencies (e.g., Schwartz and Gottlieb, 1976; Harari et al., 1985) found that the bystander effect is inversely affected by the apparent danger of the situation, such that when the costs of not helping are greater than the costs of helping, people are more likely to intervene in a dangerous situation. To observe the bystander effect in a naturalistic setting, Harari et al.'s (1985) replication study simulated a violent crime – rape – on a college campus. In their study, the male subjects observed the crime under either an individual condition or a group condition, and their intervention rate was measured. Unlike previous laboratory studies on the bystander effect (e.g., Borofsky et al., 1971; Field, 1978), Harari et al.'s replication in a realistic setting enhanced "realism, demand characteristics, social desirability, and generalizability" (1985: 654) in explaining the bystander effect.

1.2.1 REPLICATION IN LINGUISTICS

In formal linguistics (e.g., syntax and semantics), one linguist's introspective judgments about meaning and grammaticality of a certain language might be disagreed with by another linguist, with such a disagreement calling into question the reliability and generalizability of the theoretical work. In order to avoid this, studies in formal linguistics often utilize tasks asking native speakers about the plausibility or acceptability of sentence meaning. These judgments contribute to testing linguistic theory. For instance, the use of evaluation tasks (e.g., asking about acceptability or preference on a three- or four-point scale) with the same or different populations allows formalists to replicate the previous study, which might eventually contribute to testing or enhancing the explanatory power of theories. Some research in formal linguistics, then, lends itself to both approximate replication and conceptual replication.

In SLA research, conceptual replications are generally viewed as the easiest to realistically carry out. Leow (1995), for example, replicated his own (1993) original study with a different, but comparable, population and in a different modality (aural versus written). His original study investigated the effects of the complexity of written input (simplified versus unsimplified texts), linguistic item (present perfect versus present subjunctive verbs), and language experience (first semester versus fourth semester students) on learner intake. Participants at both learning levels were assigned written input that was either simplified with present perfect or present subjunctive verbs, or unsimplified with present perfect or present subjunctive verbs. In an analysis of pre-tests and post-tests, Leow (1993) found no differences in intake due to complexity of input or linguistic items, whereas language experience was a significant factor in determining the number of linguistic items that learners take in. Leow's (1995) replication using aural data corroborated his original results using written data with regard to complexity of input and language experience, but not linguistic item. In the aural modality, learners took in significantly more present perfect forms than present subjunctive forms in the input. This difference in results between aural and written input stresses the importance of considering the role of modality when investigating cognitive processes in SLA.

While Leow's (1993, 1995) work raises awareness of the potential contributions of replication studies to L2 research, there are many subfields within SLA where studies are rarely replicated. For example, there is only one study that is explicitly labeled as a replication in the abstract in the *Journal of Second Language Writing*. This study, by Allison et al. (1999), was a contextualized critique and approximate replication of Reid's (1996) exploratory work investigating the prediction of L2 sentences by native and nonnative English speakers, and resulted in different findings from the original study. Given the degree of controversy surrounding many of the key questions in the field of L2 writing, for instance the efficacy of feedback for the development of grammatical accuracy (e.g., Ferris and Roberts, 2001; Chandler, 2003; Hyland, 2003) and varying operationalizations of errors and their type classifications (e.g., Casanave, 1994; Ishikawa, 1995; Polio, 2003; among many others), a number of areas of L2 writing research, like SLA in general, would significantly benefit from replication research (see Polio, Chapter 2 this volume; Porte and Richards, 2012).

1.2.2 INSUFFICIENTLY DETAILED METHODS IN SLA ARTICLES

Researchers who intend to replicate a study need first to establish the rationale for its replication. One way to begin this process is by explaining the significance for the field of the original study and establishing its worthiness of replication (*Language Teaching Review Panel*, 2008). Sometimes, it may not be feasible to replicate a study if there are methodological issues that cannot be addressed without making multiple methodological changes which render the new study too different from the original. Even conceptual replication research can be difficult to carry out. Insufficient reporting of the kind of details that would allow replication is a problem with many studies. First, the language proficiency of subjects is not always stated in exact terms, so the equivalence of sample populations is difficult to determine in replication studies. For instance, Thomas (1994: 314) was one of the first to describe the problem of impressionistic judgments of L2 proficiency in SLA studies, noting that some publications did not provide enough information about participants' proficiency (e.g., the subjects "were more or less beginners" – Ellis, 1988: 260; "have some degree of oral reading ability" – Carlisle, 1991: 83; "spoke English with a noticeable foreign accent in the authors' opinion" – Flege and Bohn, 1989: 41). In other cases, assessment criteria, such as placement tests, what each program/assessment level represents, and so on, are often reported vaguely, if at all. Even when researchers use standardized proficiency measures, there is often considerable variation between researchers, for example, in what constitutes an "advanced" learner, making it difficult to directly compare subjects across studies. Second, in many methodology sections in journal articles there is not enough space for detailed information regarding the settings and contexts of experimental conditions. Also, coding systems vary widely and are not always represented in sufficient detail. To address the latter concern, Mackey and Gass suggest making more "use of existing coding schemes, because this would facilitate comparison between studies" (2005: 230). However, sometimes existing coding schemes are refined to capture new knowledge or they may need to be revised to address the research questions, at least if the prevalence of research using new or custom-made coding systems is anything to go by. Third, the variability of operationalizations applied to concepts of the same name is a problem. For example, according to Polio (2003), it is notoriously difficult to find a common denominator for the concept of "linguistic accuracy" in L2 writing research, which makes establishing a starting point problematic in a replication study. Finally, lack of direct access to examples of materials used in the original study is often a serious barrier to successful replication although the establishment of an SLA database of instruments may go some way toward mitigating this problem (Marsden and Mackey, 2010: www. iris-database.org).

   Another problem with replication studies is the uncertainty that arises when the replication results are different from the results in the original study. Such situations raise the question of whether the results of the original or the replication study are correct. For example, DeKeyser et al. (2002) tackle the issue of operationalizations of learning conditions in Input Processing (IP) research, pointing out that replication studies carried out by VanPatten and colleagues (VanPatten, 1990; VanPatten and Cadierno, 1993; VanPatten and Oikkenon, 1996; Wong, 2001) confirm VanPatten's theoretical claims about IP, whereas replications carried out in other contexts (Collentine, 1998; Benati, 2001; Farley, 2001; Cheng, 2002) resulted in alternative interpretations. DeKeyser et al. (2002) pointed out that vaguely defined constructs can cause operationalizational issues, and can produce overgeneralization and overinterpretation of results.

1.3 The catch-22 of replication in the field

Porte, in his Introduction, suggested an additional factor contributing to the general paucity of replication research is its relatively unglamorous status in professional journals and in the academic community in general. According to Valdman, "in replication one loses the aura of glamour and the exhilaration of innovation" associated with original research (1993: 505). Original research is often more valued by tenure/promotion/reward committees and journal editors, and major universities in the United States require that dissertations should be original work. For example, the Department of Linguistics at the University of Hawai'i at Manoa encourages PhD students as follows: "The third and final part of the PhD program involves preparing and defending a dissertation that makes a significant original contribution to knowledge in the candidate's chosen field." The Department of Linguistics and Germanic, Slavic, Asian, and African languages at Michigan State University has similar originality requirements: "The dissertation is based on original research that makes a significant contribution to knowledge in some area of theoretical and/or applied linguistic." Although those requirements do not include any explicit indication that replication studies are not allowed, students might be dissuaded from replicating a previous study in choosing their dissertation topic by the requirement of originality.

This sort of value judgment might be passed on from faculty to graduate students, leading to a preference for original research (*Language Teaching* Review Panel, 2008). Despite replication being considered a basic tenet of scientific advancement (Smith, 1975), replication research in the field of SLA finds itself in the proverbial "catch 22" situation. On the one hand, replication is essential to verify important findings:

- Replication is an important step in validating research and is considered a criterion for the acceptance of new theories and knowledge (*Language Teaching* Review Panel, 2008).
- Replication is, of course, crucial in order to distinguish the spurious from the real ... (Polio and Gass, 1997: 500).

On the other hand, current practices in the field prevent replication research from gaining more acceptance as a useful procedure. This is unfortunate for many reasons. For example, in addition to verifying existing findings, replication research can serve as a learning tool, providing valuable experience for novice researchers or graduate students, as noted elsewhere in this volume (see Abbuhl, Chapter 5, and also Fitzpatrick, Chapter 6). Polio and Gass (1997) also suggested that faculty should encourage graduate students to conduct a replication study, by including it as a requirement in a course syllabus, such as research methods.

1.4 Identifying studies for replication

To qualify as a candidate for replication, a study should address appropriate, theoretically interesting, and currently relevant research questions. Or, it should address studies that are generally accepted in the field, but might have been insufficiently investigated in the original studies. It is not uncommon to find gaps in existing research. If an original study failed to control for important variables or discovered a variable post hoc that was not controlled for in the original research but should have been, then a replication study that takes those variables into account may be in order. In other cases, a study may be selected for replication because it would be interesting to assess whether its results would hold in different settings (e.g., laboratory results extending to the classroom) or different languages, or with learners of different ages (children versus adults). Authors often provide suggestions for replications in the "limitations" section of their papers, which open the door for many more replication opportunities. Issues typically mentioned include things like a limited number of participants/tokens, only one L1 background or setting being considered, as well as potentially intervening variables such as learners' diverse backgrounds. Although replication studies often make changes to the original research design, it is important to stick to the previously established constructs of the research objects (e.g., L2 writing, L2 attention, L2 anxiety). However, these are often redefined for local contexts rather than further tested as originally operationalized (*Language Teaching* Review Panel, 2008). Replication studies using the original research design are useful in reexamining the theoretical relationship among constructs. For instance, in a situation where the original research identified multiple explanations for the results, a conceptual replication can manipulate nonsignificant variables and operationalizations of the original study to examine the strength of the causal relationship among variables.

1.5 SLA: Ripe for replication

Areas of research within SLA that are ripe for replication are relatively easy to identify. Inconsistent findings across different studies are a good starting point. One currently hot topic is research on the effects of implicit and explicit conditions on language learning (including the relationship between explicitness and awareness). While many studies have attempted to look at the relationship between awareness and L2 learning (e.g., Leow, 1997, 2000; Rebuschat and Williams, 2006), the researchers have reported different results, sometimes possibly due to the methodological differences in measuring awareness and learning (see Section 1.5.1).

Testing findings in different instructional contexts is also an interesting area for replication studies. Currently, most studies on the effects of feedback are "laboratory based," where learners and native speakers typically (although not always) interact in dyads, which is why it is important to repeat the studies in classroom contexts, with multiple participants and usually only one instructor. Since laboratory environments, where intervening variables are controlled, are very different from regular learning situations, such as classrooms, caution is necessary before assuming research from one context applies to another (Hulstijn, 1997). Also, research investigating the effects of instructional interventions on learning outcomes would benefit greatly from careful verification of its tools and practices, as well as from assessing the value of other methods (such as online measures, concurrent or retrospective protocols, etc.) and their applications. The following section further describes replication studies in two particular areas: SLA in the classroom and interactive SLA.

1.5.1 POSSIBLE REPLICATION AREAS

Explicit and implicit learning

Research on explicit and implicit learning has focused largely on evidence from qualitative research (e.g., Leow, 1997, 2000) and psycholinguistics (e.g., Rebuschat and Williams, 2006). These studies investigate the role of learners' awareness in adults' L2 learning, but different findings are reported. Leow (1997, 2000) found that awareness and attention play a significant role in L2 processing and accuracy whereas Rebuschat and Williams (2006) reported that adult learners were able to learn some syntactic regularities incidentally without conscious awareness of the forms. Different methodologies used to measure awareness seem to result in the contrastive findings: think-aloud protocol data and two tasks (a multiple-choice recognition task and a written production task) were used in Leow's (2000) study, while a grammaticality judgment task on artificial grammar was used in Rebuschat and Williams's (2006) study. Since the studies in this area use different methods (e.g., subjective measure, online/offline verbal report) and coding systems (dichotomous, continuous) to measure awareness, consciousness, and learning, the reported results are hard to compare. Additional evidence from a series of replication studies using systematically unified coding systems and perhaps also incorporating new technologies in psycholinguistics and neurolinguistics that measure the original constructs in new ways (e.g., eye-tracking for measuring attention, event-related potential [ERP] for measuring products) may provide converging evidence related to the differences in these types of learning.

Individual differences

Measuring individual differences in learners before carrying out experimental research can be crucial for understanding data obtained from studies. Factors, such as working memory span, anxiety, motivation, personality, language aptitude, willingness to communicate, and drift, could all be profitably assessed in replication research in order to dissociate, for example, the benefits of instructional methodologies from individual differences. Trofimovich et al. (2007) asked whether individual differences in factors such as learners' phonological memory, working memory, attention control, and analytical ability could determine their ability to notice and benefit from recasts. Unlike Mackey et al. (2010), which found learners with larger working memory and phonological memory spans are more likely to notice the error targeted by recasts than learners with smaller spans, Trofimovich et al. (2007) found no association of working and phonological memory with noticing rates. Trofimovich et al. (2007) attributed these contradictory results to different measures for noticing employed in the two studies. As the authors noted in their limitations, their participants received nonnaturalistic interactional feedback through computerized tasks, which uniformly provided native speaker responses to both target-like and erroneous utterances. It would be worthwhile replicating this important study in the original, as well as in a new context with multiple measures for noticing and naturalistic tasks.

Technology in L2 learning

Replication research in the area of computer-assisted language learning (CALL) would also contribute to determining potentials of new technology and its use in specific areas. The reexamination of the effectiveness of various software tools for language learning (e.g., speech-recognition software), the effects of synchronous as against asynchronous interaction in L2 development (e.g., Sotillo, 2000; Abrams, 2003; Sachs and Suh, 2007), and the effects of computer-mediated communication versus face-to-face interaction (e.g., Peterson and Mackey, 2009) will contribute to improving the applicability issue in CALL. Conceptual replications will allow technological improvements and innovations to be considered. For example, Sagarra (2007) showed that oral recasts provided via computer were beneficial to L2 learners, pointing to a relationship between computer-delivered recasts, working memory, and the modified output. Sagarra argued for further research about the way the interactional feedback is delivered via computer, indicating that it is necessary to see whether the same result could be obtained even when computer-administered recasts are delivered in a less controlled way. CALL research, like much of SLA research, has been carried out using a variety of methods of delivery and coding, and would benefit from having its central findings tested in a series of replications with established delivery and coding methods.

Study abroad

Study-abroad research is replete with hard-to-control variables, such as prior knowledge and aptitude, so determining tendencies in outcomes of studies abroad requires numerous replications in order to establish generalizability of phenomena (e.g., interpreting oral proficiency interviews [OPIs]). Collentine (2004) compared the effects of study abroad (SA) and formal instruction "at home" (AH) experiences by using the OPI, and found that while the AH group performed better than the SA group in terms of grammatical and lexical features, the SA group showed much development in terms of fluency.

As Collentine explicitly suggests, a different type of data collection instrument could be added to future replications. Because the episodes related to the OPI are more closely associated with experience in the SA context than in the AH context, this might have influenced the SA group's performance. Replicating this study and adding another data-collection instrument, such as role plays and spontaneous writing tasks, would be helpful in generalizing the findings.

L2 processing

The differences and/or similarities between L1 processing and L2 processing have received attention from both psycholinguistics and applied linguistics. However, depending on language typology, learner proficiency, age, and other cognitive variables, inconsistent results (e.g., syntactic processing, lexical processing) have been produced. Replication research on L2 processing in comparison to L1 processing will provide insightful perspectives in understanding learners' L2 acquisition and development. Papadopoulou and Clahsen (2003) investigated L2 sentence processing using Greek relative clauses to see if L2 learners with different L1 backgrounds exhibit L1-based preferences, and found that they did not. They wondered whether their findings could be extended to other kinds of ambiguous sentences. Thus, replicating this study using the original and adding a different target structure would be useful and interesting for the field.

1.6 Spotlight on a study: Classroom research

When conducting classroom-based SLA research, it is important to know whether findings from one context can be generalized to other contexts. Mackey et al. (in press) evaluated communicative tasks in terms of their effectiveness at promoting the development of English question forms in EFL and ESL contexts. The two main research questions guiding the investigation were:

1   Are communicative tasks or traditional practice activities most effective for L2 learning?
2   Are communicative tasks or traditional practice activities perceived to be more beneficial by L2 learners?

In this study, communicative tasks were compared with traditional classroom activities in two different classroom contexts: EFL in Japan (*n*=37) and ESL in the United States (*n*=23). The study was comprised of pre-test, treatment, and post-test, and a follow-up stimulated recall session. For each context, one group of participants was given communicative tasks (find the differences, problem solving, interview with the researcher) during the treatment session and one group was taught the same material using a traditional, grammar-based approach. The study was executed using researcher–teacher partnerships, with instructors in both the United States and Japan, to develop pedagogically valid classroom tasks that were based on theory and research in SLA, while also being comparable to the teachers' usual activities.

Quantitative analyses of learner production in pre- and post-tests were carried out, and triangulated with qualitative introspective data collected in stimulated recall interviews. Findings suggest that in ESL classrooms in the United States, communicative tasks were more effective than traditional classroom activities in promoting L2 development. However, in the university EFL classrooms in Japan, where learners have little prior experience with grammar instruction in a communicative context, more learning was observed from learners who carried out the traditional classroom activities, compared to those who participated in the communicative task condition.

To some extent, it seems that learners' prior experiences in the classroom, as well as their cultural expectations and values associated with different approaches to teaching and learning, played a role in the effectiveness of communicative tasks. However, an observed mismatch between learners' perceptions and the quantitative results suggests that learners' reported perceptions of certain classroom activities are only one aspect of the activity's effectiveness.

Overall, Mackey et al. (in press) showed that communicative tasks are an effective teaching tool in ESL classrooms, particularly if they have already been used as part of the regular classroom routine. Communicative tasks might also be effective in EFL classrooms if the procedures and goals of the task activities are introduced and learners receive instruction on "how" to do the task, as well as opportunities to practice participating in tasks. Importantly, this study suggests that research findings from one context, that is, ESL or EFL, cannot be automatically generalized to another context, thus demonstrating the importance of mixed-methods research. Conceptual replication of this study would be helpful because, clearly, EFL classrooms in Japan are not representative of those in other countries. Also, the ESL comparison was made with one particular context on the East Coast of the United States and, again, ESL is practiced in a wide range of rich and diverse settings. Furthermore, the teachers and researchers in the partnerships were familiar with each other and all worked in higher education settings. Testing such partnerships between unfamiliar teachers and researchers, using teachers with different levels of training and experience, would be interesting and helpful. If research like this is to have any impact on classroom instructions, it should first be replicated in its original context, and then scrutinized to see if the findings were particular to the Japanese and specific U.S. contexts.

1.7 Spotlight on a study: Input and interaction

Another area of SLA in need of replication is research in input, interaction, and feedback, including how these conditions and processes affect learning, the relationship between feedback and so-called learner-internal variables, and the laboratory–classroom interface. An example of an input and interaction study that would be a good candidate for replication will now be discussed (Philp, 2003).

1.7.1 PHILP (2003)

Philp (2003) conducted a study based on Schmidt's noticing hypothesis (Schmidt, 1990, 1993, 1995, 2001), which states it is only what the learner *notices* about the input that holds potential for learning because intake – that is, "a process that mediates between target language input and the learner's internalized set of rules" (Gass, 1988: 206) – is conditional upon noticing. Based on the hypothesized importance of noticing in SLA, Philp's study investigated whether learners notice recasts, specifically in the context of dyadic interaction. The research questions of the study were threefold:

1 Is the ability to recall a recast constrained by the level of the learner?
2 Is the ability to recall a recast constrained by the length of the recast?
3 Is the ability to recall a recast constrained by the number of changes made during the recast?

Like Mackey (1999), Mackey and Oliver (2002), and Mackey and Silver (2005), Philp (2003) operationalized learning as the development of question formation. The participants in the study were 33 adult ESL students (18 female and 15 male) who ranged in age from 17 to 30. Learners had varying proficiency levels and were enrolled in six- to eight-week intensive English courses at an Australian university. Each learner was involved in five native speaker (NS) – nonnative speaker (NNS) dyadic interaction sessions over two weeks, for a total of 100 minutes of interaction. Three NSs, including the researcher, acted as partners in NS–NNS dyads. Participants were randomly assigned to NSs and rotated so that all participants were paired with all NSs over the five sessions. Cued immediate recall was used as a measure of a particular level of noticing.

The results of the study indicated that learners noticed over 60–70% of recasts. However, recast length, the number of changes made in the recast, and the readiness of the learner were all factors that appeared to constrain the noticing of feedback provided through recasts in the context of interaction.

There are several reasons to replicate this study. The first is that the results from the learner population may not be generalizable to other populations. The study was conducted in a university environment, and all participants were highly motivated to learn English and use it in the future. Learners with lower motivation levels may not notice as many recasts as a highly motivated population. Another reason to replicate Philp (2003) would be to generalize the findings to another context more representative of natural or classroom language use. The setting in this study was very controlled, focusing on NS–NNS dyads in a laboratory context. It would be interesting, and important, to investigate how learners notice recasts in classroom settings. Finally, there are some limitations to the immediate–recall method used by Philp (2003). The subjects did not have the ability, or possibly the opportunity, to comment on certain types of input (e.g., morphological information), even if noticing may have occurred. Additionally, individual working memory limitations may also have prevented subjects from recalling input that they did actually notice.

There are two replication options for Philp (2003). An approximate replication of this study would involve the same study design, conditions, and materials, but a different instructional setting (e.g., a classroom with a different language). A conceptual replication would replicate the study design in either a laboratory or classroom setting, changing the concurrent protocols to stimulated recalls of recorded data and controlling for types of data (e.g., morphological) that learners find difficult to describe or comment on. Furthermore, the same study design which employs qualitative methods, such as stimulated recall, survey data, or ethnographic research, combined with quantitative methodology, would make the study more robust and the results more generalizable in relation to the original theory, as well as in relation to other cases of similar phenomena (Firestone, 1993).

Bigelow et al. (2006) replicated Philp's (2003) design with low-literacy learners. Taking into account Philp's findings that factors such as length of recast and the number of changes in the recast seem to constrain noticing, Bigelow et al. investigated whether the ability to recall a recast is related to:

1   the literacy level of the learner
2   the length of the recast
3   the number of changes made by the recast.

Specifically addressing literacy as an independent variable, they examined whether learners with higher literacy have better recall of longer recasts and/or recasts with more changes. The participants in the study were eight Somali ESL learners between the ages of 15 and 27. Out of 35 initial participants, they received the four highest and four lowest scores on a Native Language Literacy Screening Device, and they were all at Stage 5 on the Pienemann and Johnston (1987) developmental scale of question formation. Each participant had two one-on-one sessions with the researcher during which they engaged in four "spot-the-difference" tasks and received recasts for "trigger utterances." Bigelow et al. (2006) found that the ability to recall a recast is related to the literacy level of the learner, and that learners with higher literacy have better recall of recasts with more changes than learners with lower literacy. The ability to recall a recast was not related to the length of the recast or to the number of changes in the recast, and learners with higher literacy did not have better recall of longer recasts than learners with lower literacy. However, as a result of the small number of participants, none of the results in this study were statistically significant. While this study in particular did not yield significant results, it is a good model for replicating Philp (2003), as it addresses the issue of population generalizability and expands the analysis to control for factors, such as recast length and the number of changes to the recast, that Philp noted as an influence in the post-hoc analyses. Unlike the original study, Bigelow et al.'s findings did not show that length of recasts or number of changes in recasts had a significant impact on learners' performance.

Other potential replications of Philp (2003):

• *Extending target structures* In Philp (2003), syntax (question formation) was used as a target form. However, it is possible that learners' noticing of recasts would be different when the targets are phonological, lexical, and pragmatic elements. Also, other syntactic elements that have different syntactic complexity (e.g., present or past counterfactual) would involve different levels of learners' noticing during interaction.
• *Relationship between noticing and L2 development* In Philp's study, the observation was limited to learners' noticing of recasts

as feedback. However, it would also be worthwhile to examine the relationship between noticing and L2 development. As Philp mentioned, it is unclear "whether the internal processing of noticing, comparison, and integration occur following recasts" (2003: 119). A replication study could further investigate the relationship between learners' noticing rate and substantial English question formation development.

1.8 Qualitative replication

As discussed elsewhere in this book, traditionally, replication was used primarily in "hard" and social sciences and involved studies focused on quantitative methods. In quantitative research, generalizing from a sample to the general population is a cornerstone of conducting investigations, and replication advances exactly that aspect of research. In other words, for quantitative research, replication helps establish the validity of claims for greater population ranges, thus promoting the generalizability of original study results. Qualitative research, on the other hand, is not traditionally structured around the same principles as quantitative research, which is why generalizability does not play the same role that it does in quantitative research (Mackey and Gass, 2005).

However, some types of qualitative research do value the criterion of generalizability, although the concept is understood differently. According to Maxwell (1992), for example, generalizability in qualitative research is based on the assumption that it is useful to begin to understand similar situations or individuals, rather than represent a large target population. This assumption means that qualitative results can be generalized within a limited paradigm, consisting of similar settings and people in the particular study. It is important to point out that not all qualitative research fits into this model, because differences across cases and contexts can be found. The concept of generalizability in quantitative studies is often replaced with what is known as transferability in qualitative research, which refers to the degree to which qualitative results can be generalized to other contexts or settings (Lincoln and Guba, 1985: 124). Thus, findings in qualitative studies are generalizable or transferable to a new setting when their contexts are sufficiently congruent. Because external conditions of L2 learning vary across cases and contexts, transferability assigns "the responsibility to readers to determine whether there is a congruence, fit, or connection" between one study context and the readers' own context (Duff, 2006: 75). Therefore, consideration of transferability eventually facilitates the "understanding of how general principles operate within a field beyond what the notion of transferability suggests" (Duff, 2006: 75).

Since the assumptions of much qualitative study are quite different from those of quantitative research, the purpose of qualitative study is also different. Newman and Benz (1998) noted that the most common purposes of qualitative research are theory initiation and theory building, making them different from those of quantitative research, which has theory testing and modification as its objectives. This distinction suggests that while qualitative research cannot be generalized from the research sample to a population, it can be used to generalize a theory, or to demonstrate the utility of research findings for building or expanding theories, as well as from case to case, demonstrating the transferability of concrete findings to other similar cases and/or conditions in question (Firestone, 1993).

In other words, then, the concept of quantitative replication can be applied to some types of qualitative research, cautiously, and recognizing that qualitative research replications are not, for a number of reasons, traditionally necessary. First of all, according to the meta-analysis of methodology in original applied linguistics research articles conducted by Lazaraton (2000), 88% of original research articles from four major SLA and applied linguistics journals (namely, *The Modern Language Journal, Language Learning, Studies in Second Language Acquisition*, and *TESOL Quarterly*) reported findings from quantitative research, whereas only 12% reported partially or solely qualitative findings. In other words, there is not enough qualitative research being published to begin with – a difficulty also reported by Pennycook (1994). However, since 2000, a number of journals have dedicated special issues to various topics of qualitative research, which is an encouraging fact for qualitative researchers in general, and for those who might attempt replicating qualitative research in particular.

Not only are qualitative replications hard to publish, but they are hard to conduct to begin with. For example, in an edited article, Cumming et al. (1994) report on a number of complications in qualitative research experienced by seasoned applied linguists. Cumming et al. (1994) identify three particular approaches to qualitative research that contribute to these complications: i) a descriptive approach that analyzes learner language (e.g., analysis of interlanguage), verbal reports, and texts, and provides an insightful perspective on a learner's L2 development; ii) an interpretive approach which analyzes classroom interaction and gives quality information on what really goes on in language classrooms; and iii) an ideological approach that describes inequity in education and examines the relationship between

L2 learning and social factors (e.g., race, class). Generalizability – the underlying reason for replication research – is crucial to descriptive research, but it seems less so for interpretive and ideological approaches. Replicating studies that descriptively analyze aspects of learner language and verbal reports/texts is certainly likely to shed light on the generalizability of qualitative findings (see also Firestone, 1993); however, the goals of interpretive and ideological research are not to provide the replicable validity of phenomena. Instead, the goals of those kinds of research are to provide interpretations (which have the potential to be skewed) or to make a strong point for a given ideological view. Critical research, for all intents and purposes, can indeed "define data and analytic procedures in a way consistent with its pedagogic and analytical project" (Pierce, 1995); in other words, it is perfectly acceptable for critical research to be biased in one way or another. Such a situation essentially obviates the need for, and perhaps explicitly rejects, the goals of transferability and generalizability. Thus, it seems that conducting replications of interpretively and ideologically oriented studies contradicts the essential nature of those respective research stances. It is important to point out, though, that the difficulty of replication of those studies may be encouraging an accumulation of research findings where validity and/or generalizability are impossible to test and are not considered, by the researchers, to be testable (see Porte and Richards, 2012).

Clearly, however, there is a fine line between contradicting research stances and producing a body of research that is not questioned or questionable, and which some would argue renders it unscientific.

To illustrate this issue with concrete examples, let us consider two specific studies. Hinkel's (1994) study is descriptive in nature, comparing native speaker and nonnative speaker evaluations of four short essays (two written by native speakers and two by advanced ESL learners). The participants read the texts and answered a number of questions about the essay, thus demonstrating their background knowledge about the principles of L2 writing. The results of the analysis showed that the nonnative speaker participants, despite many years of exposure to the L2 general linguistic and writing conventions, still used a different set of pragmatic principles when interpreting native and nonnative speaker written texts, as opposed to the pragmatic interpretations used by the native speakers. The study has very clear pedagogical implications, since differences in pragmatic perceptions of texts need to be addressed through classroom instruction. A replication of Hinkel's original study would be quite valuable to the field of L2 writing research, as it would likely produce additional data testing the validity of Hinkel's claims and potentially expand their generalizability to the theoretical background used for the original research, as well as to other cases. Thus, this study could serve as an example to show that a qualitative research study can be replicated, making a contribution to the understanding of L2 writing, as long as we are aware that exact replication may not be possible. Indeed, as Porte and Richards (2012) argue, it might be worthwhile to think about this issue in terms of the ways qualitative research projects can build on one another, and contribute to a developing understanding of the area. This can be illustrated with reference to Norton's (2005) study, which lies outside the scope of replication-friendly research. In her article "Towards a model of critical language teacher education," Norton makes a case for introducing a new model for training language teachers, thus representing the critical branch of qualitative research at its finest. The scope of the article covers not only suggested practices and methods of teaching per se, but also professional identities imposed onto teachers in training. Norton strongly suggests reorganizing teacher-training programs, and encourages giving future teachers more opportunities to "choose" their own identities, which, according to her line of argumentation, would enhance their sense of legitimacy in their own classrooms and thus positively affect the quality of education across various communities. While Norton's points critique an existing problem in teacher-training reality, her study does not offer any ground for a replication, and it is unlikely that it would benefit from one, even if such grounds were indeed present. Since Norton's stance does not attempt to portray an objective picture of the reality in the first place, replicating this piece of critically oriented and groundbreaking research would not be useful for any particular goal. However, building on it and questioning its interpretation is both possible and desirable.

2 Conclusions

First, we clearly need greater acknowledgment of the fact that replications are important for the ongoing development of our field. Replications build upon foundations laid before us, exploring questions that may have not been answered sufficiently in existing research. Graduate study settings present an ideal environment for carrying out replication research. The field of SLA needs to evolve in terms of its training, as well as the value it places on replications, encouraging graduate students to carry out this necessary type of research. The chapters on graduate student training in this volume are particularly important in this respect. Next, we need a better understanding of the many facets of replication work, and again, education is critically important in this regard. Finally, we need to strive to improve the perceived value of replication research, which means that both seasoned and junior researchers need to conduct more replication studies in a variety of areas within the field of SLA. For this to happen, more journals need to follow the trail blazed by *Language Teaching* and *Studies in Second Language Acquisition*, and provide a legitimate and rigorous forum in which replication studies can be published.

References

Abrams, Z. I. (2003). The effect of synchronous and asynchronous CMC on oral performance in German, *The Modern Language Journal*, **87**, 157–67.

Allison, D., Varghese, S. and Wu, S. M. (1999). Local coherence and its limits: A second look at second sentences, *Journal of Second Language Writing*, **8**, 77–97.

American Psychological Association. (2010). *Publication Manual of the American Psychological Association* (6th edn.), Washington, DC: American Psychological Association.

Benati, A. (2001). A comparative study of the effects of processing instruction and output-based instruction on the acquisition of the Italian future tense, *Language Teaching Research*, **5**, 95–127.

Bigelow, M., Delmas, R., Hansen, K. and Tarone, E. (2006). Literacy and the processing of oral recasts in SLA, *TESOL Quarterly*, **40**, 665–89.

Borofsky, G. L., Stollack, E. G. and Messe, L. A. (1971). Sex differences in bystander reactions to physical assault, *Journal of Experimental Social Psychology*, **7**, 313–18.

Carlisle, R. S. (1991). The influence of environment on vowel epenthesis in Spanish/English interphonology, *Applied Linguistics*, **12**, 76–95.

Casanave, C. P. (1994). Language development in students' journals, *Journal of Second Language Writing*, **3**, 179–201.

Chandler, J. (2003). The efficacy of various kinds of error feedback for improvement in the accuracy and fluency of L2 student writing, *Journal of Second Language Writing*, **12**, 267–96.

Cheng, A. (2002). The effects of processing instruction on the acquisition of *ser* and *estar*, *Hispania*, **85**, 308–23.

Collentine, J. (1998). Processing instruction and the subjunctive, *Hispania*, **81**, 576–87.

Collentine, J. (2004). The effects of learning contexts on morphosyntactic and lexical development, *Studies in Second Language Acquisition*, **26**, 227–48.

Cumming, A., Tarone, E., Cohen, A. D., Connor, U., Spada, N., Hornberger, N. H., Pennycook, A. and Auerbach, E. (1994). Alternatives in TESOL research: Descriptive, interpretive, and ideological orientations, *TESOL Quarterly*, **28**, 673–703.

Darley, J. M. and Latané, B. (1968). Bystander intervention in emergencies: Diffusion of responsibility, *Journal of Personality and Social Psychology*, **8**, 377–83.

DeKeyser, R., Salaberry, R., Robinson, P. and Harrington, M. (2002). What gets processed in processing instruction? A commentary on Bill Van-Patten's "Processing Instruction: An Update," *Language Learning*, **52**, 805–23.

Department of Linguistics and Germanic, Slavic, Asian, and African Languages at Michigan State University. (n. d.). *Graduate Studies: The PhD Program*. Retrieved 13 January 2011 from http://linglang.msu.edu/linguistics/grad/phd.php

Department of Linguistics at University of Hawai'i at Manoa. (December 2010). *Student Manual for the PhD Program in Linguistics*. Retrieved 13 January 2011 from www.ling.hawaii.edu/graduate/pdfs/PhDmanual.pdf

Duff, P. (2006). Beyond generalizability: Contextualization, complexity and credibility in applied linguistics research, in Chalhoub-Deville, M., Chapelle, C. and Duff, P. (eds.), *Inference and Generalizability in Applied Linguistics: Multiple Research Perspectives*, Amsterdam: John Benjamins, pp. 65–95.

Ellis, R. (1988). The effects of linguistic environment on the second language acquisition of grammatical rules, *Applied Linguistics*, **9**, 257–74.

Farley, A. P. (2001). Authentic processing instruction and the Spanish subjunctive, *Hispania*, **84**, 289–99.

Ferris, D. and Roberts, B. (2001). Error feedback in L2 writing classes: How explicit does it need to be?, *Journal of Second Language Writing*, **10**, 161–84.

Field, H. S. (1978). Attitudes toward rape: A comparative analysis of police, rapists, crisis counselors, and citizens, *Journal of Personality and Social Psychology*, **36**, 156–79.

Firestone, W. A. (1993). Alternative arguments for generalizing from data as applied to qualitative research, *Educational Researcher*, **22**, 16–23.

Flege, J. E. and Bohn, O. S. (1989). An instrumental study of vowel reduction and stress placement in Spanish-accented English, *Studies in Second Language Acquisition*, **11**, 35–62.

Gass, S. (1988). Integrating research areas: A framework for second language studies, *Applied Linguistics*, **9**, 198–217.

Gass, S. M. and Selinker, L. (2008). *Second Language Acquisition: An Introductory Course* (3rd edn.), New York: Routledge.

Gross, M. T. (1997). The need for replication studies – Is it really a done deal?, *Journal of Orthopaedic and Sports Physical Therapy*, **25**, 161–2.

Harari, H., Harari, O. and White, R. V. (1985). The reaction to rape by American male bystanders, *The Journal of Social Psychology*, **125**, 653–8.

Hinkel, E. (1994). Native and non-native speakers' pragmatic interpretations of English texts, *TESOL Quarterly*, **28**, 353–76.

Hulstijn, J. H. (1997). Second language acquisition research in the laboratory: Possibilities and limitations, *Studies in Second Language Acquisition*, **19**, 131–43.

Hyland, K. (2003). Genre-based pedagogies: A social response to process, *Journal of Second Language Writing*, **12**, 17–29.

Ishikawa, S. (1995). Objective measurement of low-proficiency EFL narrative writing, *Journal of Second Language Writing*, **4**, 51–69.

Kessler, R. C. and Stipp, H. (1984). The impact of fictional television suicide stories on U.S. fatalities: A replication, *The American Journal of Sociology*, **90**, 151–67.

Krause, C., Haarala, C., Sillanmäki, L., Koivisto, M., Alanko, K., Revonsuo, A., Laine, M. and Hämäläinen, H. (2004). Effects of electromagnetic field emitted by cell phones on the EEG during an auditory memory task: A double blind replication study, *Bioelectromagnetics*, **25**, 33–40.

Krause, C., Sillanmäki, L., Koivisto, M., Häggqvist, A., Saarela, C., Revonsuo, A., Laine, M. and Hämäläinen, H. (2000). Effects of electromagnetic field emitted by cell phones on the EEG during a memory task, *Neuroreport*, **11**, 761–4.

Language Teaching Review Panel. (2008). Replication studies in language learning and teaching: Questions and answers, *Language Teaching*, **41**, 1–14.

Latané, B. and Darley, J. M. (1968). Group inhibition of bystander intervention in emergencies, *Journal of Personality and Social Psychology*, **10**, 215–21.

Latané, B. and Darley, J. M. (1970). *The Unresponsive Bystander: Why Doesn't He Help?*, New York: Appleton-Century-Crofts.

Latané, B. and Nida, S. (1981). Ten years of research on group size and helping, *Psychological Bulletin*, **89**, 308–24.

Latané, B. and Rodin, J. (1969). A lady in distress: Inhibiting effects of friends and strangers on bystander intervention, *Journal of Experimental Social Psychology*, **5**, 189–202.

Lazaraton, A. (2000). Current trends in research methodology and statistics in applied linguistics, *TESOL Quarterly*, **34**, 175–81.

Leow, R. P. (1993). To simplify or not to simplify: A look at intake, *Studies in Second Language Acquisition*, **15**, 333–55.

Leow, R. P. (1995). Modality and intake in second language acquisition SLA, *Studies in Second Language Acquisition*, **17**, 79–89.

Leow, R. P. (1997). Attention, awareness and foreign language behavior, *Language Learning*, **47**, 467–505.

Leow, R. P. (2000). A study of the role of awareness in foreign language behavior: Aware versus unaware learners, *Studies in Second Language Acquisition*, **22**, 557–84.

Lincoln, Y. and Guba, E. G. (1985). *Naturalistic Inquiry*, Beverly Hills, CA: Sage.

Mackey, A. (1999). Input, interaction, and second language development, *Studies in Second Language Acquisition*, **21**, 557–87.

Mackey, A., Adams, R., Stafford, C. and Winke, P. (2010). Exploring the relationship between modified output and working memory capacity, *Language Learning*, 60, 501–33.

Mackey, A., Fujii, A., Biesenbach-Lucas, S., Weger-Guntharp, H., Abbuhl, R., Jacobsen, N. D., Fogle, L., Lake, J. B., Sondermann, K., Tagarelli, K., Takada, M. and Watanabe, A. (in press). Classroom, foreign language and second language context and communicative activities, in McDonough, K. and Mackey, A. (eds.), *Interaction in Diverse Educational Settings*, Amsterdam: John Benjamins.

Mackey, A. and Gass, S. M. (2005). *Second Language Research: Methodology and Design*, Mahwah, NJ: Lawrence Erlbaum Associates.

Mackey, A. and Oliver, R. (2002). Interactional feedback and children's L2 development, *System*, 30, 459–77.

Mackey, A. and Silver, R. E. (2005). Interactional tasks and English L2 learning by immigrant children in Singapore, *System*, 33, 239–360.

Marsden, E. and Mackey, A. (2010). *Research Grant. Instruments for Research into Second Language Learning: The Establishment of a Digital Repository*. Economics and Social research Council (ESRC), UK. www.iris-database.org

Maxwell, J. A. (1992). Understanding the validity in qualitative research, *Harvard Educational Review*, 62, 279–300.

Muma, J. R. (1993). The need for replication, *Journal of Speech and Hearing Research*, 36, 927–30.

Newman, I. and Benz, C. R. (1998). *Qualitative-Quantitative Research Methodology: Exploring the Interactive Continuum*, Carbondale, IL: Southern Illinois University Press.

Norton, B. (2005). Teacher training: Towards a model of critical language teacher education, *Language Issues*, 17, 12–17.

Ortega, L. (2008). Foreword, in Wa-Mbaleka, S., *A Meta-Analysis Investigating the Effects of Reading on Second Language Vocabulary Learning*, Saarbrücken, Germany: VDM Verlag, pp. iii–v.

Papadopoulou, D. and Clahsen, H. (2003). Parsing strategies in L1 and L2 sentence processing: A study of relative clause attachment in Greek, *Studies in Second Language Acquisition*, 25, 501–28.

Pennycook, A. (1994). Critical pedagogical approaches to research, in Cumming, A. (ed.), *Alternatives in TESOL Research: Descriptive, Interpretive, and Ideological Orientation*, TESOL Quarterly, 28, 690–3.

Peterson, K. and Mackey, A. (October 2009). Interaction, Modality and Learning: Comparing the Effectiveness of Computer-Generated and Face to Face Recasts, Paper presented at Second Language Research Forum (SLRF), Michigan State University, MI.

Phillips, D. P. (1982). The impact of fictional television stories on U.S. adult fatalities: New evidence on the effect of the mass media on violence, *The American Journal of Sociology*, 87, 1340–59.

Philp, J. (2003). Constraints on "Noticing the Gap," *Studies in Second Language Acquisition*, 25, 99–126.

Pienemann, M. and Johnston, M. (1987). Factors influencing the development of language proficiency, in Nunan, D. (ed.), *Applying Second Language Acquisition Research*, Adelaide, Australia: National Curriculum Resource Centre, AMEP, pp. 45–141.

Pierce, B. N. (1995). The theory of methodology in qualitative research, *TESOL Quarterly*, **29**, 569–75.

Polio, C. (2003). Research on second language writing: An overview of what we investigate and how, in Kroll, B. (ed.), *Exploring the Dynamics of Second Language Writing*, Cambridge: Cambridge University Press, pp. 35–65.

Polio, C. and Gass, S. (1997). Replication and reporting: A commentary, *Studies in Second Language Acquisition*, **19**, 499–508.

Porte, G. (2010). *Appraising Research in Second Language Learning: A Practical Approach to Critical Analysis of Quantitative Research* (2nd edn.), Amsterdam/Philadelphia: John Benjamins.

Porte, G. and Richards, K. (2012). Focus article: Replication in second language writing research, *Journal of Second Language Writing*, **21**, 3.

Rebuschat, P. and Williams, J. N. (2006). Dissociating implicit and explicit learning of natural language syntax, in Sun, R. and Miyake, N. (eds.), *Proceedings of the 28th Annual Conference of the Cognitive Science Society*, Mahwah, NJ: Lawrence Erlbaum Associates, pp. 25–94.

Reid, J. (1996). U.S. academic readers, ESL writers, and second sentences, *Journal of Second Language Writing*, **5**, 129–61.

Sachs, R. and Suh, B.-R. (2007). Textually enhanced recasts, learner awareness, and L2 coutcomes in synchronouns computer-mediated interaction, in Mackey, A. (ed.), *Conversational Interaction in Second Language Acquisition: A Series of Empirical Studies*, Oxford: Oxford University Press, pp. 197–227.

Sagarra, N. (2007). From CALL to face-to-face interaction: The effect of computer-delivered recasts and working memory on L2 development, in Mackey, A.(ed.), *Conversational Interaction in Second Language Acquisition: A Series of Empirical Studies*, Oxford: Oxford University Press, pp. 229–48.

Santos, T. (1989). Replication in applied linguistics research, *TESOL Quarterly*, **23**, 699–702.

Schmidt, R. W. (1990). The role of consciousness in second language learning, *Applied Linguistics*, **11**, 129–58.

Schmidt, R. W. (1993). Awareness and second language acquisition, *Annual Review of Applied Linguistics*, **13**, 206–26.

Schmidt, R. W. (1995). Consciousness and foreign language learning: A tutorial on the role of attention and awareness in learning, in Schmidt, R. W. (ed.), *Attention and Awareness in Foreign Language Learning*, Honolulu, HI: University of Hawai'i, pp. 1–63.

Schmidt, R. W. (2001). Attention, in Robinson, P. (ed.), *Cognition and Second Language Instruction*, Cambridge: Cambridge University Press, pp. 3–32.

Schneider, B. (2004). Building a scientific community: The need for replication, *Teachers College Record*, **106**, 1471–83.

Schwartz, S. H. and Gottlieb, A. (1976). Bystander reactions to a violent theft: Crime in Jerusalem, *Journal of Personality and Social Psychology*, 34, 1188–99.

Smith, H. (1975). *Strategies of Social Research*, Englewood Cliffs, NJ: Prentice-Hall.

Sotillo, S. (2000). Discourse functions and syntactic complexity in synchronous and asynchronous communication, *Language Learning and Technology*, **4**, 82–119.

Thomas, M. (1994). Review article: Assessment of L2 proficiency in second language acquisition research, *Language Learning*, 44, 307–36.

Trofimovich, P., Ammar, A. and Gatbonton, E. (2007). How effective are recasts? The role of attention, memory, and analytical ability, in Mackey, A. (ed.), *Conversational Interaction in Second Language Acquisition: A Series of Empirical Studies*, Oxford: Oxford University Press, pp. 171–95.

Valdman, A. (1993). Replication study (editorial introduction), *Studies in Second Language Acquisition*, **15**, 505.

VanPatten, B. (1990). Attending to form and content in the input: An experiment in consciousness, *Studies in Second Language Acquisition*, **12**, 287–301.

VanPatten, B. and Cadierno, T. (1993). Explicit instruction and input processing, *Studies in Second Language Acquisition*, **15**, 225–43.

VanPatten, B. and Oikkenon, S. (1996). Explanation versus structured input in processing instruction, *Studies in Second Language Acquisition*, **18**, 495–510.

Wong, W. (2001). Modality and attention to meaning and form in the input, *Studies in Second Language Acquisition*, **23**, 345–68.

2 Replication in published applied linguistics research: A historical perspective

Charlene Polio

In 1996, Susan Gass and I were asked to participate in a colloquium at the TESOL convention titled "Professional ethics in TESOL-related research." We chose to talk about issues related to the reporting of research. At the time, I was conducting a study (Polio et al., 1998) that involved the calculation of accuracy in L2 writers' texts. I was struggling to find a valid and reliable measure of accuracy among a wide variety of ways found in published research to operationalize the construct. It was not surprising that different studies used different measures. What was surprising was that many of the studies neither described the measures in any detail nor reported reliability on any or each of the individual measures (Polio, 1997). Polio et al. (1998) had two goals. One was to investigate a research question similar to a previous study conducted by Kroll (1990) regarding the effect of extra time on L2 writing, and the other was to examine the effects of written error correction over the course of a semester. Without a reliable measure of linguistic accuracy, treatment effects might be undetectable. The lack of detail and reliability also led to a concern that the studies using such measures were unreplicable. After the colloquium, Susan Gass and I published a commentary on replication in *Studies in Second Language Acquisition* (Polio and Gass, 1997).

The goal of this chapter is to provide a historical perspective on the role of replication in applied linguistics both before and after the commentary was published. I first address what has been said about replication in applied linguistics and discuss how replication can be defined. I then provide a summary and discussion of studies that claim to be some type of replication. Finally, using the example of written error correction studies, I deal further with the problem of determining what counts as replication and discuss the relationship between replication (and replicability) and how this has added or, may in the future add, to what we know about written error correction.

1 Discussions of replication

Polio and Gass (1997) noted two commentaries prior to 1997 on the topic of replication within applied linguistics. In 1989, Santos, in a commentary in *TESOL Quarterly*, argued for more replication in applied linguistics. She said, "What is considered standard procedure in other disciplines that hypothesize, quantify, and generalize is ignored in ours" (1989: 699). She noted that of the 100 quantitative studies in *TESOL Quarterly* and *Language Learning*, none had been replicated. She also noted that none of the studies in those journals were "explicitly" replications (1989: 699), but she reported that two studies in the issue in which her commentary appeared did report replicating an earlier study. Santos's use of the word "explicit" raises the question of what is considered a replication, and I return to this point below. She went on to elucidate two benefits of replication. The first being to the field:

> Research is an accretive process; it is the accumulation and consolidation of knowledge over time. Replication of research confirms or calls into question existing findings; without it, a discipline consists of scattered hypotheses and insufficiently substantiated generalizations.
>
> (Santos, 1989: 700)

In addition, she argued that replication would encourage both communication among researchers and explicitness in reporting.

In 1993, Albert Valdman, the editor of *Studies in Second Language Acquisition* (*SSLA*), introduced a new section of the journal devoted to replication and invited researchers to submit manuscripts. This coincided with the publication of Tyler and Bro (1993), which examined native speakers' (NSs) comprehension of nonnative speakers' (NNSs) written texts. They intended to replicate Tyler and Bro (1992), which examined how the order of ideas in a text and discourse-structuring miscues affected comprehension. NSs were shown four types of texts that included either a misordering of ideas, discourse-structuring miscues, both, or neither. In the first study, NSs read texts on paper and assessed them for comprehensibility. In the replication, two features were changed: The texts were presented on a computer, and a second measure of text comprehension was added. When reading the text on a computer, the participants were not able to go back and reread the texts, making the research, Tyler and Bro claimed, "more relevant to the effects of the targeted features on listening comprehension" (1993: 509). In addition, the use of a computer allowed the researchers to measure reading speed. They found that, as in the first study, discourse-structuring miscues, and not the order of ideas, had an effect on comprehension, but that the ordering of ideas did show some effect on reading time.

Valdman did not explicitly define replication, but stated:

> Re-running experimental studies under different conditions while main-taining *central variables constant* promises to eliminate much uncontrolled variance. If the same or another team of researchers fails to obtain nearly the same results on a second trial, then it may suspect that the key vari-ables were not properly identified in the original study. [italics added]
>
> (Valdman, 1993: 505)

It appears, then, that a replication, according to the above quote, means that the central variables are held constant, but what that means is definitely open to interpretation. Tyler and Bro (1993) cer-tainly had the same independent and dependent variables, that is, text cues and organization, and text comprehension, respectively, but they changed both somewhat. The researchers seemed to be trying to improve the design of the study by measuring the time on task and adding a measure of comprehensibility, certainly an improvement in my opinion. They also tried to extend their results saying that read-ing in the computer format was more similar to the processing of oral texts, which I believe is open to debate. This relatively early study, as I will show, is quite representative of many studies claiming to be rep-lications: It tries both to improve the study *and* to extend the results.

Since 1993, only four articles have been published in the replica-tion section of *Studies in Second Language Acquisition* (Leow, 1995; Muñoz, 1995; VanPatten and Oikkenon, 1996; Leow, 2000). In the current submission guidelines for *SSLA*, no mention is made of a spe-cific replication section, but the guidelines do state that the journal welcomes replications (http://assets.cambridge.org/SLA/SLA_ifc.pdf). At first glance, then, it would seem that the publication of replications, in *SSLA* at least, has ceased. As shown below, however, this is not the case.

More recently, *Language Teaching* published a lengthy commen-tary on replication, in part to encourage submissions to the replica-tion section of the journal (*Language Teaching* Review Panel, 2008). The panel responded to several issues about replication including the lack of replications, the advantages of different types of replications, difficulties in conducting replications (echoing Santos, 1989, and Polio and Gass, 1997), and the identification of studies and topics for replication.

I note here that not all researchers in applied linguistics agree on the importance of replication, and opposition to the relevance of replication in the field has been voiced, most notably by Block (1996), who rejected a positivist approach to SLA. He claimed that replication is done in an attempt to control extraneous variables and to generalize findings, but that controlling extraneous variables is not necessarily a desirable activity. I will assume that it is desirable and I agree with Gregg et al., who stated, "Extraneous variables are to be eliminated where possible, in science and elsewhere, precisely because they are extraneous" (1997: 545). In addition, I agree with Norris and Ortega, who suggested that "purposeful replication" (2006: 8) can be indicative of a field's maturity, and Porte (2010), who stated that replication is necessary to generalize results precisely because of the different contexts in which language learning occurs.

Finally, with the growing interest in meta-analysis, discussions of the relationship between meta-analysis and replication are increasing (e.g., Norris and Ortega, 2006; Oswald and Plonsky, 2010). Meta-analysis is addressed elsewhere in this volume, but we need to remember replications are essential for meta-analyses, and that meta-analyses themselves can and should be replicated (see Plonsky, Chapter 4, this volume).

2 Definitions of replication

In the *Language Teaching* commentary and in the Introduction to this book, three principal types of replications are mentioned: exact, approximate, and conceptual. Commentaries from other fields classify types of replications differently. Kelly et al. (1979), in examining studies in communication, defined four types of replications depending on whether the dependent variable, independent variable, both variables, or neither are changed. Hendrick (1990) proposed a complex classification related to whether contextual variables (such as participant characteristics and physical setting) or procedural characteristics (the independent variable) are changed. These three sets of definitions are provided in Table 2.1. What is clear is that agreement on the definitions does not exist. For example, *systematic replication* has a very specific meaning for Hendrick, who defined it as determining ranges for a procedural variable in which one would expect the same and different results, whereas the *Language Teaching* Review Panel defines it as the change of "one key variable" (2008: 3). Collins (2002) was the only researcher in the studies that I found who called her study a *systematic replication*, but according to Kelly et al. (1979), the two studies that she reports would be instrumental and constructive. The definitions of exact replications are fairly similar in that all agree that the treatment and measurement of variables remain exactly the same. The *Language Teaching* Review Panel pointed out that even participant characteristics need to be kept the same, while also admitting that it is usually impossible to do so. Yet, as shown below, studies that kept both the treatment and measurements the same, using a new population, were not found in my search. Thus, no exact replications were found, even with a more liberal definition of the term.

Table 2.1 Types of replications

Article	Type	Definition
Kelly, Chase, and Tucker (1979)	Literal	Both the manipulation (i.e., treatment, intervention, independent variable) and measurement of variables are kept the same.
	Operational	The manipulation is kept the same, but the dependent variables are measured differently, thus resulting in a different operationalization of a construct.
	Instrumental	The manipulation is changed but the measurement of the dependent variable stays the same.
	Constructive	Both the manipulation and the measurement of the dependent variable are changed.
Hendrick (1990)	Conceptual	This type of replication is "an attempt to convey the same crucial structure of information in the independent variables to the subjects" (p. 45) but with a change in "primary information focus" (p. 44) and possibly task variables.
	Partial	Changes to the procedural variables are made whereas other parts of the study are kept the same.
	Exact	The contextual variables are kept as close to the original as possible, and so are the procedural variables.
	Systematic	This type of replication involves a range of variation in the procedural variables to "bracket the original set of results" (p. 48).

(cont.)

Table 2.1 (continued)

Article	Type	Definition
Language Teaching Review Panel (2008)	Exact	Everything, including the subjects, is kept the same.
	Approximate or systematic	One "key variable (such as the learners' proficiency, L1 background, or learning context) is changed" (p. 3).
	Constructive or conceptual	This may involve changing the operationalization of a construct, the study design, or a "nonmajor" (p. 3) variable.

For the remainder of this chapter, I will use the terms provided in the Introduction to this volume but break down "approximate" into two categories, operational and instrumental, both proposed by Kelly et al. (1979) to allow for better contrast of the studies. Kelly et al. classified replications according to what has been changed: nothing (literal, the same as exact), operational (the measure of the dependent variable), instrumental (the manipulation of the independent variable), or both (constructive, the same as conceptual) and I will therefore use the terms exact, approximate/operational, approximate/instrumental, and conceptual.

Van der Veer, van IJzendoorn, and Valsiner (1994) pointed out that exact (or literal) and conceptual replications are two points on a continuum and not a dichotomy. The goals of a more exact replication are to confirm previous results whereas the goals of a more conceptual replication are to extend the generalizability of the results. Kelly et al. saw their four-part classification as a continuum from literal (to confirm results) to constructive (to extend results). Even using Kelly et al.'s relatively straightforward definition, however, the terms *same* and *different* are problematic and relative. Furthermore, Kelly et al.'s classification does not discuss contextual or participant variables. Given that it would be nearly impossible to maintain the exact same contextual (e.g., location and time of day) and participant variables in applied linguistics research, such a concern may not seem relevant. However, many of the replication studies identified in Table 2.2 are causal-comparative studies and thus the participant characteristics are the independent variables. Ultimately, what counts as a replication is less important than determining what type of replication is most beneficial to the field, and I return to this point in my conclusion.

3 Replication studies: Where are we now?

I approach this review in two ways. First, in an attempt to provide a picture of replication over the past 20 years, I examine studies that claim to be some type of replication. Second, I examine studies on a specific topic (written error correction) and discuss the extent to which they may be replications of other studies. This reverse approach is used because others (Neulip and Crandall, 1993) have stated that replications that are not called "replications" commonly appear in print. Written error correction, specifically, was chosen both because there is a large number of empirical studies on the topic and because of the controversy surrounding the topic.

3.1 Studies that claim to be some type of replication

I began by doing a search from 1990–2009 in six applied linguistics journals (*Applied Linguistics, Language Learning, The Modern Language Journal, Second Language Research, Studies in Second Language Acquisition, TESOL Quarterly,* and *Language Teaching*)[1] for any studies that included the word or a form of the word "replicate." This resulted in the 24 studies shown in Table 2.2. Note that although ten of the 24 studies are from *SSLA*, only four studies were in the replication section of the journal. *SSLA* had by far the greatest number of replication studies, which may be related to Valdman's (1993) commentary encouraging replication. Direct comparisons among journals, however, should not be made because some publish more qualitative research than others. In addition, other journals and edited volumes may include replications not reported here.

There were no exact replications, even using a liberal definition. In other words, something in the dependent and independent variables was always changed. I found it somewhat surprising that I found no studies in which only the population was changed, and the dependent and independent variables were kept the same. However, as mentioned above, causal-comparative studies (i.e., studies looking at group differences) are common and thus changing the participants would be the same as changing the independent variable. Furthermore, changing the population often necessitates a change in the instrument because of, for example, a different proficiency level or L1.

Table 2.2 Studies presented as a "replication"

Study	Study replicated*	Type claimed to be	Research question/ topic	What was changed	Type**	Same or different results	Comments
Studies in Second Language Acquisition							
Schneider and Connor (1990)	Connor and Schneider (1988)	Not stated.	Is there a relationship between raters' judgments of essays and type of topic progression?	Addition of a third group of essays with a different Test of Written English score. Controlled for length of essay.	Approximate/ instrumental?	Mixed.	Guidelines for coding given in the Appendix.
Edge (1991)	Eckman (1981)	Partial and extension.	How much production can be accounted for by Eckman's rules and how can speech not accounted for by Eckman's rules be explained?	Increased sample size. Different elicitation tasks. Inclusion of native speaker controls.	Approximate/ operational.	Mixed.	Participants were kept at a similar proficiency level.
Tyler and Bro (1993)	Tyler and Bro (1992)	Extension.	How do discourse miscues and order of ideas in a text affect comprehension?	Modality. Additional measure of comprehension.	Conceptual.	Same.	Also included reading time as a dependent variable.

Leow (1995)	Leow (1993)	Not stated.	What effect do simplification, type of linguistic feature, and proficiency level have on learners' intake?	Modality of input from written to aural for treatment.	Approximate/ instrumental.	Mixed.	In the replication section of *SSLA*.
Muñoz (1995)	Chaudron and Parker (1990)	Partial replication.	What is the effect of discourse and structural markedness on noun phrase use?	Addition of new discourse context (in materials). Different L1 group. Different modality.	Conceptual.	Different.	In the replication section of *SSLA*.
Juffs and Harrington (1995)	White and Juffs (1998)	Not stated.	Is there a difference between native English speakers and advanced Chinese learners of English on judgment tasks involving long-distance *wh*-extraction?	Slight change in stimulus.	Approximate/ operational.	Same.	Addition of another research question and condition. Note that the study replicated was listed as "in press" in Juffs and Harrington but appeared in print at a later date.

(cont.)

Table 2.2 (continued)

Study	Study replicated*	Type claimed to be	Research question/topic	What was changed	Type**	Same or different results	Comments
VanPatten and Oikkenon (1996)	VanPatten and Cadierno (1993)	Partial replication.	What is the effect of explicit information on processing instruction?	Addition and deletion of a treatment group.	Approximate/ instrumental.	Different treatment groups, so not comparable.	In the replication section of *SSLA*.
Wong (2001)	VanPatten (1990)	Partial replication.	Can learners pay attention to form and meaning in the aural and written modes?	Different population requiring a different treatment and instrument (but kept quite similar).	Conceptual?	Same for aural, different for written.	
Robinson (2005)	Reber, Walkenfeld, and Hernstadt (1991) Knowlton and Squire (1996)		What is the correlation between IQ and implicit and explicit learning in an artificial grammar? What is the relationship between chunk strength and grammaticality judgments?	Population more experienced language learners. Different L1.	Approximate/ instrumental.	Mixed.	

(cont.)

			What is the effect of individual differences in relation to chunk strength in learning? (Also added a question related to real language learning.)			
Barcroft and Sommers (2005)	Barcroft (2001)	Not stated.	Does acoustic variability affect vocabulary learning?	Additional measures of vocabulary learning. Different acoustic conditions.	Conceptual.	Mixed.
Henry, Culman, and VanPatten (2009)	Fernández (2008)	Conceptual.	What is the effect of explicit instruction on German L2 learners' processing of word order and object pronouns?	German instead of Spanish.	Approximate/ instrumental (as much as possible).	Different.

Table 2.2 (continued)

Study	Study replicated*	Type claimed to be	Research question/topic	What was changed	Type**	Same or different results	Comments
Applied Linguistics							
Tauroza and Allison (1990)	Pimsleur, Hancock, and Furey (1977)	Not stated.	What is an estimate of speech rates in British English?	A wider variety of speech contexts. Additional measure.	Conceptual.	Different.	
TESOL Quarterly							
Roller and Matambo (1992)	Carrell (1983)	Partial.	Will participants use context to improve comprehension? Will there be an interaction effect among familiarity, language, and use of context?	Different L1. Higher proficiency level.	Approximate/ instrumental.	Mixed.	Lee (1986) also replicated Carrell with a different population and with the recall in the L1.
Harley (2000)	Harley, Howard, and Hart (1995)		Does age affect whether learners pay more attention to prosodic or syntactic cues?	Learner L1 changed from Cantonese to Polish (tried to ensure comparability by keeping	Approximate/ instrumental (appears to be the same instrument).	Same.	

Bigelow, Delmas, Hansen, and Tarone (2006)			length of residence the same, but no group of grade 2 students).			
Philp (2003)	Partial replication.	Is a learner's ability to recall a recast related to the length of the recast and the number of changes made? (as in Philp) Is there an interaction with literacy level? (added)	Participants had two different literacy levels. Exact same task used but slight procedural differences: number and length of sessions.	Approximate/ instrumental.	Different.	Very small sample size.
Second Language Research						
Kanno (1996) Kellerman and Yoshioka (1999)	Not stated.	Is the empty category principle available to L2 learners?	Different L1 (Dutch learners of Japanese) in different environment. Some changes to stimulus.	Conceptual.	Different.	

(cont.)

Table 2.2 (continued)

Study	Study replicated*	Type claimed to be	Research question/topic	What was changed	Type**	Same or different results	Comments
Tremblay (2006)	Bruhn de Garavito (1999a, 1999b)	Partial replication.	Can L2 learners acquire the properties of Spanish reflexive passives and reflexive impersonals?	Participants were advanced (instead of near-natives). Some different test items. All participants learned Spanish in Canada (not abroad in different countries).	Conceptual.	Different.	
The Modern Language Journal							
Moeller and Reschke (1993)	Hahn, Stassen, and Reschke (1988)	Not stated.	What is the effect of grades on performance on an oral proficiency test?	Changes not specified except for larger sample size.	Unknown.	Same.	
Polio and Gass (1998)	Gass and Varonis (1994)	Not stated.	Does interaction lead to better comprehension of nonnative speakers by native speakers?	Similar population but more homogeneous with regard to proficiency.	Difficult to classify: procedural changes and minor changes in participants.	Different.	

(cont.)

				Some procedural changes: no nonverbal feedback in noninteraction dyads.		
Bateman (2002)	Robinson-Stuart and Nocon (1996)	Not stated.	What is the effect of student ethnographic interviews on students' attitudes toward Spanish and Spanish speakers?	Setting and participants. Questionnaires and treatment were changed somewhat.	Conceptual.	Same.
Jiang (2004)	Jiang (2002)	Not stated.	Is an L2 word mapped on to an L1 word in terms of semantic content? (semantic transfer hypothesis)	Different L1. More controlled materials (and necessity of changing materials because of population).	Conceptual.	Same.

Table 2.2 (Continued)

Study	Study replicated*	Type claimed to be	Research question/ topic	What was changed	Type**	Same or different results	Comments
Mullock (2006)	Gatbonton (2000)	Partial replication.	What is teachers' pedagogical knowledge base?	Different context: intact classes. Different stimulated recall procedure. Different setting.	Approximate/ instrumental (coding was the same).	Different.	The author refers to the study as a *qualitative* study.
Language Learning							
DeKeyser (2000)	Johnson and Newport (1989)	Not stated.	Is there a correlation between age of acquisition and ultimate attainment? Do adults who are successful learners have high verbal ability?	Different population. Changes in method: a few items deleted, changed or added.	Approximate/ instrumental?	Mixed.	Excellent explanation of minor changes to instrument.
Collins (2002)	Bardovi-Harlig and Reynolds (1995)	Systematic.	Is French ESL learners' use of tense/ aspect markers predicted by the aspect hypothesis?	Study 1: L1 of learners, same. Study 2: L1, instrument.	Study 1: Approximate/ instrumental. Study 2: Conceptual.	Mixed.	This study discusses its status as a replication.

Replication in published applied linguistics research   63

Schauer (2006)	Bardovi-Harlig and Dörnyei (1998)	Not stated.	Do EFL and ESL learners differ in their recognition and rating of pragmatic and grammatical errors? (added: Do ESL learners become more pragmatically aware when living in the target culture?)	Different L1 and country. Addition of interviews. Addition of a time variable (participants tested at beginning and end of stay).	Approximate/instrumental: population and thus independent variable differs, but same instrument used to measure dependent variable.	Same.
Language Teaching						
Crossley and McNamara (2008)	Crossley, Louwerse, McCarthy, and McNamara (2007)	Approximate.	How do authentic and simplified texts found in L2 materials differ with regard to a variety of features?	Larger sample size. Materials from a higher level of L2 textbooks directed at a more homogeneous audience.	Approximate/instrumental.	Mixed.

Table 2.2 (continued)

Study	Study replicated*	Type claimed to be	Research question/ topic	What was changed	Type**	Same or different results	Comments
Eckerth (2009)	Foster (1998)	Approximate.	What is the effect of task type and participant structure on the amount of talk, comprehensible input, and modified output?	Different L2. Some changes in procedure. Some changes in task. Addition of stimulated recall.	Approximate/ operational.	Mixed.	Discussed *why* the Foster study was chosen to replicate. Target study author invited to comment on outcomes.

*The studies listed in this column are included in the reference list as secondary citations only (i.e., I did always return to the original source).

**A question mark indicates that the type of replication is open to debate.

The most common types of replications were approximate/instrumental, where the measurement of the dependent variable was the same. In other words, the researchers were able to use the same instrument for measuring the dependent variable. This would include both elicitation device and the scoring procedure. So, for example, Collins (2002) used almost exactly the same elicitation and scoring procedure as Bardovi-Harlig and Reynolds (1995) in the first study reported in her article. DeKeyser (2000), in replicating Johnson and Newport (1989), wanted to replicate their study using a different population. He made some changes in the test used for grammatical judgments by making the test shorter and changing and adding a few items. I have classified this study as an approximate/instrumental replication despite small changes to the instrument because the elicitation method and most of the sentences were the same. What is particularly helpful in the DeKeyser study is his comparison of the two instruments, provided in the appendix of his article.

It is noteworthy that the DeKeyser (2000) replication and some of the others are a way for researchers to, in a sense, methodologically clean up other studies by eliminating small problems in a study's design. A similar example is Jiang (2004), who, in replicating his own work (Jiang, 2002), improved the materials in his lexical study by controlling for word length and frequency. His study, however, used a new population with a different L1, thus requiring new materials and making his study a conceptual replication.

Another study that attempted to improve an experimental design through replication was Polio and Gass (1998). They were interested in the fact that Gass and Varonis (1994) found no effect for interaction on native speakers' comprehension of nonnative speakers. The nonnative speakers in the Gass and Varonis study, who were from a variety of proficiency levels, had to describe the placement of objects on a board to native speakers under two conditions, with and without interaction with the native speaker. Polio and Gass differed from Gass and Varonis in that they used a similar but more homogeneous population to reduce variation. Furthermore, through the use of a physical divider, the participants were seated so that they could not see each other, thus ensuring no nonverbal interaction in the non-interaction group. They also increased the number of objects discussed by the dyads (when describing the placement of objects on a board) and increased the sample size. Essentially, a similar population and task was used with these minor changes, but the study is difficult to classify with regard to type of replication. In other words, the same instrument was used, but the number of objects being described was increased. It comes close to being an exact replication in that the major variables were operationalized in the same way, but the sample size and procedures were changed. In the end, the study did find, contrary to Gass and Varonis, that interaction improved the comprehension of nonnative speakers for native speakers, so the small improvements had an effect, and too much variability in Gass and Varonis may have masked group differences.

During my search for replication studies, I found several articles that included more than one study, one of which was a replication of another study in the same article including Bongaerts et al. (1997), Kroll et al. (2002), and Sachs and Polio (2007). In Kroll et al., a surprising result was found, namely that low-proficiency L2 learners were slower than more proficient L2 learners in a word-naming task in their L1. Thus, they replicated the study using groups who had a greater differential in proficiency than in the first study. Sachs and Polio also reported on two studies of written error correction. In their case, they noted flaws in their first study that led to a new study using a different design (i.e., they went from a repeated measures study to a nonrepeated measures study). Certainly, replicating one's own study because of surprising results or possible design flaws is beneficial to the field and should be encouraged, a point made by the *Language Teaching* Review Panel (2008). Furthermore, publishing more than one study within an article allows readers to more closely consider the evolution of a study while also highlighting design problems of the replicated study. The realities of article length limitations, however, can make reporting on two studies in sufficient detail impossible, especially when authors are encouraged to fully report their design. Journal editors, I would hope, can allow for longer articles when more than one study is reported.

A surprising result or a design flaw (including controlling for extraneous variables as mentioned earlier) are two such reasons to replicate a study. Indeed, as mentioned earlier, a desire to improve on a study's design, because of an internal validity problem, or because the researcher wants to use a more reliable or valid measure, seemed to be one motivation for replicating a study. Also, extending the results to a new population, an external validity issue, was another reason to replicate a study, using an approximate/instrumental or conceptual replication. For example, Bigelow et al. (2006) replicated Philp's (2003) study of recasts, using participants of varying literacy levels. What is impressive is that they tried to keep the task variables the same despite a very different population. They did, however, have to change some of the procedural variables, namely the timing and length of the sessions. Nevertheless, a study such as theirs was successful in pushing the field toward a deeper understanding of factors affecting feedback.

The studies discussed here were included because they used some form of the word "replicate" in the text. Some of the studies even referred to what type of replications they were, with the most common type being called "partial," a term not defined by Kelly et al. (1979) or the *Language Teaching* Review Panel (2008). Nor do the uses coincide with Hendrick's (1990) definition of "partial." Rather, the authors seem to mean simply that the study is not an exact replication. Collins is the only researcher who discusses what type of replication her study is. She says that her study is a "systematic" (2002: 50) replication, but according to the Kelly et al. classification system, one of her studies would be an approximate/instrumental replication and the other, conceptual. In the end, the important issue is whether or not certain types of replications are more beneficial to the field than others. If we engage in replication to confirm or disconfirm the hypotheses of earlier studies, changing only one variable will better help us understand where there is a difference from the earlier study if one is found (hence an approximate/instrumental or an approximate/operational replication). When both variables are changed, it is more difficult to isolate the source of the difference, but because of the nature of social science research (i.e., changing one variable necessitates changing another), this is often unavoidable.

Another consideration in replication is the choice to replicate a study with statistically significant or nonsignificant findings (controversies related to significance testing notwithstanding, e.g., Cohen, 1994; Nassaji, Chapter 3, this volume). For example, a study that had no statistically significant findings but was then replicated and found to have such significant findings, perhaps because of a more sensitive measure, would be extremely important if only the measure was changed. When too much is changed, the source of difference may be unknown. One interesting replication of a nonsignificant finding is Barcroft and Sommers (2005), who examined the effect of acoustic variability on vocabulary learning. They replicated Barcroft (2001), who found no effect of acoustic variability on vocabulary learning. Although somewhat risky, they changed the independent variable, by increasing the acoustic variability, as well as the dependent variable, by adding another measure. Because they still found no statistically significant differences, the results strengthened the original findings. The risk was, however, that had they found a difference, it would not be clear as to whether the source of the difference was the independent or the dependent variable. Note, however, that they conducted two other studies, reported in the same article, with a further increase in acoustic variability, and that they did find an effect on vocabulary learning. Barcroft and Sommers is a particularly good example of how replication can clarify a finding, despite the fact it might have been better to have changed only one variable in their first experiment. I return to this issue of replicating studies with statistically significant versus nonsignificant findings below in my discussion of written error correction.

With regard to what types of studies have been replicated, the only discernable trend from Table 2.2 is that more studies focusing on SLA and using psycholinguistics research methods have been replicated, as opposed to studies focusing on discourse or pedagogy, for example. This is not surprising given that such studies are more controlled than studies done in other areas of applied linguistics. Thus, small changes, allowing the studies to be called "replications," can be made.

Some studies that did not use psycholinguistic research methods are Schauer (2006), who studied pragmatics; Mullock (2006), who conducted classroom research; and Bigelow et al. (2006) and Polio and Gass (1997), who studied interaction. Certain types of classroom research should certainly be amenable to replication (e.g., Loewen, 2005) and indeed would be important to extend the external validity of the studies. Thus, I now reverse the inquiry by examining studies of written error correction.

3.2 Studies of written error correction

As mentioned above, I have chosen to look at the area of written error correction with regard to replication both because there has been a substantial body of research conducted on the topic and because the area is so controversial. Despite the many empirical studies, there remains widespread disagreement (e.g., Truscott and Hsu, 2008) about the usefulness of written error correction in L2 learning, which began with the publication of Truscott's (1996) argument against the effectiveness of written error correction. None of the studies in Table 2.2 dealt with written error correction, which could simply be related to the journals that I chose to search, but I would like to look more closely at the written error correction studies to see if any of them are replications and to speculate on how the issue might benefit from replication in the future.

I have divided the studies into three groups chronologically: before 1996, 1996–2006, and 2007–present. The studies in group one were cited by Truscott (1996), those in group two were included in his meta-analysis (2007), and those in group three were identified through a literature search. In some ways, 1997 was a turning point because research on written error correction exploded after the publication of Truscott's (1996) article. In addition, in 1997, Polio and Gass called for better reporting of research methods. Polio (1997) lamented the lack of detail and reliability in reporting measures of linguistic accuracy. In 1998, Wolfe-Quintero et al. (1998) was published and also addressed measures of accuracy, as well as complexity and fluency, in L2 writing. One would hope that the publication of these four pieces would have resulted in more rigorous research.

In studies of written error correction, the independent variable, the correction, can be operationalized in a variety ways (see Ellis, 2009, for a summary), mostly related to the type of feedback (e.g., underlining or actual correction) and the amount (e.g., focused on specific errors or provided on all errors), but the definitions are not controversial, as there are indeed different ways to correct errors, and for the most part, they are well defined in the studies. If studies use the same methods of error correction, but with different populations or different measures of language improvement, can we say that they are some type of replications of one another? All the studies in Table 2.3 have the same general question regarding the effectiveness of written error correction but vary with regard to how they operationalize correction (including the type, length, and focus of the treatment) and how they operationalize language improvement (including varying measures of accuracy and whether or not other constructs, such as fluency and complexity, are considered). In addition to different populations, the studies use different prompts for the pre-test, treatments, and post-tests. In Table 2.3, I have included the authors' research questions, the context, the operationalization of the independent variable (i.e., some form of feedback), the operationalization of the dependent variable (i.e., some measure of language improvement), the reliability of the dependent variable, and my assessment of whether or not there is enough information to replicate the study.

Beginning with the last two issues, reliability and amount of information, the situation has improved somewhat. Only two out of ten studies (Fazio, 2001, and Ferris, 2006) completed after 1997 do not report any reliability, whereas only two out of six before 1998 did. Some of the studies reporting reliability, however, calculated only intrarater reliability (e.g., Ellis et al., 2008, and Truscott and Hsu, 2008) and some reported that only a portion of the data was coded by more than one rater (e.g., Sheen, 2007). Although achieving acceptable intrarater reliability should reduce one source of error, it is not as beneficial as achieving interrater reliability, which could show that the results are at least generalizable to other researchers' assessments of writing. In my opinion, any study reporting only intrarater reliability, as well as any study reporting none, would be good candidates for replication.

Table 2.3 *Studies of written error correction*

Study	Research question(s) (only those in the study related to written error correction)	Context	Independent variable	Dependent variable	Interrater reliability of dependent variable(s)	Enough information to replicate?
Before 1996						
Lalande (1982)	What is the effect of coding errors vs. correction of error on accuracy?	60 intermediate German students at a U.S. university divided by intact classes into two treatment groups.	Type of feedback: error correction of all errors with required revision vs. error coding with required revision. Feedback given on three essays over the course of a semester.	Accuracy: number and type of errors.	None reported.	Error coding system for feedback and calculating accuracy included. Topics for writing not provided.
Semke (1984)	Does correcting errors on students' freewriting assignments improve students' accuracy and fluency?	141 first-year German students at a U.S. university divided by intact classes into one of four treatment groups.	Type of feedback: comments only; corrections only; corrections with comments; student correction. Feedback given on weekly journal assignments over ten weeks.	General proficiency: cloze test. Accuracy: ratio of errors per words. Fluency: number of words produced in ten minutes.	None reported.	The study design is described well, but the measure of accuracy is not. Reader is referred to Brière (1966). Test instructions provided.

Robb, Ross, and Shortreed (1986)	What is the effect of direct versus indirect feedback?	134 Japanese college freshmen EFL students divided by intact classes into four groups.	Type of feedback: corrected, coded, highlighted, number of errors noted in margin. Feedback given on weekly essays over about seven months.	19 measures collapsed through a factor analysis into accuracy, complexity, and fluency. Five narrative compositions written over the academic year.	Average of .87 on objective measures and .81 on holistics. Individual reliabilities not given (based on five sets of essays).	No details on coding of errors for treatment. Few details on what types of errors were corrected. No guidelines for calculating accuracy measure given. Assessment topics not given.
Kepner (1991)	What is the effect of error versus content feedback?	60 Spanish L2 students at a second-year university level divided into low and high verbal ability (based on English) randomly assigned to feedback group.	Surface-level error correction (with rules) vs. message-related feedback given on eight journal entries during the semester.	Higher-level propositions and surface-level errors.	.92 on propositions and .97 on errors.	No guidelines or examples of feedback given. No details on writing assignments. Reader is referred to Quellmalz (1985, 1987) and Brière (1966) for coding of propositions and errors, respectively.

(cont.)

Table 2.3 (continued)

Study	Research question(s) (only those in the study related to written error correction)	Context	Independent variable	Dependent variable	Interrater reliability of dependent variable(s)	Enough information to replicate?
Sheppard (1992)	What is the effect of error versus content feedback?	26 upper-intermediate ESL students divided by intact classes with the same instructor and course content.	Feedback on seven essays over the semester with revisions required. No information on treatment given.	Accuracy: percentage of correct verb forms (person, tense, number, aspect); percentage of correct sentence boundaries (periods, semi-colons, question marks). Complexity: dependent clauses per sentence.	None reported.	Topics for assessment and treatment essays unknown. No details on treatment given.

Study	Research question	Participants	Type of feedback/treatment	Measures	Reliability	Assessment
Frantzen (1995)	Does supplementing a content course with grammar exposure (i.e., grammar reviews and error correction) result in language improvements?	44 second-year university Spanish students divided by intact classes with same instructors.	Type of feedback and class review: experimental group had grammar reviews on 11 different topics. Feedback on two essays during the semester: either circling/underlining or correction; revision required.	Same topic for pre- and post-test on a personal experience. Grammatical accuracy on several categories of errors errors/obligatory contexts. Fluency: length; type/token ratio and others.	None reported.	Assessment essay topic provided in full. Topics for grammar review provided. List of measures provided without any guidelines. No information on feedback guidelines.
1998–2007 Polio, Fleck, and Leder (1998)	Does feedback on grammar and editing instruction improve students' accuracy in writing?	65 U.S. university EAP students randomly divided into two groups.	Type of feedback and grammar/editing instruction: feedback given to the experimental group on 14 journal entries; revision of seven required; grammar review of six different topics. Control group wrote 28 entries with no feedback.	Accuracy: error-free T-units (EFT)/total T-units (TT) and words in EFT over total words on narrative essays.	Between .83 and .91 for EFT/TT (depending on coders) and .80 and .85 for words in error-free T-units (WEFT)/total words (TW).	Topics for assessment essays given. Instructional materials not provided. No guidelines for feedback. Extensive guidelines for calculating accuracy measures (with readers also referred to Polio, 1997).

(cont.)

Table 2.3 (continued)

Study	Research question(s) (only those in the study related to written error correction)	Context	Independent variable	Dependent variable	Interrater reliability of dependent variable(s)	Enough information to replicate?
Fazio (2001)	What is the effect of content-based feedback, form-focused feedback, and a combination on accuracy in journal writing?	112 fifth-grade French as a second language classrooms in Montreal randomly assigned to groups.	Type of feedback: content-based (statement and questions); form-focused (all errors underlined and correct form given); both. No revision required, but students were told to review feedback. Students wrote journal entries on any topic they wished. Students wrote at least one entry a week of varying length over the course of three and a half months.	Accuracy: number of errors in "grammatical spelling as a function of the total number of occurrences of the structure" (p. 242) calculated on five entries throughout the time period.	None reported.	No guidelines for coding or feedback given.

Chandler (2003)	Does error correction improve accuracy in student writing?	31 music students in a high-intermediate ESL class divided into two groups by intact classes.	The experimental group had their errors underlined and had to revise them. The control group did not. Five autobiographical essays written over the semester.	Accuracy: number of errors per 100 words. Fluency: minutes per 100 words.	76% on error identification.	Topics given. Examples of errors on which feedback was given and used for calculating accuracy.
Bitchener, Young, and Cameron (2005)	Does the type of corrective feedback improve accuracy on new pieces of writing?	53 post-intermediate ESL students in Australia divided into three groups by intact classes.	Type of feedback: feedback on content and organization; direct correction; direct correction plus 5-minute conference. Limited to simple past, articles, and prepositions. On four letters on various topics.	Accuracy: percentage of correct uses each of prepositions, articles, and simple past in obligatory contexts.	94% agreement rate for error identification and categorization.	Sample writing task (for feedback and for final assessment) provided. A sample essay with feedback provided.
Ferris (2006)	Does written error correction help students improve their writing in the short and long term?	92 ESL undergraduates.	A variety of feedback types based on teacher marking strategy on four second-drafts throughout the semester.	Type of change made by student.	None reported.	This study is more descriptive than experimental, but was included in Truscott (2007).

(cont.)

Table 2.3 (continued)

Study	Research question(s) (only those in the study related to written error correction)	Context	Independent variable	Dependent variable	Interrater reliability of dependent variable(s)	Enough information to replicate?
2007–present						
Sheen (2007)	Does focused written corrective feedback affect learners' acquisition of English articles? Is there any difference for the effect of direct correction with and without metalinguistic feedback?	111 ESL communication college students divided into three groups by intact classes.	Type of feedback: none; direct correction (provision of correct form); direct metalinguistic correction (provision of correct form with metalinguistic comment) on articles only (with "a few errors other than those involving articles" p. 264). Two treatment sessions on the rewriting of two stories that students had copied and heard.	Accuracy on a picture description based on a series of pictures. Coded using Pica's (1983) target-like use calculation.	Second researcher coded 25% of data and on the three tests (pre, post, delayed) with between 78.4% and 83.3% reliability.	Treatment narratives provided. Method of feedback described. Pictures not provided for pre- and post-test. Very detailed guidelines on coding errors.

Bitchener (2008)	What is the effect of different types of feedback on English article use?	75 low-intermediate level students studying at a private language school in New Zealand divided by intact classes into four groups.	Direct feedback plus oral and written metalinguistic explanation; direct feedback and written metalinguistic explanation; direct feedback; no feedback on two narrative describing pictures.	Accuracy: suppliance in obligatory context on narratives describing a series of pictures, the same used for treatment.	91%	Treatment described clearly with examples. Picture for assessment described but not provided.
Ellis, Sheen, Murakima, and Takashima (2008)	Does written error correction lead to more accurate use of articles? Is there a difference between unfocused and focused written error correction?	49 students divided by intact classes into three groups. Intermediate students studying general English at a Japanese university.	Focused correction (first- and second-mention articles); unfocused (on a variety of errors); Control: no feedback on narrative treatment as in Sheen (2007).	Suppliance in obligatory context on a narrative describing a series of pictures.	.97 intrarater reliability on portion of data.	Treatment described in detail with one story provided in Appendix. Coding of articles straightforward. Examples of feedback given Picture not provided for pre- and post-tests.

(cont.)

Table 2.3 (continued)

Study	Research question(s) (only those in the study related to written error correction)	Context	Independent variable	Dependent variable	Interrater reliability of dependent variable(s)	Enough information to replicate?
Truscott and Hsu (2008)	Does feedback have an effect on short-term and subsequently delayed writing?	47 EFL graduate students at a university in Taiwan in three classes. Equivalent experimental and control groups were formed based on test scores.	Underlining of error vs. feedback on a narrative describing a series of pictures.	Accuracy: number of errors. Writing 1: original essay while looking at feedback. Writing 2: a new narrative also based on a series of pictures.	.967 intrarater reliability only.	Samples of student writing provided, but not the writing prompt. Both series used for the pictures is described. Description of which errors were and were not marked given.

| Hartshorn et al. (2010) | What is the effect of dynamic corrective feedback on students' writing? | 47 students divided into two groups by intact classes Advanced-low to advanced-mid ESL students studying at university language center. | Feedback on ten-minute essays written nearly every class day for 15 weeks on a variety of topics. Feedback using coded symbols and students were required to revise until all errors were corrected. | Accuracy: EFT/TT; Rhetorical competence: a modified TOEFL iBT rubric. Fluency: number of words per 30 minutes. Complexity: average number of words per t-unit. Students wrote two opinion essays. | EFT/TT: .97 Not reported for fluency or words per t-unit. Rhetorical competence: See discussion in article. | Rubric for rhetorical competence provided in Appendix. Error feedback list provided. No guidelines on accuracy or complexity. Topics written about during treatment not given, but pre- and post-test topics given. |

Reporting interrater reliability on only a portion of the data is still somewhat problematic (see Polio, 1997) but understandable given logistic constraints. Nevertheless, it makes replication even more necessary, particularly when nonsignificant results are found. Errors in measurement do not necessarily render statistically significant results invalid, but they could certainly hide otherwise significant differences.

In evaluating the quality of the research on written error correction, we also need to consider the amount of information provided. Porte, in his book on appraising research, states that readers need "continually to consider the degree to which the study as described could reasonably be repeated by another researcher in the same or a different context" (Porte, 2010: 65). In reviewing the 16 studies on error correction, I would argue that none included enough detailed information on the treatment, the writing prompts, and the measure to conduct an exact replication in a different setting with a new population. Furthermore, the studies varied in what they reported, with some providing treatment guidelines and examples (Bitchener et al., 2005), some providing detailed guidelines for assessing accuracy (Polio et al., 1998), and some providing the exact prompts (Chandler, 2003). All of these details are necessary for replication, and an added benefit of calculating interrater over intrarater reliability is that more detailed guidelines need to be established so others can follow them. That said, journals often have space limitations and potential replicators can certainly contact the authors for more details about their studies.

Looking more closely at the independent and dependent variables, we can consider if any of these studies are replications of one another. All the studies examined written error correction, albeit with different operationalizations, and all assess learners' writing improvement, albeit using different methods. So can they all be called conceptual replications of each other? If they were, we might expect that after so many studies, we might be able to form clear conclusions about the role of written error correction, but I believe that we cannot. The source of the problem is fourfold. First, several of the studies have design flaws such that a more exact replication would be pointless. Second, there are major design differences regarding what piece of writing is examined (i.e., a revision of something already written or a brand-new text). Third, differences regarding what constitutes writing improvement exist (i.e., some studies examine only accuracy whereas others include a variety of measures). Fourth, as mentioned earlier, differences in the treatment (error correction) and length of the treatment exist as well. Each of these points is addressed with regard to replication.

Studies showing statistically significant results with internal validity problems are good candidates for replication, with, of course, the flaws corrected. For example, two studies purportedly demonstrating the effectiveness of error correction had design problems that could have caused an improvement in writing to be attributable to other factors. Chandler's (2003) experimental group, receiving direct correction, actually wrote twice as much as the control group. In Bitchener et al. (2005), the group receiving correction and conferencing attended class more often than the other participants. It might be helpful to replicate both of these studies correcting these problems so as to avoid speculation as to why these studies found a benefit for error correction but others did not.

Some studies examined the effect of error correction on a revised piece of writing, whereas others examined the effect of error correction on a new piece of writing. Such different types of studies are without a doubt not comparable, a point emphasized by Truscott and Hsu (2008), particularly if students are allowed to look at the feedback, as in Fathman and Whalley (1990). Note that any studies where students were able to look at their corrections while revising were not included in Table 2.3 because I felt that they did not really address the issue of the effectiveness of written error correction since students could simply copy the corrections. Truscott (1996; Truscott and Hsu, 2008) believes this as well, but nevertheless chose to do what might be called a replication of Fathman and Whalley (1990) in Truscott and Hsu (2008). He conducted a study in which students received feedback and wrote essays similar to those in Fathman and Whalley, but he also examined the students' errors on new narratives. They found, as in the Fathman and Whalley study, that students' writing improved in the short term, but that there were no long-term effects. The point that Truscott and Hsu were trying to make in their study was that there was no evidence that short-term improvements would lead to long-term improvements, and that studies of short-term changes did nothing to move forward the field of written error correction. And although a replication of Fathman and Whalley did not add to the evidence for or against written error correction, Truscott and Hsu's point was well made.

Another problem making the studies difficult to compare is related to what constitutes measures of writing improvement. Certainly, different accuracy measures can result in different findings (Polio, 1997), but also, some studies measure only accuracy whereas others also examine complexity and fluency. I agree fully with Truscott (1996) that an improvement in accuracy alone does not constitute writing improvement. Students can focus so much on errors that their writing becomes less sophisticated in other areas. Thus, to appropriately assess improvement, complexity and fluency, at the very least, need to be studied, but most studies do not measure all constructs. One exception is Robb, Ross, and Shortreed (1986), who used many different measures of fluency, accuracy, and complexity. In what appears to be a well-designed study, they did not find differences among error treatment groups in most measures. On one hand, this study seems like an excellent candidate for a closer replication as it was well designed and widely cited, and we can only speculate as to why, as far as I know, it has not been replicated. My guess is that such a study is a huge undertaking that might not prove very rewarding if no statistically significant results were found. A study that did find such results for error correction is Sheen (2007), but this study assessed only accuracy. This study could be replicated keeping everything the same but adding measures of complexity and fluency to assess the writing. If improvements in all areas were found, or even an improvement in accuracy with other areas of writing remaining the same, then we could make a much stronger argument for the effectiveness of written error correction.

Finally, differences in the treatment and length of the treatment make it difficult to compare studies and to argue that any of the studies are replications of each other unless written error correction is defined broadly. But consider three similar studies that examined the correction of English articles in writing: Sheen (2007), Bitchener (2008) and Ellis et al. (2008). Sheen included three conditions: no feedback, direct correction (provision of correct form), and direct metalinguistic correction (provision of correct form with metalinguistic comment). Bitchener had four groups: direct feedback plus oral and written metalinguistic explanation; direct feedback and written metalinguistic explanation; direct feedback; and no feedback. Finally, Ellis et al. had three somewhat different groups: focused correction (on first- and second-mention articles); unfocused correction (on a variety of errors); and no feedback. Yet even these three studies, which were more similar to one another than others in Table 2.3, differed not only with regard to population but also in how they assessed accuracy. Bitchener and Ellis et al. used a suppliance in obligatory context measure whereas Sheen used target-like use (see Pica, 1983, for a discussion of these measures). Ellis et al. and Sheen used a similar treatment in that they had students reproduce narratives that they had read to elicit articles that were then corrected, whereas Bitchener did not do this. In addition, Sheen and Ellis et al. included an indirect measure (i.e., not a writing test) of accuracy. All three studies showed that some type of error correction on articles was effective. Given the similarities of the studies, it may be safe to conclude that correction of articles in some form does lead to more accurate use of articles, and this may be of some interest to students who lament about their article errors. For those involved in the written error correction debate, however, even these robust findings may be of limited consequence. An improvement on articles reveals little about the rest of the participants' writing, which easily could have suffered because of a focus on only articles (for a full discussion, see Xu, 2009). Thus, in this case, we have a fairly clear finding but it does not rectify the lack of consensus in the written error correction debate.

Finally, of all the studies in Table 2.3, the recent Hartshorn et al. (2010) seems to be the best designed study showing a positive effect for written error correction in that no flaws are immediately evident and in that they considered a variety of measures when assessing improvement in writing. This study would be an excellent candidate for replication. If the same results were found with another population, then I would finally feel confident in saying that at least one type of written error correction is effective.

4 Where do we go from here?

I return to Santos's statement:

> Research is an accretive process; it is the accumulation and consolidation of knowledge over time. Replication of research confirms or calls into question existing findings; without it, a discipline consists of scattered hypotheses and insufficiently substantiated generalizations.
>
> (Santos, 1989: 700)

With regard to written error correction, the research is fairly scattered and has not benefited from replication. Only by replicating the well-designed studies and cleaning up some of the flawed studies will there ever be convincing findings on their effectiveness. It may be that only when we try to replicate a study can we truly assess it. In the studies of written error correction, I found no *purposeful* replications, and this is certainly a problem that should be rectified. As stated above, both the Robb et al. (1986) and the Hartshorn et al. (2010) studies were well designed, yet the former had nonsignificant and the latter statistically significant results. These findings are not necessarily contradictory as they had very different treatment methods. I return to a question asked earlier: Is it better to replicate studies with statistically significant or nonsignificant findings? It takes only one study with such significant findings to negate studies with nonsignificant findings as they may have contained a flaw, such as a weak treatment or unreliable measure. Furthermore, several studies with nonsignificant results do not prove a lack of effect (e.g., for written error correction) because it is impossible to prove that something does not exist. However, although it may be more difficult to get nonsignificant results published, a large number of well-designed studies show the lack of effect for a practice such as error correction – that is, the status quo lends some support for arguing against its effectiveness. Alternatively, if one were to replicate Hartshorn et al. (2010) and find no effect, say with a new population, one might be able to question the treatment's effectiveness in a new context. Thus, I do not think that replicating one type of study over the other is preferable. What matters is the replication is well designed and improves flaws related to internal validity in the original study. Note that only four of the 16 error correction studies used random assignment when many could have, and this would be one design problem that could be rectified.

With regard to the type of replication that is most beneficial, I would argue that the two types of approximate replications (instrumental and operational) are the most useful, as well as exact replications that study a different population, so as to increase the external validity of a study. When too much is changed, it is difficult to reconcile the source of any differences among studies, as is the case with written error correction studies. Finally, as mentioned above, much, but not all, of the replicated research is psycholinguistic research, perhaps because such research strives to control variables and perhaps because replication is encouraged in that area. Some researchers have argued that laboratory research has no ecological validity (see Gass et al., 2005, for a discussion of this issue). We need to consider the importance of replicating laboratory studies in the classroom as well as replicating classroom research itself.

For the former, any of the laboratory studies on interaction would be good candidates to replicate in a classroom. Indeed, Gass et al. (2005) repeated a laboratory interaction study in a classroom and found the same results. Other laboratory studies using treatments that could be differentially administered to a control and an experimental group in one class would be excellent candidates as well. For the latter, experimental classroom research administering different treatments to different classrooms (e.g., Collins et al., 1999) could be replicated in new contexts. Much classroom research is descriptive (e.g., Lyster and Ranta, 1997; Zyzik and Polio, 2008) and some does not include a control group (e.g., Rodgers, 2006). Nevertheless, repeating such descriptive research in new settings would definitely strengthen the conclusions of those studies showing that the results were not idiosyncratic to one university or one program.

To return to the example of written error correction, the debate regarding its effectiveness has raged on since 1996 with little benefit from replication. If there is a lesson to be learned from this research[2], it is that well-designed replications in all areas of applied linguistics should be encouraged so that we do not end up with contradictory results from poorly designed studies.

Notes

1   These journals were chosen because they are widely read journals in the field. In addition, *SSLA* and *Language Teaching* have dedicated strands for replication studies.

2   Another possible problem with the research on written error correction is that, with the exception of Hartshorn et al. (2010), it is not theoretically motivated, but such discussion is beyond the scope of this chapter.

References

Barcroft, J. (2001). Acoustic variation and lexical acquisition, *Language Learning*, **51**, 563–90.

Barcroft, J. and Sommers, M. S. (2005). Effects of acoustic variability on second language vocabulary learning, *Studies in Second Language Acquisition*, **27**, 387–414.

Bardovi-Harlig, K. and Dörnyei, Z. (1998). Do language learners recognize pragmatic violations? Pragmatic vs. grammatical awareness in instructed L2 learning, *TESOL Quarterly*, **32**, 233–59.

Bardovi-Harlig, K. and Reynolds, D. (1995). The role of lexical aspect in the acquisition of tense and aspect, *TESOL Quarterly*, **29**, 107–31.

Bateman, B. E. (2002). Promoting openness toward culture learning: Ethnographic interviews for students of Spanish, *The Modern Language Journal*, **86**, 318–31.

Bigelow, M., Delmas, R., Hansen, K. and Tarone, E. (2006). Literacy and the processing of oral recasts in SLA, *TESOL Quarterly*, **40**, 665–89.

Bitchener, J. (2008). Evidence in support of written corrective feedback, *Journal of Second Language Writing*, **17**, 102–18.

Bitchener, J., Young, S. and Cameron, D. (2005). The effect of different types of corrective feedback on ESL student writing, *Journal of Second Language Writing*, **14**, 191–205.

Block, D. (1996). Not so fast: Some thoughts on theory culling, relativism, accepted findings and the heart and soul of SLA, *Applied Linguistics*, **17**, 63–83.

Bongaerts, T., Van Summeren, C., Planken, B. and Schils, E. (1997). Age and ultimate attainment in the pronunciation of a foreign language, *Studies in Second Language Acquisition*, **19**, 447–65.

Brière, E. (1966). Quantity before quality in second language composition, *Language Learning*, **16**, 141–51.

Bruhn de Garavito, J. L. S. (1999a). The *se* construction in Spanish and near-native competence, *Spanish Applied Linguistics*, **3**, 247–95.

Bruhn de Garavito, J. L. S. (1999b). The Syntax of Spanish Multifunctional Clitics and Near-native Competence. Unpublished PhD dissertation, McGill University, Montreal, Canada.

Carrell, P. (1983). Three components of background knowledge in reading comprehension, *Language Learning*, **33**, 183–205.

Chandler, J. (2003). The efficacy of various kinds of error feedback for improvement in the accuracy and fluency of L2 student writing, *Journal of Second Language Writing*, **12**, 267–96.

Chaudron, C. and Parker, K. (1990). Discourse markedness and structural markedness: The acquisition of English noun phrases, *Studies in Second Language Acquisition*, **12**, 43–64.

Cohen, J. (1994). The earth is round (p < .05), *American Psychologist*, **49**, 997–1003.

Collins, L. (2002). The roles of L1 influence and lexical aspect in the acquisition of temporal morphology, *Language Learning*, **52**, 43–94.

Collins, L., Halter, R., Lightbown, P. and Spada, N. (1999). Time and the distribution of time in L2 learning, *TESOL Quarterly*, **33**, 655–80.

Connor, U. and Schneider, M. (March 1988). Topical Structure and Writing Quality: Results of an ESL Study. Paper presented at the 22nd Annual TESOL Convention, Chicago, IL.

Crossley, S., Louwerse, M., McCarthy, P. and McNamara, D. (2007). A linguistic analysis of simplified and authentic texts, *The Modern Language Journal*, **91**, 15–30.

Crossley, S. and McNamara, D. (2008). Assessing L2 reading texts at the intermediate level: An approximate replication of Crossley, Louwerse, McCarthy and McNamara (2007), *Language Teaching*, **41**, 409–29.

DeKeyser, R. M. (2000). The robustness of critical period effects in second language acquisition, *Studies in Second Language Acquisition*, **22**, 499–533.

Eckerth, J. (2009). Negotiated interaction in the L2 classroom, *Language Teaching*, **42**, 109–30.

Eckman, F. (1981). On predicting phonological difficulty in second language acquisition, *Studies in Second Language Acquisition*, **4**, 18–30.

Edge, B. A. (1991). The production of word-final voiced obstruents in English by L1 speakers of Japanese and Cantonese, *Studies in Second Language Acquisition*, **13**, 377–93.

Ellis, R. (2009). A typology of written corrective feedback types, *English Language Teaching Journal*, **63**, 97–107.

Ellis, R., Sheen, Y., Murakima, M. and Takashima, H. (2008). The effects of focused and unfocused written corrective feedback in an English as a foreign language context, *System,* **36**, 353–71.

Fathman, A. and Whalley, E. (1990). Teacher response to student writing: Focus on form vs. content, in Kroll, B. (ed.), *Second Language Writing: Research Insights for the Classroom*, Cambridge: Cambridge University Press, pp. 178–90.

Fazio, L. (2001). The effect of corrections and commentaries on the journal writing accuracy of minority- and and majority-language students, *Journal of Second Language Writing*, **10**, 235–49.

Fernández, C. (2008). Reexamining the role of explicit information in processing instruction, *Studies in Second Language Acquisition*, **30**, 277–305.

Ferris, D. (2006). Does error feedback help student writers? New evidence on the short- and long-term effects of written error correction, in Hyland, K. and Hyland, F. (eds.), *Feedback in Second Language Writing: Contexts and Issues*, Cambridge: Cambridge University Press, pp. 81–104.

Foster, P. (1998). A classroom perspective on the negotiation of meaning, *Applied Linguistics*, **19**, 1–23.

Frantzen, D. (1995). The effects of grammar supplementation on written accuracy in an intermediate Spanish content course, *The Modern Language Journal*, **79**, 329–44.

Gass, S., Mackey, A. and Ross-Feldman, L. (2005). Task-based interactions in classroom and laboratory settings, *Language Learning*, **55**, 575–611.

Gass, S. and Varonis, E. (1994). Input, interaction and second language production, *Studies in Second Language Acquisition*, **16**, 283–302.

Gatbonton, E. (2000). Investigating experienced ESL teachers' pedagogical knowledge, *Canadian Modern Language Review*, **56**, 585–616.

Gregg, K. R., Long, M. H., Jordan, G. and Beretta, A. (1997). Rationality and its discontents in SLA, *Applied Linguistics*, **18**, 4, 538–58.

Hahn, S., Stassen, T. and Reschke, C. (1988). Grading classroom oral activities: Effects on motivation and proficiency, *Foreign Language Annals*, **22**, 241–52.

Harley, B. (2000). Listening strategies in ESL: Do age and L1 make a difference?, *TESOL Quarterly*, **34**, 769–77.

Harley, B., Howard, J. and Hart, D. (1995). Second language processing at different ages: Do younger learners pay more attention to prosodic cues to sentence structure?, *Language Learning*, **45**, 43–71.

Hartshorn, K. J., Evans, N. W., Merrill, P. F., Sudweeks, D. S. and Anderson, N. J. (2010). Effects of dynamic corrective feedback on ESL writing accuracy, *TESOL Quarterly*, **44**, 84–109.

Hendrick, C. (1990). Replications, strict replications, and conceptual replications: Are they important?, *Journal of Social Behavior and Personality*, **5**, 41–9.

Henry, N., Culman, H. and VanPatten, B. (2009). More on the effects of explicit information in instructed SLA: A partial replication and a response to Fernández (2008), *Studies in Second Language Acquisition*, **31**, 559–75.

Jiang, N. (2002). Form–meaning mapping in vocabulary acquisition in a second language, *Studies in Second Language Acquisition*, **24**, 617–37.

Jiang, N. (2004). Semantic transfer and its implications for vocabulary teaching in a second language, *The Modern Language Journal*, **88**, 416–32.

Johnson, J. S. and Newport, E. L. (1989). Critical period effects in second language learning: The influence of maturational state on the acquisition of English as a second language, *Cognitive Psychology*, **21**, 60–99.

Juffs, A. and Harrington, M. (1995). Parsing effects in second language sentence processing: Subject and object asymmetries in wh-extraction, *Studies in Second Language Acquisition*, **17**, 483–516.

Kanno, K. (1996). The status of a non-parametrized principle in the L2 initial state, *Language Acquisition*, **5**, 317–35.

Kellerman, E. and Yoshioka, K. (1999). Inter- and intra-population consistency: A comment on Kanno (1998), *Second Language Research*, **15**, 1, 101–9.

Kelly, C., Chase, L. and Tucker, R. (1979). Replication in experimental communication research: An analysis, *Human Communication Research*, **5**, 338–42.

Kepner, C. (1991). An experiment in the relationship of types of written feedback to the development of second-language writing skills, *The Modern Language Journal*, **75**, 305–13.

Knowlton, B. and Squire, L. (1996). Artificial grammar learning depends on implicit acquisition of both abstract and exemplar-specific information, *Journal of Experimental Psychology: Learning, Memory, and Cognition*, **22**, 169–81.

Kroll, B. (1990). What does time buy? ESL student performance on home versus class compositions, in Kroll, B. (ed.), *Second Language Writing: Research Insights for the Classroom*, Cambridge: Cambridge University Press, pp. 140–54.

Kroll, J. F., Michael, E., Tokowicz, N. and Dufour, R. (2002). The development of lexical fluency in a second language, *Second Language Research*, **18**, 137–71.

Lalande, J. F. (1982). Reducing composition errors: An experiment, *The Modern Language Journal*, **66**, 140–49.

Language Teaching Review Panel (2008). Replication studies in language learning and teaching: Questions and answers, *Language Teaching*, **41**, 1–14.

Lee, J. F. (1986). Background knowledge and L2 reading, *Modern Language Journal*, **70**, 350–4.

Leow, R. (1993). To simplify or not to simplify: A look at intake, *Studies in Second Language Acquisition*, **15**, 333–55.

Leow, R. P. (1995). Modality and intake in second language acquisition, *Studies in Second Language Acquisition*, **17**, 79–89.

Leow, R. (2000). A study of the role of awareness in foreign language behaviour: Aware versus unaware learners, *Studies in Second Language Acquisition*, **22**, 557–84.

Loewen, S. (2005). Incidental focus on form and second language learning, *Studies in Second Language Acquisition*, **27**, 361–86.

Lyster, R. and Ranta, L. (1997). Corrective feedback and learner uptake: Negation of form in communicative classrooms, *Studies in Second Language Acquisition*, **19**, 37–66.

Moeller, A. J. and Reschke, C. (1993). A second look at grading and classroom performance: Report of a research study, *The Modern Language Journal*, **77**, 163–9.

Mullock, B. (2006). The pedagogical knowledge base of four TESOL teachers, *The Modern Language Journal*, 90, 48–66.

Muñoz, C. (1995). Markedness and the acquisition of referential forms: The case of zero anaphora, *Studies in Second Language Acquisition*, 17, 517–27.

Neulip, J. W. and Crandall, R. (1993). Everyone was wrong: There are lots of replications out there, *Journal of Social Behavior and Personality*, 8, 1–8.

Norris, J. M. and Ortega, L. (2006). The value and practice of research synthesis for language learning and teaching, in Norris, J. M. and Ortega, L. (eds.), *Synthesizing Research on Language Learning and Teaching*, Amsterdam/Philadelphia: John Benjamins, pp. 3–50.

Oswald, F. and Plonsky, L. (2010). Meta-analysis in second language research: Choices and challenges, *Annual Review of Applied Linguistics*, 30, 85–110.

Philp, J. (2003). Constraints on "noticing the gap": Non-native speakers' noticing of recasts in NS–NNS interaction, *Studies in Second Language Acquisition*, 25, 99–126.

Pica, T. (1983). Methods of morpheme quantification: Their effect on the interpretation of second language data, *Studies in Second Language Acquisition*, 6, 69–78.

Pimsleur, P., Hancock, C. and Furey, P. (1977). Speech rate and listening comprehension, in Burt, M., Dulay, H. and Finnocchiaro, M. (eds.), *Viewpoints on English as a Second Language*, New York: Regents, pp. 27–34.

Polio, C. (1997). Measures of linguistic accuracy in second language writing research, *Language Learning*, 47, 101–43.

Polio, C., Fleck, C. and Leder, N. (1998). "If I only had more time": ESL learners' changes in linguistic accuracy on essay revisions, *Journal of Second Language Writing*, 7, 43–68.

Polio, C. and Gass, S. (1997). Replication and reporting, *Studies in Second Language Acquisition*, 19, 499–508.

Polio, C. and Gass, S. (1998). The effect of interaction on the comprehension of non-native speakers, *The Modern Language Journal*, 82, 308–19.

Porte, G. (2010). *Appraising Research in Second Language Learning: A Practical Approach to Critical Analysis of Quantitative Research* (2nd edn.), Amsterdam/Philadelphia: John Benjamins.

Quellmalz, E. (1985). Needed: Better methods for testing higher-order thinking skills, *Educational Leadership*, 43, 29–35.

Quellmalz, E. (1987). Developing reasoning skills, in Baron, J. and Sternberg, R. (eds.), *Teaching Thinking Skills: Theory and Practice*, New York: Freeman, pp. 86–105.

Reber, A., Walkenfeld, F. and Hernstadt, R. (1991). Implicit and explicit learning: Individual differences and IQ, *Journal of Experimental Psychology: Learning, Memory, and Cognition*, 17, 888–96.

Robb, T., Ross, S. and Shortreed, I. (1986). Salience of feedback on error and its effect on EFL writing quality, *TESOL Quarterly*, 20, 83–96.

Robinson, P. (2005). Cognitive abilities, chunk-strength, and frequency effects in implicit artificial grammar and incidental L2 learning: Replications of Reber, Walkenfeld and Hernstadt (1991) and Knowlton and Squire (1996) and their relevance for SLA, *Studies in Second Language Acquisition*, **27**, 235–68.

Robinson-Stuart, G. and Nocon, H. (1996). Second culture acquisition: Ethnography in the foreign-language classroom, *The Modern Language Journal*, **80**, 431–49.

Rodgers, D. M. (2006). Developing content and form: Encouraging evidence from Italian content-based instruction, *The Modern Language Journal*, **90**, 373–86.

Roller, C. M. and Matambo, A. R. (1992). Bilingual readers' use of background knowledge in learning from text, *TESOL Quarterly*, **26**, 129–41.

Sachs, R. and Polio, C. (2007). Learners' uses of two types of written feedback on an L2 writing revision task, *Studies in Second Language Acquisition*, **29**, 67–100.

Santos, T. (1989). Replication in applied linguistics research, *TESOL Quarterly*, **23**, 699–702.

Schauer, G. A. (2006). Pragmatic awareness in ESL and EFL contexts: Contrast and development, *Language Learning*, **56**, 269–318.

Schneider, M. and Connor, U. (1990). Analysing topical structure in ESL essays: Not all topics are equal, *Studies in Second Language Acquisition*, **12**, 411–17.

Semke, H. (1984). Effects of the red pen, *Foreign Language Annals*, **17**, 195–202.

Sheen, Y. (2007). The effect of focused written corrective feedback and language aptitude on ESL learners' acquisition, *TESOL Quarterly*, **41**, 255–83.

Sheppard, K. (1992). Two feedback types: Do they make a difference?, *RELC Journal*, **23**, 103–10.

Tauroza, S. and Allison, D. (1990). Speech rates in British English, *Applied Linguistics*, **11**, 90–105.

Tremblay, A. (2006). On the second language acquisition of Spanish reflexive passives and reflexive impersonals by French- and English-speaking adults, *Second Language Research*, **22**, 30–63.

Truscott, J. (1996). The case against grammar correction in L2 writing classes, *Language Learning*, **46**, 327–69.

Truscott, J. (2007). The effect of error correction on learners' ability to write accurately, *Journal of Second Language Writing*, **16**, 255–72.

Truscott, J. and Hsu, A. Y. (2008). Error correction, revision, and learning, *Journal of Second Language Writing*, **17**, 292–305.

Tyler, A. and Bro, J. (1992). Discourse structure in non-native English discourse: The effect of ordering and interpretive cues, *Studies in Second Language Acquisition*, **14**, 71–86.

Tyler, A. and Bro, J. (1993). Discourse processing effort and perceptions of comprehensibility in non-native discourse: The effect of ordering and interpretive cues revisited, *Studies in Second Language Acquisition*, **15**, 507–22.

Valdman, A. (1993). Replication study (editorial introduction), *Studies in Second Language Acquisition*, **15**, 505.

Van der Veer, R., van IJzendoorn, M. and Valsiner, J. (1994). General introduction, in Van der Veer, R., van IJzendoorn, M. and Valsiner, J. (eds.), *Reconstructing the Mind: Replicability in Research on Human Development*, Norwood, NJ: Ablex, pp. 1–9.

VanPatten, B. (1990). Attending to form and content in the input, *Studies in Second Language Acquisition*, **12**, 287–301.

VanPatten, B. and Cadierno, T. (1993). Explicit instruction and input processing, *Studies in Second Language Acquisition*, **15**, 225–43.

VanPatten, B. and Oikkenon, S. (1996). Explanation versus structured input in processing instruction, *Studies in Second Language Acquisition*, **18**, 495–510.

White, L. and Juffs, A. (1998). Constraints on wh-movement in two different contexts of non-native language acquisition: Competence and processing, in Flynn, S., Martohardjono, G. and O'Neill, W. (eds.), *The Generative Study of Second Language Acquisition*, Hillsdale, NJ: Lawrence Erlbaum Associates, pp. 111–30.

Wolfe-Quintero, K., Inagaki, S. and Kim, H. Y. (1998). Second language development in writing: Measures of fluency, accuracy, and complexity (Technical Report #17), Honolulu, HI: National Foreign Language Resource Center.

Wong, W. (2001). Modality and attention to meaning and form in the input, *Studies in Second Language Acquisition*, **23**, 345–68.

Xu, C. (2009). Overgeneralization from a narrow focus: A response to Ellis et al. (2008) and Bitchener (2008), *Journal of Second Language Writing*, **18**, 270–75.

Zyzik, E. and Polio, C. (2008). Incidental focus on form in Spanish literature classes, *The Modern Language Journal*, **92**, 50–73.

3 Statistical significance tests and result generalizability: Issues, misconceptions, and a case for replication

Hossein Nassaji

L2 research has been growing rapidly in recent years, and with this growth has come an increase in the use of significance tests. It is generally believed that such tests provide information about the generalizability of research results. That is, if the relationships or effects occurring in a certain study, in a certain context, are shown to be statistically significant using inferential statistics, those results are likely to be applied to the broader population in other contexts (Kaufman et al., 2006). However, there has been much controversy and concern over the misinterpretations and limitations of significance tests. These limitations have been extensively discussed in the fields of cognitive and social sciences (Morrison and Henkel, 1970; Carver, 1978, 1993; Thompson, 1993, 1994, 1996; Rozeboom, 1997; Daniel, 1998a; Knapp, 1998; Kline, 2004). Several authors in the field of SLA have also voiced concerns over the exclusive use of significance tests in L2 research (e.g., Crookes, 1991; Lazaraton, 1991, 2000; Larson-Hall, 2010; Oswald and Plonsky, 2010). However, the various issues and problems of such tests have not been seriously discussed in our field. Therefore, much emphasis is still placed on significance tests in L2 research, not only as a method of describing and analyzing data, but also as a mode of making generalizability conclusions based on sample data. Replication studies, on the other hand, are not common. There are a number of reasons for this, many of which have been discussed in other chapters of this volume. Another important reason, I believe, is the misunderstanding of the functions and utility of significance tests. The lack of a proper understanding of the role of such tests has led not only to their misuse, but also to a shift of attention away from exploring other methods of evaluating research results (Kline, 2004). In particular, methods that can be used to establish replicability of research findings have been less explored.

In this chapter, I will first briefly define statistical significance tests and then present a review of the misconceptions about and limitations of such tests, including those related to the generalizability of research results. Next, I will discuss some of the main suggestions that have been put forward in the literature to overcome these limitations. I will then argue that replication is the only way to determine generalizability. I will conclude by discussing different ways of exploring replicability, including external and internal replication.

1 What is a statistical significance test?

Statistical significance tests are mathematical techniques used in quantitative research to determine the probability of a given result. They are tests that are used to reject what is called the *null hypothesis*, which is the assumption that the relationship or the difference of interest does not exist in the population. The population is the entire group of people under study and a sample is a subset of the population. Significance tests assess the likelihood of the sample data, assuming that the null hypothesis is true, based on a given sample size. If the null hypothesis is rejected, the researcher then accepts what is called an *alternative hypothesis*, which asserts a certain relationship or effect exists in the population. Since it is not possible to prove the alternative hypothesis, first a null hypothesis is formulated and then a significance test is performed to determine whether it is possible to reject it.

In null hypothesis testing, there is no way to know for certain whether the null hypothesis is true or false. Therefore, the analysis should involve the use of probabilities. Significance tests assess the probability of the data based on the assumed truth of the null hypothesis. To test the null hypothesis, the significance test first computes a test statistic, which is a numerical value, calculated from the sample data based on a known sampling distribution. It then calculates a corresponding probability value (p value) for the test statistic. This value is the probability of getting a test statistic as large as the one obtained, under the assumption that the null hypothesis is true. Thus, the p value indicates how likely it is that the observed test statistic is due to sampling errors. The researcher then needs to judge whether the observed p value is small enough to justify the rejection of the null hypothesis. This will be done through the use of a criterion probability level, which is a cut-off point to decide whether or not to reject the null hypothesis. This threshold level is called the significance level (α, alpha). In social sciences, researchers usually choose an alpha (or significance level) of .05 (please note that the choice of the alpha level is arbitrary; this issue will be further discussed later). If the observed p value is equal to, or lower than, the criterion significance level ($p \leq \alpha$), the researcher will reject the assumption that the null hypothesis is true (please note the difference between the p value and the significance level). If the null hypothesis is rejected, the results are considered to be statistically significant; otherwise, it is concluded that the results are not statistically significant. There are different kinds of statistical significance tests that are used depending on the kind of data. Some of the most commonly used ones are t-tests, ANOVAs (analysis of variance), correlations, regressions, and chi-square tests.

2 Issues with significance tests

Despite the popularity of significance tests, social and psychological researchers have raised a number of issues and concerns over the use of such tests. These problems have led to different suggestions, which range from supplementing the results of significance tests with other statistical measures, such as effect sizes and confidence intervals, to minimizing and even abandoning the use of these tests in scientific research. Carver argued that significance tests are ineffective; therefore, researchers should stop using them. He stated:

> Statistical significance testing has involved more fantasy than facts. The emphasis on statistical significance over scientific significance in educational research represents a corrupt form of the scientific method. Educational research would be better off if it stopped testing its results for statistical significance.
>
> (Carver, 1978: 378)

A number of other researchers have also questioned the merits of significance tests (e.g., Morrison and Henkel, 1970; Thompson, 1993, 1994, 1996; Cohen, 1994; Rozeboom, 1997; Schmidt and Hunter, 1997; Daniel, 1998a; Knapp, 1998; Kline, 2004). Cohen, for example, argued that "NHST [null hypothesis significance testing] has not only failed to support the advance of psychology as a science but also has seriously impeded it" (1994: 997). Schmidt and Hunter presented initially a number of statements made by advocates of significance tests, such as "without significance tests we would not know whether a finding is real or just due to chance; hypothesis testing would not be possible without significance tests; significance testing ensures objectivity in the interpretation of research data" (1997: 37). After a thorough analysis of these views, however, they concluded that, "reliance on significance testing is logically indefensible" (1997: 38). Of course, issues with significance tests are not new and have been raised in the literature as early as 1960 (e.g., Rozeboom, 1960; Clark, 1963).

Given such observations, the question arises as to why significance tests are so widely relied on in scientific research. One reason are the pervasive misconceptions associated with such tests. People attribute values to these tests that they do not possess. Another reason is that many test users may not know what these tests do and what they actually tell us. Therefore, they not only misinterpret their functions but also use them inappropriately. Tyron asserted that even "statistical experts and investigators publishing in the best journals cannot consistently interpret the results of these analyses" (1998: 796). He described this situation as "extremely disturbing." Thompson pointed out that despite the availability of much information on such tests, "even today some psychologists still do not understand what statistical significance tests do and do not do" (1999: 165).

In what follows, I will review some of the main issues with significance tests, beginning with conceptual misunderstandings and then moving on to more serious problems.

2.1 Misconceptions

Misconception 1: Statistically significant means important.

One of the most common misconceptions regarding significance tests concerns the interpretation of the word *significance*. Significance is an ambiguous term; thus some may assume that a statistically significant result is also an important result, meaning a result that has practical or educational significance. However, in statistics the term significance has a technical meaning, different from its common meaning. When a result is *statistically* significant, it simply means that there is a good chance that the researcher is right in rejecting the null hypothesis. It does not indicate that the results are important or meaningful.

This misconception is very common and can be seen in the tendency to drop the word statistically and use significant difference instead of statistically significant difference in research reports. This practice is problematic because the absence of the term statistically can easily lead to the erroneous impression that the results are important and worthwhile. For this reason, a number of psychological scholars have stressed that the term statistically must always precede the word significant when describing the results of a statistical significance test (Pedhazur and Schmelkin, 1991; Carver, 1993; Thompson, 1996). Thompson (1996), for example, argued that this practice is essential because it helps to recognize that a statistically significant result has nothing to do with importance. Some researchers have even suggested that the term significance should be removed from the statistics vocabulary and only be used in everyday language to denote something important or worthwhile (Kline, 2004).

Misconception 2: Significance tests evaluate the likelihood that results were due to chance.

The second major misconception is that significance tests assess the likelihood that the results were due to chance. For example, it is usually assumed that a $p < .05$ suggests that the probability of chance causing the results is less than 5%. However, the p value represents the likelihood of getting research results based on an initial assumption that chance caused the results. Thus, it cannot be the likelihood that chance caused the results. Carver called this misconception the odds-against-chance fantasy and pointed out that "(a) the p value [is] calculated by assuming that the probability was 1.00 that chance did cause the mean difference, and (b) the p value is used to decide whether to accept or reject the idea that probability is 1.00 that chance caused the mean difference" (1978: 383). Therefore, it is illogical to assume that a p value of .05 provides a measure that the results are due to chance 5% of the time.

According to Kline, three correct interpretations of a p value are as follows:

1   The odds are less than 1 to 19 of getting a result from a random sample even more extreme than the observed one when H_0 [null hypothesis] is true.
2   Less than 5% of test statistics are further away from the mean of the sampling distribution under H_0 than the one for the observed result.
3   Assuming H_0 is true and the study is repeated many times, less than 5% of these results will be even more inconsistent with the H_0 than the observed result.

(Kline, 2004: 63)

Misconception 3: The p *value shows the probability of the null hypothesis.*

Another widely held misconception is that the p value shows the probability of the null hypothesis. Thus, a $p < .05$ is taken to indicate that the probability of the truth of the null hypothesis is less than 5%. Although this is what the researcher is looking for, it is not what the null hypothesis testing shows. Kirk pointed out:

> In scientific inference, what we want to know is the probability that the null hypothesis (H_0) is true, given that we have obtained a set of data (D); that is, p (H_0|D). What null hypothesis significance testing tells us is the probability of obtaining these data or more extreme data if the null hypothesis is true, p (D|H_0).

(Kirk, 1996: 747)

Carver called the interpretation of the p value one of the least understood aspects of null hypothesis testing and illustrated the nature of the problem by giving and comparing the following two hypothetical situations. First, the question is posed: "What is the probability of obtaining a dead person, given that the person was hanged?" The answer to this question is that it will be "very high." Now, the question is asked: "What is the probability that the person has been hanged, given that the person is dead?" Here the probability would be very low (perhaps 1%). As Carver pointed out, we do not usually make the mistake of taking the first estimate (97%) instead of the second (1%) one. However, although we are not likely to make that mistake "it is exactly the kind of mistake that is made with interpretations of statistical significance testing – by analogy, calculated estimates of p (H|D) are interpreted as if they were estimates of p (D|H), when they are clearly not the same" (1978: 384–85).

Misconception 4: A p value of .05 shows that there is a 95% likelihood that the results are caused by the treatment.

The fourth misconception is that an observed p value of .05 indicates a 95% likelihood that the results are caused by the treatment. For example, a correlation coefficient of .50, statistically significant at the .05 level is interpreted as being a 95% likelihood that the correlation is .50 in the population. However, the p value shows that there is a 95% likelihood that the correlation between the tests in the population is not zero, assuming that the samples are representative of the population (Daniel, 1998b). The misconception stems from the belief that statistical tests divide the results into real results and results caused by chance. However, statistical tests are not able to do so. Any decision based on such tests can be wrong because they can either be the result of a Type I error or a Type II error (Kline, 2004). The Type I error refers to the erroneous rejection of a null hypothesis that is actually true. The Type II error refers to the erroneous acceptance of a null hypothesis that is actually false. In any given study, there is always a risk of either a Type I or a Type II error, as these two are inversely related and, as the risk of one decreases, the risk of the other increases.

Misconception 5: The significance test tells us about the magnitude of a relationship or a difference.

Another widespread misconception is that the significance test tells us about the magnitude of a relationship or difference. For example, a p value of .0001 is taken to indicate a larger treatment effect than a p value of .04, which it does not. This misconception can be seen in

erroneous but common phrases, such as *very significant, highly significant, the most significant, the least significant,* and so on, in research
reports. Other common but erroneous statements are *marginally significant* or *approaching significance.* The *p* value, however, does not
provide any information about the magnitude of an effect. It is simply
the probability of the data under the assumption that the null hypothesis is true. Furthermore, the *p* value is a direct function of the sample
size, and it gets smaller as the sample size increases and vice versa. For
example, for a given data set, a large sample size may produce a statistically significant result, but the effect may be very small. On the other
hand, with a small sample size, there may be a statistically nonsignificant result even though the actual effect may be large.

The role of a sample size in affecting statistical significance can
be seen in Table 3.1 adapted from Daniel (1998b: 26). As the table
shows, the critical values of the correlation coefficient, *r,* for rejecting the null hypothesis at the .05 level, changes dramatically as the
sample size increases. For instance, when the sample size is 3, the critical value of *r* is .997 but when it is 1,000, it is .062. When the sample
size is fairly small, say 10, even a moderate correlation of .6 is not
statistically significant ($p < .05$). But when the sample size is 500,
even a very small correlation of .088 becomes statistically significant
(Daniel, 1998b).

Table 3.1   *The role of sample size in affecting significance level*

Sample size	Critical value of *r* at $p < .05$
3	.997
10	.632
20	.444
100	.196
500	.088
1,000	.062
5,000	.027
10,000	.0196

Therefore, significance testing seems to be testing whether the sample is large or not (Thompson, 1992; Daniel, 1998b). Since statistical significance depends so much upon the sample size, it is always
possible to find a statistically significant result if the sample size is
large enough even though the difference is very small (Anderson
et al., 2000).

Misconception 6: Failure to reject the null hypothesis means no difference or relationship.

The sixth misconception is that failing to reject the null hypothesis indicates no difference in the data. In other words, it means that the null hypothesis is true. This misconception can be widely seen in reports of experimental research that has used significance tests to compare groups. In such situations, if the test has failed to reject the null hypothesis, the typical conclusion is that the groups are the same. For example, when studies use pre-tests to compare an experimental group and a control group before the treatment and the results of the pre-test comparison turn out to be statistically nonsignificant, they are usually interpreted as indicating that the two groups were the same before the treatment. However, this interpretation is not warranted for a number of reasons. First, significance tests cannot prove the truth of a null hypothesis; they can only fail to reject it. Thus, a statistically nonsignificant result means that there is not sufficient evidence in the data to show a difference. Second, as Kline pointed out, "absence of evidence is not evidence of absence" (2004: 67). In other words, if there is no evidence to indicate that the two groups are different, this does not provide evidence that the groups are the same. Third, the null hypothesis is never true, as there is always a difference between the means of two samples, even if this difference is small. Finally, as noted earlier, the estimation of the p value is always based on the assumption that the null hypothesis is true; therefore, it cannot be taken as a measure of the truth of the null hypothesis at the same time.

Misconception 7: Statistically significant results are evidence for the success of the study.

The next misconception is that statistically significant results provide evidence for the quality of the study (Kline, 2004). In other words, a good study is the one that has found a statistically significant result. However, a statistically significant result may simply be the result of a Type I error, which occurs when the researcher rejects the null hypothesis erroneously.

The above misconception underlies the apparent bias toward favoring studies that report statistically significant results and against those that do not. This bias has been empirically documented by studies that have examined published research in academic journals and have found that the majority of the studies are those that report statistically significant results. For example, in an early survey study, Sterling (1959) examined published work in cognitive psychology journals and found that 97.3%

of the articles reported statistically significant results. Thirty years later, Sterling et al. (1995) conducted a similar study, analyzing 165 articles in four experimental psychology journals between 1986 and 1987, and found that 92.7% of the articles published used tests of significance, out of which 93.5% reported statistically significant results. The researchers concluded that, after thirty years, the situation had not changed and that articles not finding statistically significant results were still assessed adversely. They also provided an example of a rejection letter from the editor of a scientific journal, which shows such a bias:

> Unfortunately, we are not able to publish this manuscript. The manuscript is very well written and the study was well documented. Unfortunately, the negative results translate into a minimal contribution to the field. We encourage you to continue your work in this area and we will be glad to consider additional manuscripts that you may prepare in the future.
>
> (Sterling et al., 1995: 109)

Misconception 8: Failing to have statistically significant results is a research failure.

This misconception is a mirror image of the one above and suggests that failing to have statistically significant results is a failure. However, not having statistically significant results does not necessarily indicate that the study was poor. Such results can also be the outcome of good research, and therefore can be as important as statistically significant results.

Misconception 9: Statistical significance shows the probability that the results will replicate under the same conditions.

Another misconception is that statistical significance tests evaluate the replicability of research results. This misconception is related to the interpretation of the p value as the probability that the same results will be obtained if the study is repeated. For example, a $p < .05$ is taken to indicate that the probability of replicating the results is more than 95% (Kline, 1994). This belief is quite widespread and can be seen not only among researchers but also in statistics textbooks. Oakes (1986), for example, found that 60% of the 70 psychological researchers he surveyed believed that the p value minus 1 ($p - 1$) is an index of replicability. Thus, he found that the majority of the respondents agreed that an observed p value of .01 shows that the researcher gets the same result 99% of the time if the experiment is repeated.

The following quote from a statistics textbook also shows this belief (cited in Carver, 1978):

> If the statistical significance is at the 0.05 level, it is more informative to talk about the statistical confidence as being at the 0.95 level. This means that the investigator can be confident with odds of 95 out of 100 that the observed difference will hold up in future investigations.
>
> (Nunnally, 1975: 195)

This misinterpretation has been called the "replicability fantasy" by Carver (1978) and the "replication fallacy" by Kline (2004). As Carver (1978) argued, statistical testing and replicability deal with different questions. In statistical significance testing, the question is: What is the probability of getting a mean difference as large as the one obtained in the study, provided that the sample is taken from the population? However, in replicability, the question is: What is the probability that a certain mean difference, for example, can be repeated?

The researcher may be interested in the second question, and therefore may assume that significance tests provide an answer to that question. However, significance tests do not do so. What they do is to provide information about the likelihood of the data, assuming that the null hypothesis is true.

There are also other reasons why statistical significance tests cannot provide information about replicability or generalizability of research results. First, to provide information for replicability, the test should be able to provide evidence for the truth of an alternative hypothesis (Sohn, 1998). However, as discussed earlier, this is not what significance tests can do. Second, a central assumption behind inferencing from sample to population is that the sample is representative of the population. However, we do not know whether this assumption is true, and there is no way of checking it. Even when the sample is carefully selected, we do not yet know whether it is representative of the population. Another central assumption in statistical inferencing is random sampling, which is rarely achieved. Therefore, there is a gap between what statistical tests assume and how most of us collect data (i.e., from convenience samples). Finally, the p values obtained in significance tests are not a reliable measure as they can vary dramatically even when the same study is repeated over and over again. In fact, in a simulation of 25 repetitions of an experiment, Cumming (2008) found that the p value varied from .001 to .76.

This shows that the p value is a very poor indicator of generalizability or replicability.

2.2 *Other issues with significance tests*

2.2.1 THE LOGIC OF NULL HYPOTHESIS TESTING

In addition to the above misconceptions, there are other issues regarding significance tests that are worth noting. One is the logic underlying the null hypothesis testing. Cohen argued that null hypothesis testing is problematic because it is based on "a misapplication of deductive syllogistic reasoning." This problem is illustrated by Cohen (1994: 998) as follows.

The null hypothesis is often assumed to be rejected based on this kind of reasoning:

1   "If the null hypothesis is correct, then this datum (D) cannot occur. It has, however, occurred. Therefore, the null hypothesis is false."

Cohen argued that the above logic is formally correct, but this is not the reasoning that actually underlies the null hypothesis testing. The reasoning behind the rejection of the null hypothesis is probabilistic and is like the following:

2   "If the null hypothesis is correct, then these data are highly unlikely. These data have occurred. Therefore, the null hypothesis is highly unlikely."

According to Cohen, the fact that the reasoning becomes probabilistic makes the whole logic invalid, and to illustrate how, he provides the following three examples. In (1), the syllogism is sensible and the reasoning is formally correct. In (2), the syllogism is not sensible (because the major premise is wrong) but the reasoning is formally correct. However, in (3), the major premise is probabilistic and not absolute; thus, it is now sensible, but because of that, the reasoning becomes formally incorrect, leading to a conclusion that does not make sense.

1   "If a person is a Martian, then he is not a member of Congress. This person is a member of Congress. Therefore, he is not a Martian."
2   "If a person is an American, then he is not a member of Congress. (WRONG) This person is a member of Congress. Therefore, he is not an American."

3   "If a person is an American, then he is probably not a member of Congress. (TRUE)
This person is a member of Congress.
Therefore, he is probably not an American."

Cohen argued that the reasoning in (3) is exactly like the reasoning underlying hypothesis testing, which is:

"If H_0 is true, then this result (statistical significance) would probably not occur.
This result has occurred.
Then H_0 is probably not true."

Thus, if (3) is invalid, the reasoning of the null hypothesis testing is invalid too.

2.2.2 THE DIRECTION OF INFERENCING AND THE ISSUE OF GENERALIZABILITY

When doing research, researchers are often interested in results that can be generalized to the larger population. Statistical significance tests are believed to be capable of doing so. That is, they are perceived to allow us to determine whether the specific sample results are likely to hold in the population (Kaufman et al., 2006). In other words, they are believed to help us infer from the sample to the population, by finding out about the probability of the null hypothesis given the observed differences in the results. However, as noted earlier, many authors (Carver, 1978; Cohen, 1994; Kirk, 1996; Snyder and Thompson, 1998; Kline, 2004) have pointed out that significance testing informs us about the probability of the data given the null hypothesis is true, not the probability of the null hypothesis given the data. Cohen, in particular, stressed that, although the main reason for using a statistical test is to be able to reject the null hypothesis (H_0), "when one tests H_0 one is finding the probability that the data (D) could have arisen if H_0 were true," and that these two scenarios are completely different (Cohen, 1994: 998). In other words, "the direction of statistical inference in statistical significance tests is from the population to the sample, and not from the sample to the population" (Snyder and Thompson, 1998: 337). There are, of course, methods such as Bayesian inferencing that is believed to provide this kind of sample-to-population inferencing, by specifying a prior probability for the null hypothesis. And, for that reason, a number of scholars have recently argued for the use of such statistics as an alternative to traditional significance tests (see Pruzek, 1997, and Bolstad, 2007, for a discussion of this method). However, Bayesian methods have rarely been used in psychological research, and thus, they do not have well-established procedures for analyzing all kinds of data.

2.2.3 THE ARBITRARINESS OF THE SIGNIFICANCE LEVEL

Another problem concerns the arbitrariness of the significance level. As stated earlier, a key concept in the null hypothesis testing is the notion of a significance level, a criterion point used by researchers to decide whether or not to reject the null hypothesis (e.g., .05). However, the selection of the significance level is arbitrary and subjective and there is no logical rule for it. Because of this, the significance level leads to arbitrarily rejecting the null hypothesis, or categorically classifying the results into statistically significant and nonsignificant results (Anderson et al., 2000).

Furthermore, the decision about the significance level is usually made before the statistical test is performed. Thus, it is possible that the significance level chosen can overemphasize the evidence against the null hypothesis. This particularly happens in situations where the research involves multiple statistical comparisons (i.e., multiple significance tests). The use of multiple tests increases the chances of a Type I error. In such cases, an additional statistical procedure is usually recommended, called the Bonferroni correction. This procedure adjusts the value of the criterion downward to account for the repeated comparisons in the study. The Bonferroni correction can be helpful, in that, by reducing the alpha level, it decreases the chances of erroneously rejecting the null hypothesis. However, by doing so, it can increase the likelihood of a Type II error, which is not discovering an actual effect. For this reason, the use of the Bonferroni correction is controversial.

2.2.4 INAPPROPRIATE USES OF SIGNIFICANCE TESTS

Furthermore, although significance tests are widely used in research, this does not mean they are used appropriately. A very common problem here is the misuse of such tests due to a lack of understanding, or not observing, the assumptions they are based on. Every significance test makes certain assumptions about the data that must be satisfied for that test to be of any value. For instance, parametric tests, such as *t*-tests and ANOVA, require the assumptions of normality of distribution and homogeneity of variance. Normality of distribution holds that the data come from a normally distributed population. Homogeneity of variance refers to the idea that samples from which the data are collected come from populations that have a similar variance. If these assumptions are not met, the results of such tests are not reliable and can lead to erroneous conclusions.

As Larson-Hall (2010) pointed out, researchers do not usually report whether the assumptions behind their tests have been satisfied. However, there is evidence to suggest that such assumptions are often violated. For example, in a survey study, Lazaraton et al. (1987) found that most L2 researchers and professionals they surveyed reported that ANOVA was a difficult statistical test to carry out and interpret. However, in a subsequent survey of empirical studies in L2 research journals, Lazaraton (2000) found that over 40 percent of the studies had used ANOVA. She considered this situation surprising and concluded that it was quite likely that most of these studies had violated some of the assumptions of ANOVA. Since then, the situation may have improved in terms of researchers' knowledge of statistical tests. Currently there are more books on statistics, and SLA researchers have greater access to more sophisticated statistical analyses (Loewen and Gass, 2009). However, there is still little evidence to suggest that these tests are used more appropriately now. As Lazaraton (2009) pointed out, greater access to books or statistics does not necessarily mean proper use.

One frequent example of the violation of assumptions is in the use of the chi-square test. The chi-square is a significance test to examine the relationship between two sets of categorical (or frequency) data. Like ANOVA, this test requires certain assumptions to be met. For example, one such assumption is that of independence of observation, which requires that each subject should contribute data to only one cell in the chi-square table. The independence of observation is violated if data from the same subject are entered into different cells of the table (between-cell violation), or if the same participant contributes more than his or her own share to the same cell (within-cell violation) (Hatch and Lazaraton, 1991). It is not hard to find many cases in L2 research where the chi-square analysis has been used when the data did not fulfil one or both of these assumptions. One scenario, for example, is when the chi-square is used to compare sets of data collected from the same group of learners. For example, a study may examine through a chi-square test whether there is any relationship between the type of questions teachers ask and the learners' responses to those questions. In such cases, responses from all students may be combined and entered in one of the cells of a chi-square table. However, this can be problematic because one learner may have contributed more data than the other learners to the same cell (thus violating the within-cell independence of observation assumption). Another case is when the chi-square test is used as a repeated measure test

(Larson-Hall, 2010). For example, the researcher may compare a set of categorical data collected from a group of learners at time one (e.g., a pre-test) to another set of data from the same group of learners at time two (e.g., a post-test). Although the data collected are categorical, and a chi-square test may seem appropriate, the use of chi-square tests in such cases is problematic because the two sets of data come from the same participants, hence violating the independence of observation assumption. How to deal with these situations is beyond the scope of the chapter, but interested readers can consult Larson-Hall (2010: Chapter 8) for suggestions.

3 Recommendations

With the misconceptions and problems associated with statistical significance tests, the question arises as to what we should do. Given these problems, a number of scholars in cognitive and social sciences have suggested that the use of such tests should be seriously minimized or entirely abandoned (Morrison and Henkel, 1970; Carver, 1978, 1993; Cohen, 1994; Rozeboom, 1997; Kline, 2004). As noted earlier, in his early analysis of the situation, Carver described the use of significance tests in educational research as an unhealthy practice and therefore recommended that this use should be discontinued. In 1993, he revisited the issue and reached the same conclusion, stating "[s]tatistical significance testing is still being used in a manner that corrupts the scientific method" (1978: 278). Schmidt described statistical tests as ineffective and as activities that have "retarded the growth of cumulative knowledge in psychology." Thus, he argued, "we must abandon the statistical significance test" (Schmidt, 1996: 115–16). More recently, Kline, in his review of the criticisms about significance tests, pointed out that "the criticisms have sufficient merit to support the minimization or abandonment of NHST in the behavioural sciences" (2004: 61–62).

Of course, the positions taken by these scholars may sound too extreme. It may be argued that although there are issues with statistical tests, with some being more serious than others, there still remains a role for significance tests in scientific research. For example, although significance tests do not prove a claim or are not able to make a prediction, if they are used and interpreted appropriately, they can point to results that might be worth noting and can be further studied (Frick, 1996). This leads to a more conservative position, which suggests that we should be aware of the pitfalls of significance tests and use them appropriately.

However, we should know that even when such tests are used appropriately, their value is highly restricted. For example, as discussed above, although significance tests may provide information about the probability of the data under the assumption of a true null hypothesis, they do not provide information about the truth of a null hypothesis or the plausibility of an alternative hypothesis. They also do not provide information about the strength or the importance of the evidence in the data. More importantly, they do not offer any evidence about the external validity or the generalizability of research results.

To alleviate the shortcomings of significance tests, there are a number of suggestions. One is the use of other statistical measures, such as effect sizes and confidence intervals in conjunction with significance test results (Cohen, 1994; Schmidt and Hunter, 1997; Daniel, 1998a; Kline, 2004; Thompson, 2005). Effect sizes are standardized measures that estimate the magnitude of an effect. Therefore, they provide an additional and essential piece of information that significance tests do not. As noted earlier, significance tests provide information about the presence of a difference or a relationship, but do not provide information about the size of an effect. Effect sizes provide this information. There are different types of effect sizes and different ways of calculating them (see Olejnik and Algina, 2000). One well-known measure is Cohen's *d*. The calculation of Cohen's *d* is achieved by determining the difference between the mean (average score) of different conditions or groups in the study (i.e., the experimental group and the control group) and dividing that difference by their standard deviations. The values of an effect size range from 0.00 to 1.00. Conventionally, an effect size of 0.2 is considered small, an effect size of 0.5 is considered medium, and an effect size of 0.8 is considered large. Since effect sizes are standardized measures, they do not rely solely on sample size. Therefore, they not only show the relative strength of an effect, but also allow for a comparison of the effects of an experimental treatment across studies.

Because effect sizes are important, the sixth edition of the publication manual of the American Psychological Association (APA, 2010) has recommended the use of this measure in statistical studies. In the field of SLA, a number of authors have also stressed the importance of including effect sizes in statistical research (e.g., Crookes, 1991; Lazaraton, 1991; Larson-Hall, 2010). There are also applied linguistics journals which require the publication of effect sizes in major statistical analyses (e.g., *Language Learning*). Despite this, however, effect sizes are still not required in submissions to many L2 journals (Norris and Ortega, 2010).

In addition to effect size measures and p values, there is the use of confidence intervals (Cohen, 1994; Schmidt and Hunter, 1997; Kline, 2004; Thompson, 2005). The p value is used to determine whether a null hypothesis should be rejected or not. Confidence intervals, however, reveal the margin of error in the data by showing the boundaries within which the value of the population may fall. Thus, they provide additional and complementary information about the precision of sample estimates and the probability of how close they are to the population parameters: the wider the interval, the lower this probability. The confidence level conventionally used for confidence intervals in most studies is 95%, which means that there is a 95% certainty that the population value may fall within the given confidence interval. For example, if the confidence interval of a mean value of 2.3 is between 1.6 and 3.8 at the 95% confidence level, it means that we can be 95% confident that the population mean may fall somewhere between 1.6 and 3.8. Thus, in this case, the confidence intervals provide not only the information that significance tests provide, but also add to that information by showing the probability of obtaining similar values if the study is repeated. Because of its importance, the sixth edition of the APA manual (APA, 2010) requires the inclusion of confidence intervals in addition to effect sizes.

A further suggestion is the use of meta-analysis. Meta-analysis is not an alternative, like effect sizes and confidence intervals, that a researcher can use in a single study. Rather, it is a method that synthesizes and summarizes research results from multiple studies. In meta-analysis, the effects of variables are examined in terms of the strength of the differences they make on research outcomes (Fitz-Gibbon, 1985). These differences are estimated in the form of effect sizes calculated for individual studies and then averaged across studies (see Glass et al., 1981; Hedges and Olkin, 1985; Borenstein et al., 2009; Plonsky, Chapter 4, this volume). Meta-analysis is a useful method because it allows researchers to examine the degree to which a set of related findings converge or diverge across studies. Furthermore, it can reveal some of the underlying regularities, or possible effects, that may exist in the data but are not exposed in individual studies due to the small sample size. Since studies are combined in meta-analysis, such hidden effects are easily detected.

4 The need for replication

However, although the above measures and procedures are very useful, they still provide little information about the likelihood of replicability or generalizability of research findings. Both effect sizes and confidence intervals provide important information about the strength of an effect, and in the case of the latter, also about the precision of sample estimates. However, the results reported still remain pertinent to only a particular sample and condition. Thus, there is no way of knowing whether these effects hold in other similar conditions or populations. Furthermore, the results of these analyses are affected by a number of other variables, including the reliability of the measures, variations in sample size, and the kind of treatments and variables investigated. As for meta-analysis, although it increases our confidence in the rigor of the research evidence by reviewing and combining research results from multiple studies, which can in turn facilitate replication and knowledge generalization (see Plonsky, Chapter 4, this volume), this method has its own limitations. Meta-analysis often makes use of significance tests, particularly chi-square tests, to examine homogeneity among studies (Rosenthal and Rubin, 1982; Hedges and Olkin, 1985). In such cases it suffers, though to a lesser degree, from the problems associated with statistical significance tests. In addition, meta-analysis does not improve the quality of the original studies. That is, if the original studies are problematic, the results of the meta-analysis will be problematic to the same extent. Moreover, the conditions of most studies in a meta-analysis are not the same, which makes comparison difficult. For example, there may be studies that report conflicting results, contain divergent effect sizes, provide different measures and definitions of the same variable, or include insufficient descriptive statistics needed for meta-analysis. These then add to the challenges of conducting a systematic meta-analytic review (Oswald and Plonsky, 2010). Finally, the studies included in a meta-analysis are mostly published studies. Therefore, the review is unlikely to include a representative sample of all the research conducted.

Thus, no matter whether results from single studies are statistically significant or not, whether they are supplemented with effect sizes and confidence intervals, or whether the strength of the evidence has been evaluated across multiple studies through meta-analysis, we still do not know whether the findings reported in those studies can be applied to other learners or hold in other situations. Indeed, when it comes to generalizability, the only reliable solution is replication. Thus, L2 researchers should try to explore the various ways of determining replicability of their findings. There are different ways of conducting replicability analyses, which I will briefly discuss next.

4.1 External and internal replication

In general, there are two main ways of assessing replicability of research results: internally and externally. Internal replication is the kind of replication conducted by the original researcher, using the same sample. It does not involve re-performing the study. External replication involves redoing the study with new participants: New data are collected from new samples. The most informative method of replication is external replication. However, as Thompson (1996) noted, researchers may not always be willing, or able, to spend the time redoing a study. In those cases, an alternative option would be internal replication.

SLA researchers are typically more familiar with external replication. Detailed descriptions and information about the different types of such replication have also been provided in other chapters of this volume (see, in particular, Porte's Introduction). Hence, I will not discuss external replication and instead focus here on internal replication.

There are three common methods of internal replication: cross-validation, bootstrap, and jackknife (Thompson, 1994). These methods involve dividing the sample into different subsamples and combining them in different ways in order to determine whether the results are the same across subsamples, taking into account the variability among individual subjects that make up the sample. Cross-validation is a re-sampling procedure that tests the predictive power of the statistical analyses of interest by comparing and cross-validating the performance of one subset of data against the other subset(s). In the simplest form, the sample is randomly divided into two almost equal parts and then separate analyses are conducted on each half. One subset of data, which is called the training set, is used to generate the intended statistical estimates, and the other subset, called the validation, or the test set, is used to assess the accuracy of the prediction of the training set. In cross-validation, it is possible to compare and confirm the findings of the first subsample of the data against the second, and then again the second against the first subsample, in which case the procedure is called a double cross-validation (Thompson, 1994). If the sample size is large enough, the data set can even be split into three sets: the training set, the test set, and another validation set. The second validation set is used to tune the model and help reduce the error rate of the prediction. Another form of cross-validation is n-fold cross-validation. In this procedure the whole data set is randomly partitioned into n subsets (folds) of almost equal sizes (n, for example, can be 5). Each time, one of the subsets is used as the validation, or test set, and the other sets are combined as the training set. The cross-validation is then repeated n times on the data.

The other two re-sampling methods are the bootstrap and the jackknife. The bootstrap is a computer-based simulation method that involves re-sampling the data by repeating and recombining the data in different ways. In this method, through a procedure called data replacements, a large mega-sample is created from the original sample by repeatedly copying the original sample into a large combination sample (Thompson, 1993, 1994). Different subsamples with different configurations are then randomly drawn from the mega-sample. These new samples, called bootstrap samples, are individually analyzed each time they are drawn, and the results are then compared and confirmed with each other. Such comparisons provide useful information about the variability within the data and also whether the results can be generalized within subsamples involving different subjects and configurations (for a more detailed discussion of this method, see Efron and Tibshirani, 1993).

The jackknife (also known as a "leave-one-out" method) is another technique of internal replication. Like the bootstrap, this method also involves re-sampling different subsamples and calculating and comparing the analyses of interest in these subsamples. However, unlike the bootstrap, which involves data copying, or replacement, the jackknife technique involves data omission by systematically removing subsamples from the data, one at a time, and then recalculating the intended statistics for the remaining data. Doing this provides important information about sampling variability, which in turn increases the degree of confidence in the data's replicability (see Thompson, 1993, 1994, for a more detailed discussion of this method).

However, we should bear in mind that although the above methods of internal replication are helpful in providing important cross-validation information about the findings, they have their own limitations. The first is that they usually need a reasonably adequate sample size to allow for resampling. In any analysis, including a replicability analysis, if the researcher wants to minimize the effects of within-individual idiosyncrasies, a relatively large sample size is needed (Thompson, 1994). In the case of the jackknife method, the sample size can itself become a limitation if it is too large because a large number of cross-validations are then needed. The second problem is that the findings are still limited to the properties of one sample since the analyses involve the same sample (Robinson and Levin, 1997). Also, since repeated analysis is conducted on the same sample, it maximizes the potential effects of sampling errors. Furthermore, although methods of internal replication assess variations in subjects, they do not explore variations in terms of measurement or context, and because of this, such analyses can lead to overstated evidence for replicability (Thompson, 1994).

Given these limitations, it is important not to rely solely on internal replication as a measure of result generalizability. We must eventually undertake external replication, as it is the most reliable type of replication. Since external replication involves collecting and analyzing new data, it minimizes sampling errors and also provides direct information about the extent to which the results of an original study can hold in different contexts with different samples (see replication study models by Eckerth and by Rott, in this volume).

5 Conclusion

In this chapter, I reviewed a number of misconceptions and limitations of significance tests and the suggestions for dealing with these limitations, including reporting effect sizes and confidence intervals, as well as conducting meta-analyses. I argued that these procedures provide crucial pieces of information that statistical significance tests do not, but they still do not provide information about the generalizability of research results. The only way to determine generalizability is through replication. Statistically significant results from single studies are at best suggestive, even when the tests are used appropriately, and other types of measures, such as effect sizes and confidence intervals, are deployed to complement their results. Therefore, what we eventually need is replication, and for that reason replication studies must be more widely used and encouraged in L2 research. Cronbach and Snow might summarize the essence of the arguments put forward in this chapter:

> *All* the findings of statistical studies are shadows on the wall of the cave. Some are likely to recur, but we do not know which ones ... One can make it a rule to attend only to results that have actually recurred in a second sample.
>
> (1977: 52)

References

American Psychological Association. (2010). *Publication Manual of the American Psychological Association* (6th edn.), Washington: Author.

Anderson, D. R., Burnham, K. P. and Thompson, W. L. (2000). Null hypothesis testing: Problems, prevalence, and an alternative, *The Journal of Wildlife Management*, **64**, 912–23.

Bolstad, W. M. (2007). *Introduction to Bayesian Statistics*, Hoboken, NJ: Wiley.

Borenstein, M., Hedges, L. V., Higgins, J. P. T. and Rothstein, H. R. (2009). *Introduction to Meta-analysis*, Hoboken, NJ: Wiley.

Carver, R. P. (1978). The case against statistical significance testing, *Harvard Educational Review*, **48**, 378–99.

Carver, R. P. (1993). The case against statistical significance testing, revisited, *The Journal of Experimental Education*, **61**, 287–92.

Clark, C. A. (1963). Hypothesis testing in relation to statistical methodology, *Review of Educational Research*, **33**, 455–73.

Cohen, J. (1994). The earth is round (p < .05), *American Psychologist*, **49**, 997–1003.

Cronbach, L. J. and Snow, R. E. (1977). *Aptitudes and Instructional Methods: A Handbook for Research on Interactions*, New York: Irvington.

Crookes, G. (1991). Power, effect size, and second language research. Another researcher comments, *TESOL Quarterly*, **25**, 762–5.

Cumming, G. (2008). Replication and *p* intervals: *p* values predict the future only vaguely, but confidence intervals do much better, *Perspectives on Psychological Science*, **3**, 286.

Daniel, L. G. (1998a). The statistical significance controversy is definitely not over: A rejoinder to responses by Thompson, Knapp, and Levin, *Research in the Schools*, **5**, 63–5.

Daniel, L. G. (1998b). Statistical significance testing: A historical overview of misuse and misinterpretation with implications for the editorial policies of educational journals, *Research in the Schools*, **5**, 23–32.

Efron, B. and Tibshirani, R. J. (1993). *An Introduction to the Bootstrap*, New York: Chapman and Hall.

Fitz-Gibbon, C. T. (1985). The implications of meta-analysis for educational research, *British Educational Research Journal*, **11**, 45–9.

Frick, R. W. (1996). The appropriate use of null hypothesis testing, *Psychological methods*, **1**, 379–90.

Glass, G. V., McGaw, B. and Smith, M. L. (1981). *Meta-analysis in Social Research*, Beverly Hills, CA: Sage Publications.

Hatch, E. and Lazaraton, A. (1991). *The Research Manual: Design and Statistics for Applied Linguistics*, New York: Newbury House.

Hedges, L. V. and Olkin, I. (1985). *Statistical Methods for Meta-analysis*, New York: Academic Press.

Kaufman, R., Kaufman, R. A., Guerra, I. and Platt, W. A. (2006.) *Practical Evaluation for Educators: Finding What Works and What Doesn't*, Thousand Oaks, CA: Corwin Press.

Kirk, R. E. (1996). Practical significance: A concept whose time has come, *Educational and Psychological Measurement*, **56**, 746–59.

Kline, R. B. (2004). *Beyond Significance Testing*, Washington, DC: American Psychological Association.

Knapp, T. R. (1998). Comments on the statistical significance testing articles, *Research in the Schools*, **5**, 39–41.

Larson-Hall, J. (2010). *A Guide to Doing Statistics in Second Language Research Using SPSS*, New York: Routledge.

Lazaraton, A. (1991). Power, effect size, and second language research. A researcher comments, *TESOL Quarterly*, **25**, 759–62.

Lazaraton, A. (2000). Current trends in research methodology and statistics in applied linguistics, *TESOL Quarterly*, **34**, 175–81.

Lazaraton, A. (2009). The use of statistics in SlA: A response to Loewen and Gass (2009), *Language Teaching*, **42**, 415–16.

Lazaraton, A., Riggenbach, H. and Ediger, A. (1987). Forming a discipline: Applied linguists' literacy in research methodology and statistics, *TESOL Quarterly*, **21**, 263–77.

Loewen, S. and Gass, S. (2009). The use of statistics in L2 acquisition research, *Language Teaching*, **42**, 181–96.

Morrison, D. E. and Henkel, R. E. (1970). *The Significance Test Controversy*, Chicago: Aldine.

Norris, J. M. and Ortega, L. (2010). Research synthesis, *Language Teaching*, **43**, 461–79.

Nunnally, J. C. (1975). *Introduction to Statistics for Psychology and Education*, New York: McGraw-Hill.

Oakes, M. (1986). *Statistical Inference: A Commentary for the Social and Behavioural Sciences*, New York: Wiley.

Olejnik, S. and Algina, J. (2000). Measures of effect size for comparative studies: Applications, interpretations, and limitations, *Contemporary Educational Psychology*, **25**, 241–86.

Oswald, F. L. and Plonsky, L. (2010). Meta-analysis in second language research: Choices and challenges, *Annual Review of Applied Linguistics*, **30**, 85–110.

Pedhazur, E. J. and Schmelkin, L. P. (1991). *Measurement, Design, and Analysis: An Integrated Approach*. Hillsdale, NJ: Lawrence Erlbaum Associates.

Pruzek, R. M. (1997). An introduction to Bayesian inference and its applications, in Harlow, L. L., Muliak, S. A. and Steiger, J. H. (eds.), *What If There Were No Significance Tests?*, Mahwah, NJ: Lawrence Erlbaum Associates, pp. 287–318.

Robinson, D. H. and Levin, J. R. (1997). Reflections on statistical and substantive significance, with a slice of replication, *Educational Researcher*, **26**, 21–6.

Rosenthal, R. and Rubin, D. B. (1982). A simple, general purpose display of magnitude of experimental effect, *Journal of Educational Psychology*, **74**, 166–9.

Rozeboom, W. W. (1960). The fallacy of the null hypothesis significance test, *Psychological Bulletin*, **57**, 416–28.

Rozeboom, W. W. (1997). Good science is abductive, not hypothetico-deductive, in Harlow, L. L., Mulaik, S. A. and Steiger, J. H. (eds.), *What If There Were No Significance Tests?*, Mahwah, NJ: Lawrence Erlbaum Associates, pp. 335–92.

Schmidt, F. L. (1996). Statistical significance testing and cumulative knowledge in psychology: Implications for training of researchers, *Psychological methods*, **1**, 115–29.

Schmidt, F. L. and Hunter, J. E. (1997). Eight common but false objections to the discontinuation of significance testing in the analysis of research data, in Harlow, L. L., Muliak, S. A. and Steiger, J. H. (eds.), *What If There Were No Significance Tests?*, Mahwah, NJ: Lawrence Erlbaum Associates, pp. 37–64.

Snyder, P. A. and Thompson, B. (1998). Use of tests of statistical significance and other analytic choices in a school psychology journal: Review of practices and suggested alternatives, *School Psychology Quarterly*, **13**, 335–48.

Sohn, D. (1998). Statistical significance and replicability, *Theory and Psychology*, **8**, 291–311.

Sterling, T. D. (1959). Publication decisions and their possible effects on inferences drawn from tests of significance – or vice versa, *Journal of the American Statistical Association*, **54**, 30–34.

Sterling, T. D., Rosenbaum, W. L. and Weinkam, J. J. (1995). Publication decisions revisited: The effect of the outcome of statistical tests on the decision to publish and vice versa, *The American Statistician*, **49**, 108–12.

Thompson, B. (1992). Two and one-half decades of leadership in measurement and evaluation, *Journal of Counseling and Development*, **70**, 434–8.

Thompson, B. (1993). The use of statistical significance tests in research: Bootstrap and other alternatives, *Journal of Experimental Education*, **61**, 361–77.

Thompson, B. (1994). The pivotal role of replication in psychological research: Empirically evaluating the replicability of sample results, *Journal of Personality*, **62**, 157–76.

Thompson, B. (1996). Aera editorial policies regarding statistical significance testing: Three suggested reforms, *Educational Researcher*, **25**, 26–30.

Thompson, B. (1999). If statistical significance tests are broken/misused, what practices should supplement or replace them?, *Theory and Psychology*, **9**, 165–81.

Thompson, B. (2005). Effect sizes versus statistical significance, in Swanson, R. A. and Holton III, E. F. (eds.), *Research in Organizations: Foundations and Methods of Inquiry*. San Francisco, CA: Berrett-Koehler Publishers, pp. 57–73.

Tyron, W. W. (1998). The inscrutable null hypothesis, *American Psychologist*, **53**, 796.

4 Replication, meta-analysis, and generalizability

Luke Plonsky

SLA is a relatively young field that has been primarily concerned with collecting data and producing original research. The field has spread itself out, covering a vast theoretical territory and addressing a wide range of questions related to both theory and practice. The result of this condition, also observed in other fields, is an overreliance on individual studies to advance theory and inform future research (e.g., Schmidt, 1996). Recently, however, SLA researchers have begun to at least take an interest in, and value, replication and meta-analysis as tools that can be used to reach greater precision and reliability of findings over time. Although replication in SLA has not yet shown the signs of coming of age like meta-analysis (see Oswald and Plonsky, 2010), the relationship between and benefits shared by these methods make it fitting – and of great potential benefit to the field – that they should enter the mainstream of SLA research together. First, implied in both replication and meta-analysis is a rejection of the assumption that a single or one-shot study can provide a definitive answer to any of the questions posed by SLA research, a position echoed throughout this volume and shared by colleagues across the sciences (e.g., Sun et al., 2010). Second, and perhaps somewhat less often recognized, is the symbiotic nature of these approaches, one of which contributes to the purposeful accumulation of data and another that provides a retrospective account of that data. Third, and most central to the discussion in this chapter, is the inherent concern of both replication and meta-analysis in determining the generalizability of findings across different contexts, learners, target structures, and so on (see Chalhoub-Deville et al., 2006, for a thorough discussion of generalizability and related issues in applied linguistics).

The three-part section that follows will expand on the relationship between replication and meta-analysis and the capacity of both, individually and in coordination, to establish and determine generalizability in L2 research. The next section will make a case for replication at the meta-analytic level, drawing on examples from the L2 literature. Finally, toward greater consistency, interpretability, and replicability of meta-analyses, in the last section I will propose an instrument for assessing the research and reporting practices of L2 meta-analyses.

1 Replication and generalizability

Whether expressed explicitly or not, most quantitative, primary research in SLA seeks to generalize. I think we can all agree on this. The extent to which applied linguists agree – in theory and in practice – on the conclusiveness of claims about generalizability from a particular study, however, will vary. Imagine a quasi-experiment designed to test the effect of an instructional intervention on learners' acquisition of a particular grammatical structure. And let's say the study found a statistically and practically significant effect for the treatment. Even if, for the sake of this exercise, we ignore some excellent arguments in favor of replication research presented elsewhere in this volume, such as the unreliability of p values (see Nassaji, Chapter 3, this volume) or low power due to small samples typical of applied linguistics research (Plonsky, 2011b; Plonsky and Gass, 2011; Polio and Gass, 1997), we as a field still ought to give serious consideration to the extent to which it is appropriate to generalize these findings. More concretely, would we expect the findings to apply to other learners of the same L2 at different proficiency levels or in a different educational setting or from a different L1 background? And how about with a different L2 target structure or a similar structure in a different L2? These questions, typical of much of L2 research, are questions of generalizability that require replication. For this reason, we must accept and even embrace a more incremental and, at times, patience-testing pace toward cumulative knowledge. Such an approach will lead more slowly to advances but it is one that principally engenders precision, because it tests rather than assumes external validity, and, by extension, efficiency of research efforts and resources.

To be sure, the incremental and replication-based approach advocated here represents a marked change from the current culture of topic selection, study execution, and what is perceived as progress in SLA. Whereas, historically, priority has been given to novelty and extensive research efforts, the focus here is on intensive research aimed at filling gaps, determining generalizability of findings, and thereby moving theory forward perhaps less rapidly but with greater accuracy.

1.1 Meta-analysis and generalizability

If replication research contributes to generalizability by retesting and reexamining hypotheses, examining the validity of previous findings across different learner populations, L2s, linguistic structures, and so forth, the purpose of meta-analysis is to consolidate the data collected across all studies and variables related to a particular question or hypothesis to determine the extent of the relationships in question. In this way, the capacity of meta-analysis is not only constrained by the number, quality, and breadth of replication research, it depends on such research exclusively; without replications, at least in the conceptual sense, there are no meta-analyses.

In the context of this discussion, it may seem obvious that meta-analysis should play an important role in determining generalizability. Nevertheless, there are at least two related conditions that limit the capacity of meta-analysis to inform generalizability. First is the fact that the data that undergo meta-analysis are not always sufficiently representative of the different populations, contexts, and structures to which one might generalize the meta-analytic result (see Matt and Cook, 2009). With a median sample of only 16 studies among 27 L2 meta-analyses reviewed by Oswald and Plonsky (2010), however, it is unlikely that the findings of previous meta-analyses, most of which synthesize bodies of research on adult learners of English as a second language or adult learners of another foreign language studied in the United States, can be interpreted as generalizable considering the wide array of language-learner populations. Moreover, L2 meta-analysts frequently cite specific areas to which their findings should not be generalized due to lacking or absent primary data. For example, in their meta-analysis of the relationship between test format and performance, In'nami and Koizumi (2009) found that only three primary studies had collected data from learners with first languages (L1s) other than English. Recognizing this limitation in the corrective feedback literature, the potential threat to external validity that it introduces, and the need for replication research as a remedy, Russell and Spada state that "there is a need not only for a greater volume of studies on corrective feedback, but also for studies that investigate similar variables in a consistent manner" (2006: 156).

The second impediment to meta-analysis as a tool for informing generalizability has less to do with the availability of data – although that, of course, is a prerequisite – and more to do with how the published results of meta-analyses are consumed and interpreted. More specifically, the prominence given to the overall finding or *grand mean* (i.e., the mean of the means) often overshadows the rich set of secondary results produced by most meta-analyses. Although this summary statistic, the distillation and culmination of years and massive amounts of data, usually provides an answer to a question of much import, the greatest capacity of meta-analysis in terms of informing theory and hypothesis testing may be its ability to provide a quantitative indication of the more subtle relationships between variables measured across primary studies (Lipsey and Wilson, 2001). This task is accomplished by means of *subgroup analyses* (also referred to as *sensitivity analyses*), or separate meta-analyses of effect sizes based on substantive (e.g., explicitness of instruction) and/or methodological variables (e.g., length of intervention, study quality) that are used to group and average effects. It is also this portion of a meta-analysis that tests and speaks mostly directly to parameter estimates and generalizability (Littell et al., 2008). For example, in order to answer whether or to what extent there may be a relationship between the effects of corrective feedback and different classroom contexts as well as the type of instrument used to measure those effects (i.e., questions of generalizability), Lyster and Saito (2010) separately meta-analyzed subgroups of studies based on whether they were carried out in second or foreign language settings and whether the measure for the dependent variable was a free constructed response, a constrained constructed response, or a metalinguistic judgment. Depending on what is available in the primary literature, many meta-analysts are able to use subgroup analyses to address questions related to generalizability not explicitly posed by any constituent study. And by doing so, they are able to fulfill the purpose of meta-analysis according to Hall et al. to "summarize *and* add new knowledge" (1994: 24–25, emphasis added). From the L2 literature, Bowles (2010) was able to test the relationship between proficiency and the reactivity of think-aloud protocols, which had not been examined in any previous study. Likewise, Plonsky's (2011a) meta-analysis tested the relationship between strategy instruction and several variables that had been hypothesized to relate to its effectiveness but had never been controlled for in primary studies, such as number of strategies taught, length of interventions, and whether the study was conducted in a laboratory or classroom setting.

1.2 Replication, meta-analysis, and generalizability

So far this chapter has described the trajectory toward determining generalizability as somewhat linear: primary research is conducted and replicated to incorporate novel variables/values, the findings of which may then be meta-analyzed as a means to quantify an overall relationship as well as the validity of that relationship among different populations, outcome types, and so forth. In theory, this might be sufficient to move the field forward. In a young discipline such as SLA, however, it is more likely, practical, and desirable for this process to play out

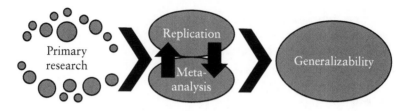

Figure 4.1   A model of the contributions of primary research, replication research, and meta-analysis to generalizability

in a more iterative fashion. That is, not only do replications inform future meta-analyses, but meta-analyses can and should inform future replications, as illustrated in Figure 4.1. This can take place somewhat implicitly when, as exemplified above, meta-analysts identify areas lacking attention in the empirical research base. A meta-analyst can also be more explicit in attempting to influence future replications by suggesting a *prospective meta-analysis*, an a priori outline for future research that specifies the number and types of studies needed to fill gaps in the literature (see Berlin and Ghersi, 2005).

Of course, there is no guarantee that the studies prescribed by the prospective meta-analysis will be carried out, but there are at least three potential benefits to such practice in addition to a more robust and representative set of primary data that can later be meta-analyzed. First, clear direction for a given subdomain may decrease researcher idiosyncrasy (e.g., in study design, sampling). Second, multiple studies intentionally carried out to address a common question (i.e., replications) may reduce the expectation of individual studies to provide definitive answers (Allen and Preiss, 1993). And third, if researchers collaborate to carry out a series of planned studies to later be meta-analyzed, their research, whether published or not, may be less susceptible to the file-drawer problem (see, for example, Becker, 2005; Sutton, 2009) and therefore more accessible to the meta-analyst.

2 Replicating meta-analyses

The previous section describes a model of the cyclical and symbiotic relationship between replication and meta-analysis. In an environment where replication studies are carried out following or in response to a meta-analysis, it is somewhat intuitive that meta-analyses should be "replicated" as well. The following discussion describes several reasons why such replications of meta-analyses have contributed and will continue to contribute to progress in applied linguistics.

An initial and perhaps obvious justification for replications at the meta-analytic level is an increase in the number of primary studies investigating a common question. In Jeon and Kaya's words, "as long as the research domain under analysis is still growing, no meta-analysis can provide a conclusive picture of the domain in question" (2006: 203). To be sure, a greater number of individual studies will produce an estimate of the relationships in question that is more precise and less vulnerable to sampling error. Considering the relatively low statistical power in both primary studies and meta-analyses (see Oswald and Plonsky, 2010; Plonsky, 2011b; and Plonsky and Gass, 2011), several L2 meta-analysts have interpreted their findings cautiously, suggesting they be viewed as tentative as opposed to conclusive (e.g., Russell and Spada, 2006; Abraham, 2008). As mentioned above, L2 meta-analyses have also frequently suggested areas in need of future research. Jeon and Kaya (2006) went even further. Following their meta-analysis of L2 pragmatics instruction, the authors suggested not only additional studies but meta-analytic replications at regular intervals. And of course, beyond improving the overall meta-analytic mean, a larger sample of primary studies will also enable more refined and accurate subgroup analyses.

In addition to the accumulation of data leading to more precise meta-analytic results, replicating meta-analyses may also reveal changes over time in a particular subdomain that would otherwise go unnoticed. It is unrealistic to think that evidence will remain static (see Trikalinos et al., 2004). Consider these two scenarios: In the first scenario, as theory in a given area moves forward, increasingly nuanced relationships are investigated, leading to a decrease in effect sizes over time (Kline, 2004). For example, whereas early (quasi-)experimental studies of feedback were interested in whether or not there was a relationship between feedback and L2 gains, later studies examined this relationship at a much more finely grained level, investigating differences between different types of feedback such as recasts and prompts and even among different subtypes of recasts (e.g., Sheen, 2006). In the case of applied linguistics, meta-analyses and replications of meta-analyses may also reveal research in a particular area to transition from laboratory- to classroom-based research over time, where we might also expect to find smaller effects due to constraints on experimental control (Plonsky and Oswald, 2012). In their methodological synthesis of the interactionist tradition in SLA, Plonsky and Gass (2011) observed both of these phenomena: Among other trends, effect sizes decreased over time, and classroom-based research increased whereas laboratory-based research decreased. Conversely, we might find an increase in effect sizes over time due to improvements to instrumentation and in researchers' ability to manipulate variables (Fern and Monroe, 1996). Using replications of meta-analyses to study changes over time may also shed light on changes in methodological developments that result from suggestions or reforms of research practices proposed in previous meta-analyses. Spada and Tomita (2010), for instance, attribute in part the increase in recent years in the number of studies using measures of spontaneous and unanalyzed speech to comments made by Norris and Ortega (2000) related to data elicitation techniques in studies of L2 instruction.

Of course, changes in methods do not only occur among primary studies. We should expect to see the procedures used to carry out meta-analyses progress over time as well. To be sure, meta-analytic methods in this field are still developing, and SLA will most likely continue to follow in the methodological footsteps of other social sciences such as psychology (see Gass, 1993; Felser, 2005), moving toward greater sophistication over time. Although there is some truth to Shin's assertion that "subsequent meta-analyses have uncritically followed the methodological choices made by Norris and Ortega [2000]" (2010: 15), there is also already evidence of a maturation of meta-analytic methods taking place in SLA. Recent SLA meta-analyses, for example, have employed several novel and slightly more sophisticated techniques such as modeling (i.e., fixed vs. random effects: Taylor et al., 2006; Li, 2010), effect size weighting (e.g., Mackey and Goo, 2007; Spada and Tomita, 2010), and failsafe-N and funnel plots to examine publication bias (e.g., Abraham, 2008; Plonsky, 2011a). A third reason for replicating meta-analyses is then to produce more precise results based on more comprehensive or rigorous methods. Along these lines, Shin (2010) also suggested a reinterpretation of Norris and Ortega's (2000) findings based on an alternate set of procedures for data collection, coding, and analysis.

Finally, meta-analyses can also be replicated to answer questions that are similar to those addressed in previous meta-analyses but that are overlooked or that are either broader or narrower in scope than a previous meta-analysis. Lyster and Saito (2010) provide an example of a narrow or "local" meta-analysis (see Oswald and McCloy, 2003). Although the effects of corrective feedback had already been meta-analyzed (e.g., Russell and Spada, 2006), Lyster and Saito focused exclusively on studies of oral feedback in classroom contexts. Likewise, Plonsky (2011a) could be considered an approximate or conceptual replication of Taylor et al.'s (2006) meta-analysis of L2 reading strategy instruction. In this case, however, the replication was broader in scope, focusing on the effects of strategy instruction across multiple skill areas and outcome types (e.g., reading, speaking, grammar, vocabulary, strategy use).

For many of the reasons described above, conceptual replications make up a large portion of the meta-analyses carried out to date in applied linguistics – perhaps surprisingly so. Table 4.1 (overleaf) lists these studies, the general topics they cover, and one or more characteristics that distinguish them from other meta-analyses that overlap in primary studies included and/or substantive concerns addressed. In the case of interaction, for example, Mackey and Goo (2007) expanded on the work of Keck et al. (2006) by including a number of additional studies of interaction. Mackey and Goo also chose to examine the effects of different types of corrective feedback as separate subsets of the research on interaction. Of course, several additional studies have meta-analyzed the effects of corrective feedback, also shown in Table 4.1, yet each chose unique research questions, included a unique set of primary studies, and/or employed unique procedures to answer their questions. These decisions, in addition to the many others related to collecting, coding, and analyzing primary data among meta-analyzes of corrective feedback, have led to a variety of mean (subgrouped) effects, ranging from a small, negative effect of $d = -0.16$ for feedback on writing (Truscott, 2007) to a positive, large effect of $d = 1.69$ for recasts with a short delay (Mackey and Goo, 2007; see Oswald and Plonsky, 2010, for a discussion on the choices involved in conducting meta-analyses of L2 research and how these choices influence study outcomes). The relationship between the five meta-analyses addressing the effectiveness of L2 instruction is similar. We see two relatively inclusive studies: Norris and Ortega (2000) and Goo et al. (2009); two studies addressing somewhat narrower questions: Jeon and Kaya (2006, pragmatics instruction) and Won (2008, vocabulary instruction); and one (Spada and Tomita, 2010) that reported the findings of four separate meta-analyses investigating the interaction between types of instruction and language features. And again, although these meta-analyses can certainly be considered conceptual replications of each other, each has clearly employed its own set of operationalizations, producing a wide range of overall d values: from 0.29 (pre–post contrasts for implicit instruction on complex L2 features; Spada and Tomita, 2010) to 1.66 (pre–post contrasts, overall; Norris and Ortega, 2000).

Table 4.1   *Replications of L2 meta-analyses*

Topic	Citation	Distinguishing characteristic(s)*
Interaction	Keck et al. (2006)	Task-based interaction
	Mackey and Goo (2007)	Interaction
	Cobb (2010)	Interaction in form-focused instruction
Corrective feedback	Norris and Ortega (2000)	Different types of instruction including corrective feedback
	Russell and Spada (2006)	Effects of corrective feedback on grammar learning
	Keck et al. (2006)	Included corrective feedback but not meta-analyzed separately
	Mackey and Goo (2007)	Corrective feedback types as subsets of interaction
	Truscott (2007)	Corrective feedback and accuracy in L2 writing
	Poltavtchenko and Johnson (2009)	Written corrective feedback and L2 writing
	Li (2010)	Additional studies including dissertations
	Lyster and Saito (2010)	Classroom studies only
	Biber et al. (2011)	Feedback for L1 and L2 writing
	Kao and Wible (2011)	Focused and unfocused feedback on L2 writing
L2 instruction	Norris and Ortega (2000)	L2 instruction
	Jeon and Kaya (2006)	L2 pragmatics instruction
	Won (2008)	Vocabulary instruction
	Goo et al. (2009)	Extension/update of Norris and Ortega (2000)
	Spada and Tomita (2010)	Type of instruction by L2 feature
Strategy instruction	Taylor et al. (2006)	L2 reading strategy instruction
	Plonsky (2011a)	L2 strategy instruction across all outcomes

Table 4.1 (continued)

Topic	Citation	Distinguishing characteristic(s)*
L1 glosses, reading, and vocabulary learning	Taylor (2006)	Effect of computer-assisted language learning (CALL) vs. traditional L1 glosses on reading comprehension
	Wa-Mbaleka (2006)	Effect of reading on vocabulary learning
	Abraham (2008)	Effect of CALL glosses on reading comprehension and vocabulary learning
Technology and L2 learning	Zhao (2003)	Different forms of technology
	Grgurović (2007)	CALL/non-CALL comparison studies only
	Taylor (2006)	Effect of CALL vs. traditional L1 glosses on reading comprehension
	Abraham (2008)	Effect of CALL glosses on reading comprehension and vocabulary learning

*The distinguishing characteristics are not exhaustive. In most, if not all, cases there are several additional substantive and methodological differences between each meta-analysis listed and the others in each category.

3 Toward a standard for meta-analyses in L2 research

Several chapters in this volume have referenced the importance of transparency and thoroughness in L2 research. These characteristics of research reports are not only preferred but necessary in order to (a) delineate the substantive domain under investigation, (b) enable replications and meta-analyses, (c) appraise the appropriateness of the methods used to address a particular study's research questions, and (d) allow for consumers of research to (re-)interpret the data that are presented. True to the parallelism between primary and meta-analytic research (see, for example, Cooper, 1982, 2007; Norris and Ortega, 2006), the same benefits of transparency hold for reports of meta-analyses as well (Wilson, 2009). Therefore, as a means to guide future meta-analyses toward consistent and maximally informative and replicable reports, the final section of this chapter proposes an instrument designed to evaluate meta-analyses of L2 research. However, first, a few comments are given on the instrument's development and use and the standards it aims to uphold.

There are three conditions currently in applied linguistics that I feel prompt the need for an instrument such as this. First is the rapid expansion of meta-analysis in our field (see Oswald and Plonsky, 2010). I am aware of 38 meta-analyses of L2 research, 33 of which have been published and/or carried out (but may not be published yet) in the last five years. Second, meta-analyses tend to have a substantial impact on the subdomains they synthesize, evidenced by a much higher than average rate of citations (Cooper and Hedges, 2009). Third and most pressing is the lack of familiarity with meta-analytic methods among L2 researchers. Taken together, these three conditions suggest that the development of our field may be greatly influenced by a type of research that only a small number of individuals is able to adequately assess. The instrument below was therefore designed with consideration to journal editors, manuscript reviewers, and, of course, readers of meta-analyses who might use it as a tool or guide to evaluate the many decisions involved in carrying out and reporting on a meta-analysis and their effects on internal validity. The intended use by these different groups is reflected in the organization of the instrument, which follows the format of research reports (i.e., introduction/literature review, methods, results/discussion) instead of the steps involved in carrying out a meta-analysis, for example (i.e., defining the domain, locating primary studies, coding, etc.).

The items included in the current version of this instrument (Table 4.2), which will need to be modified based on the progression of meta-analytic methods in L2 research and the needs of researchers in the field, were drawn from several sources. The first and main source was Oswald and Plonsky's (2010) discussion of the choices and challenges inherent to carrying out meta-analyses of L2 research. I also examined a number of measures that have been proposed to assess methodological quality of systematic, secondary research from the meta-analysis literature (e.g., Cooper, 2007). In their "Proposed reporting checklist for authors, editors, and reviewers of meta-analyses of observational studies," for example, Stroup et al. (2000) include useful and relevant items such as databases and registries searched, and guidelines for future research. However, other items from Stroup et al. and other such instruments (e.g., Shea et al., 2007; Journal Article Reporting Standards Group, in *American Psychologist*, 2008; Bessa-Nogueira et al., 2008; Moher et al., 2009) were consolidated for greater parsimony or excluded due to the difference in sophistication and/or substantive interests between current meta-analytic methods in SLA and the fields from which these

Table 4.2 Proposed instrument for assessing reports of L2 meta-analyses

0–2*	Items
	Introduction/Literature review
_____	1 Does the review address a focused and clearly defined question?
_____	2 Are all (potential) moderator variables identified a priori and explained sufficiently?
_____	3 Is the relevance of the study, both theoretical and practical, presented?
_____	4 Are potential biases of primary and secondary researchers recognized?
_____	5 Are the different study designs explained with respect to their potential strengths and weaknesses?
_____	6 Are the different types of data collection instruments used in primary research explained?
	Methods
_____	1 Was the search for relevant primary research reasonably exhaustive?
_____	2 Are the inclusion/exclusion criteria sufficiently explicit and unambiguous?
_____	3 Was the presence of publication bias assessed?
_____	4 Was interrater reliability for coding measured and adequate?
_____	5 Was the quality of primary studies assessed?
_____	6 Were effect sizes from the same sample/study dealt with appropriately?
_____	7 Were effect sizes weighted appropriately?
_____	8 Were missing data dealt with appropriately?
_____	9 Were outliers dealt with appropriately?
_____	10 Are all items on the coding sheet justified and available for inspection?
	Results/Discussion
_____	1 Are the main (i.e., summary) findings presented?
_____	2 Does the review add new knowledge about the constructs of interest?
_____	3 Are the results interpreted and contextualized appropriately?
_____	4 Are the findings discussed in relation to the particular theory or model(s) being tested?
_____	5 Are practical implications discussed?
_____	6 Are the findings used to provide substantive and methodological suggestions for future research?

*0 = No; 1 = Somewhat; 2 = Yes

measures were drawn (e.g., description of how credibility intervals were calculated, statistical power of the meta-analysis; see Valentine et al., 2010, for a discussion on the importance of field-specific instruments or checklists for evaluating meta-analyses).

This instrument provides users with critical questions to ask regarding the quality of L2 meta-analyses. Answering these questions accurately and consistently, of course, requires a solid understanding of the domain being meta-analyzed and, ideally, some familiarity with research synthetic methods. For introductory readings on the latter, I suggest the following references from within applied linguistics: Norris and Ortega (2006, 2007), In'nami and Koizumi (2010), Ortega (2010), Oswald and Plonsky (2010), Plonsky and Oswald (2012).

Finally, beyond satisfying these minimally sufficient conditions for transparency, a logical next step or goal for applied linguistics would be to follow the lead of other fields, such as medicine, where meta-analytic data sets are made available online as supplementary materials. This suggestion has been voiced previously within applied linguistics (Polio and Gass, 1997) and in this volume (see chapters by Porte, Abbuhl, and Mackey), but it bears repeating in the context of replication at the meta-analytic level. In the same way, published data sets could inform consumers of primary research and would-be replicators. Providing access to meta-analytic data in a comprehensive and consistent manner would enable additional interpretations and analyses of unstudied relationships, for example, and would greatly facilitate future replications. In addition, public access to meta-analytic databases would also enable the findings of meta-analyses to be updated as soon as relevant findings are published and able to be integrated into existing data sets.

4 Conclusion

This chapter has described the symbiotic relationship between two types of research – replication and meta-analysis – and their combined contributions toward determining generalizability of empirical findings in applied linguistics. Although replication and meta-analysis share a common concern with previous research, this chapter has shown how both, used in conjunction, are necessary to move the field forward in an incremental but maximally efficient manner. This chapter also examined the prospect and utility of replication at the meta-analytic level, providing several reasons for doing so. Finally, an instrument was proposed for assessing written reports of meta-analyses that may contribute to more accurate and informative meta-analyses as well as future replications of meta-analyses in applied linguistics.

References

Abraham, L. B. (2008). Computer-mediated glosses in second language reading comprehension and vocabulary learning: A meta-analysis, *Computer Assisted Language Learning*, **21**, 199–226.

Allen, M. and Preiss, R. (1993). Replication and meta-analysis: A necessary connection, *Journal of Social Behavior and Personality*, **8**, 9–30.

Becker, B. J. (2005). Failsafe *N* or file-drawer number, in Rothstein, H. R., Sutton, A, J. and Borenstein, M. (eds.), *Publication Bias in Meta-analysis: Prevention, Assessment and Adjustments*, Hoboken, NJ: Wiley, pp. 111–26.

Berlin, J. A. and Ghersi, D. G. (2005). Preventing publication bias: Registries and prospective meta-analysis, in Rothstein, H. R., Sutton, A. J. and Borenstein, M. (eds.), *Publication Bias in Meta-analysis: Prevention, Assessment and Adjustments*, Hoboken, NJ: Wiley, pp. 35–48.

Bessa-Nogueira, R. V., Vasconcelos, B. C. E. and Niederman, R. (2008). The methodological quality of systematic reviews comparing temporomandibular joint disorder surgical and non-surgical treatment, *BMC Oral Health*, **8**, 27.

Biber, D., Nekrasova, T. and Horn, B. (2011). The effectiveness of feedback for L1-English and L2 writing development: A meta-analysis, *TOEFL iBT Re-search Report No. TOEFLiBT-14*. Princeton, NJ: Educational Testing Service.

Bowles, M. A. (2010). *The Think-Aloud Controversy in Second Language Research* (Chapter 3), New York: Routledge.

Chalhoub-Deville, M., Chapelle, C. A. and Duff, P. (eds.) (2006). *Inference and Generalizability in Applied Linguistics: Multiple Perspectives*, Amsterdam: John Benjamins.

Cobb, M. (2010). Meta-analysis of the Effectiveness of Task-Based Interaction in Form-Focused Instruction of Adult Learners in Foreign and Second Language Teaching. Unpublished doctoral dissertation. San Francisco, CA: University of San Francisco.

Cooper, H. (1982). Scientific guidelines for conducting integrative research reviews, *Review of Educational Research*, **52**, 291–302.

Cooper, H. (2007). *Evaluating and Interpreting Research Syntheses in Adult Learning and Literacy*, Cambridge, MA: National College Transition Network, New England Literacy Resource Center / World Education, Inc.

Cooper, H. and Hedges, L. V. (2009). Research synthesis as a scientific process, in Cooper, H., Hedges, L. V. and Valentine, J. C. (eds.), *The Handbook of Research Synthesis and Meta-analysis* (2nd edn.), New York: Russell Sage Foundation, pp. 3–16.

Felser, C. (2005). Experimental psycholinguistic approaches to second language acquisition, *Second Language Research*, **21**, 95–7.

Fern, E. F. and Monroe, K. B. (1996). Effect-size estimates: Issues and problems in interpretation, *Journal of Consumer Research*, **23**, 89–105.

Gass, S. (1993). Editorial. Second language acquisition: Cross-disciplinary perspectives, *Second Language Research*, **9**, 95–8.

Goo, J., Granena, G., Novella, M. and Yilmaz, Y. (2009). Implicit and explicit instruction in L2 learning: Norris and Ortega (2000) revisited and updated. Paper presented at the Second Language Research Forum, East Lansing, MI.

Grgurović, M. (2007). Research on CALL comparison studies: Can a meta-analysis inform instructed SLA?. Paper presented at the Second Language Research Forum, Urbana-Champaign, IL.

Hall, J. A., Tickle-Degnen, L., Rosenthal, R. and Mosteller, F. (1994). Hypotheses and problems in research synthesis, in Cooper, H. and Hedges, L. V. (eds.), *The Handbook of Research Synthesis*, New York: Russell Sage Foundation, pp. 17–28.

In'nami, Y. and Koizumi, R. (2009). A meta-analysis of test format effects on reading and listening test performance: Focus on multiple-choice and open-ended formats, *Language Testing*, 26, 219–44.

In'nami, Y. and Koizumi, R. (2010). Database selection guidelines for meta-analysis in applied linguistics, *TESOL Quarterly*, 44, 169–84.

Jeon, E. H. and Kaya, T. (2006). Effects of L2 instruction on interlanguage pragmatic development: A meta-analysis, in Norris, J. M. and Ortega, L. (eds.), *Synthesizing Research on Language Learning and Teaching*, Philadelphia: John Benjamins, pp. 165–211.

Journal Article Reporting Standards Working Group (2008). Reporting standards for research in psychology: Why do we need them? What might they be?, *American Psychologist*, 63, 839–51.

Kao, C.-W. and Wible, D. (October 2011). The Distinction Between Focused and Unfocused Grammar Feedback Matters: A Meta-analysis. Paper presented at the Second Language Research Forum, Ames, IA.

Keck, C. M., Iberri-Shea, G., Tracy-Ventura, N. and Wa-Mbaleka, S. (2006). Investigating the empirical link between task-based interaction and acquisition: A meta-analysis, in Norris, J. M. and Ortega, L. (eds.), *Synthesizing Research on Language Learning and Teaching*, Philadelphia: John Benjamins, pp. 91–131.

Kline, R. B. (2004). *Beyond Significance Testing: Reforming Data Analysis Methods in Behavioral Research*, Washington, DC: American Psychological Association.

Li, S. (2010). The effectiveness of corrective feedback in SLA: A meta-analysis, *Language Learning*, 60, 309–65.

Lipsey, M. W. and Wilson, D. B. (2001). *Practical Meta-analysis*, Thousand Oaks, CA: Sage.

Littell, J. H., Corcoran, J. C. and Pillai, V. (2008). *Systematic Reviews and Meta-analysis*, New York: Oxford University Press.

Lyster, R. and Saito, K. (2010). Oral feedback in classroom SLA: A meta-analysis, *Studies in Second Language Acquisition*, 32, 265–302.

Mackey, A. and Goo, J. (2007). Interaction research in SLA: A meta-analysis and research synthesis, in Mackey, A. (ed.), *Conversational Interaction in Second Language Acquisition: A Collection of Empirical Studies*, New York: Oxford University Press, pp. 407–51.

Matt, G. E. and Cook, T. D. (2009). Threats to the validity of generalized inferences, in Cooper, H., Hedges, L. V. and Valentine, J. C. (eds.), *The*

Handbook of Research Synthesis and Meta-analysis (2nd edn.), New York: Russell Sage Foundation, pp. 537–60.

Moher, D., Liberati, A., Tetzlaff, J. and Altman, D. G. (the PRISMA Group) (2009). Preferred reporting items for systematic reviews and meta-analyses: The PRISMA statement, *British Medical Journal*, **339**, 332–6.

Norris, J. M. and Ortega, L. (2000). Effectiveness of L2 instruction: A research synthesis and quantitative meta-analysis, *Language Learning*, **50**, 417–528.

Norris, J. M. and Ortega, L. (2006). The value and practice of research synthesis for language learning and teaching, in Norris, J. M. and Ortega, L. (eds.), *Synthesizing Research on Language Learning and Teaching*, Philadelphia, PA: John Benjamins, pp. 3–50.

Norris, J. M. and Ortega, L. (2007). The future of research synthesis in applied linguistics: Beyond art or science, *TESOL Quarterly*, **41**, 805–15.

Ortega, L. (2010). Research synthesis, in Paltridge, B. and Phakiti, A. (eds.), *Companion to Research Methods in Applied Linguistics*, London: Continuum, pp. 111–26.

Oswald, F. L. and McCloy, R. A. (2003). Meta-analysis and the art of the average, in Murphy, K. R. (ed.). *Validity Generalization: A Critical Review*, Mahwah, NJ: Lawrence Erlbaum, Associates, pp. 311–38.

Oswald, F. L. and Plonsky, L. (2010). Meta-analysis in L2 research: Choices and challenges, *Annual Review of Applied Linguistics*, **30**, 85–115.

Plonsky, L. (2011a). The effectiveness of second language strategy instruction: A meta-analysis, *Language Learning*, **61**, 993–1038.

Plonsky, L. (2011b). Study Quality in SLA: A Cumulative and Developmental Assessment of Designs, Analyses, Reporting Practices, and Outcomes in Quantitative L2 Research. Unpublished doctoral dissertation, Michigan State University.

Plonsky, L. and Gass, S. (2011). 30 Years of interaction: Research methods, study quality, and outcomes, *Language Learning*, **61**, 325–66.

Plonsky, L. and Oswald, F. L. (2012). How to do a meta-analysis, in Mackey, A. and Gass, S. M. (eds.), *A Guide to Research Methods in Second Language Acquisition*, London: Basil Blackwell, pp. 275–95.

Polio, C. and Gass, S. (1997). Replication and reporting: A commentary, *Studies in Second Language Acquisition*, **19**, 495–508.

Poltavtchenko, E. and Johnson, M. D. (2009). Feedback and second language writing: A meta-analysis, poster session presented at the annual meeting of TESOL, Denver, CO.

Russell, J. and Spada, N. (2006). The effectiveness of corrective feedback for the acquisition of L2 grammar: A meta-analysis of the research, in Norris, J. M. and Ortega, L. (eds.), *Synthesizing Research on Language Learning and Teaching*, Philadelphia: John Benjamins, pp. 133–64.

Schmidt, F. L. (1996). Statistical significance testing and cumulative knowledge in psychology: Implications for training of researchers, *Psychological Methods*, **1**, 115–29.

Shea, B. J., Grimshaw, J. M., Wells, G. A., Boers, M., Andersson, N., Hamel, C., Porter, A. C., Tugwell, P., Moher, D. and Bouter, L. M. (2007). Development of AMSTAR: A measurement tool to assess the methodological quality of systematic reviews, *BMC Medical Research Methodology*, **7**, 10.

Sheen, Y. (2006). Exploring the relationship between characteristics of recasts and learner uptake, *Language Teaching Research*, **10**, 361–92.

Shin, H. W. (2010). Another look at Norris and Ortega (2000), *Working Papers in TESOL and Applied Linguistics*, **10**, 15–38.

Spada, N. and Tomita, Y. (2010). Interactions between type of instruction and type of language feature: A meta-analysis, *Language Learning*, **60**, 263–308.

Stroup, D. F., Berlin, J. A., Morton, S. C., Olin, I., Williamson, G. D., Rennie, D., Moher, D., Becker, B. J., Sipe, T. A. and Thacker, S. B. (2000). Meta-analysis of observational studies in epidemiology: A proposal for reporting, *Journal of the American Medical Association*, **283**, 2008–12.

Sun, S., Pan, W. and Wang, L. L. (2010). A comprehensive review of effect size reporting and interpreting practices in academic journals in education and psychology, *Journal of Educational Psychology*, **102**, 1–16.

Sutton, A. J. (2009). Publication bias, in Cooper, H., Hedges, L. V. and Valentine, J. C. (eds.), *The Handbook of Research Synthesis and Meta-analysis* (2nd edn.), New York: Russell Sage Foundation, pp. 435–52.

Taylor, A. (2006). The effects of CALL versus traditional L1 glosses on L2 reading comprehension, *CALICO Journal*, **23**, 309–18.

Taylor, A., Stevens, J. R. and Asher, J. W. (2006). The effects of explicit reading strategy training on L2 reading comprehension: A meta-analysis, in Norris, J. M. and Ortega, L. (eds.), *Synthesizing Research on Language Learning and Teaching*, Philadelphia, PA: John Benjamins, pp. 213–44.

Trikalinos, T. A., Churchill, R., Ferri, M., Leucht, S., Tuunainen, A., Wahlbeck, K. and Ioannidis, J. P. A. (2004). Effect sizes in cumulative meta-analyses, of mental health randomized trials evolved over time, *Journal of Clinical Epidemiology*, **57**, 1124–30.

Truscott, J. (2007). The effect of error correction on learners' ability to write accurately, *Journal of Second Language Writing*, **16**, 255–72.

Valentine, J. C., Cooper, H., Patall, E. A., Tyson, D. and Robinson, J. C. (2010). A method for evaluating research syntheses: The quality, conclusions, and consensus of 12 syntheses of the effects of after-school programs, *Research Synthesis Methods*, **1**, 20–38.

Wa-Mbaleka, S. (2006). *A Meta-analysis Investigating the Effects of Reading on Second Language Vocabulary Learning*. Unpublished doctoral dissertation, Northern Arizona University, Flagstaff, AZ.

Wilson, D. B. (2009). Systematic coding, in Cooper, H., Hedges, L. V. and Valentine, J. C. (eds.), *The Handbook of Research Synthesis* (2nd edn.), New York: Russell Sage Foundation, pp. 159–76.

Won, M. (2008). *The Effects of Vocabulary Instruction on English Language Learners: A Meta-analysis*. Unpublished doctoral dissertation, Lubbock, TX: Texas Tech University.

Zhao, Y. (2003). Recent developments in technology and language learning: A literature review and meta-analysis, *CALICO Journal*, **21**, 7–27.

PART II

REPLICATION STUDIES IN GRADUATE PROGRAMS

5 Practical methods for teaching replication to applied linguistics students

Rebekha Abbuhl

It is probably no exaggeration to say that graduate school is the place where researchers are born. It is where they learn about research methods, where they see models to emulate, and where they are enculturated into the discipline. If we are to encourage replications in the field of SLA, then it is here that we need to focus our efforts, so we can help create new generations of researchers who will value replication research alongside original research.

This chapter will cover how to integrate replication research into linguistic graduate programs, including dispelling common misunderstandings of replication research, developing the skills needed to conduct (and write up) replications, and giving students opportunities and incentives to conduct this type of research.

1 Dispelling misunderstandings

One of the first tasks facing educators is to dispel some of the common misunderstandings surrounding replication research. As noted by Kane, replication research is often equated with "intellectual mediocrity, ... a lack of creativity and perhaps even a bullying spirit" (1984: 1). Consequently, graduate students may believe (or be led to believe) that replication research is not worthy of their talents. They may also have the sense that they should not even think about doing replication research, out of a fear that they would seem to be challenging an "expert," or that published research, by virtue of having been through a peer review process or of having a statistically significant result, is free from errors and thus does not need to be checked or examined again, especially by a student (see Nassaji, Chapter 3, this volume). Students may also misunderstand the scientific process itself, believing that a single study can either "prove" or "disprove" a hypothesis instead of understanding that science is concerned with the gathering of evidence across multiple studies. Even students who are interested in doing replications may not have a clear understanding of what they are, believing that it involves merely "copying" a particular study (in essence, just doing everything the same) for the sake of publishing *something*.

To help disabuse graduate students of these notions, it is essential that educators help them understand what replications are and why they are necessary (see Abbuhl, in press; Porte, this volume). As many researchers have noted, replications are essential to the sciences as they correct limitations, test the generalizability of findings, enable researchers to have increased confidence in findings, and help prevent both fraud and the acceptance of erroneous results (e.g., Connelly, 1986; Amir and Sharon, 1990; Lindsay and Ehrenberg, 1993; Long, 1993; Hubbard and Armstrong, 1994; Fahs et al., 2003; Schmidt, 2009). Findings that cannot be replicated should be treated cautiously by the field (Muma, 1993; Schmidt, 2009). An analogy with medicine could be given here: We would probably not want to trust the results of a single study on the effect of a particular medicine, especially if the researchers only examined men, or only a small number of people, or only people between the ages of 35 and 50. Before we take the medicine, we would want to know whether their results (say, a positive effect of the medicine) hold true for other populations as well.

This is true of course for the "soft" sciences as well (Easley et al., 2000). A single study – even a well-designed one with statistically significant findings – cannot be regarded as conclusive (Gardner, 1985; Lindsay and Ehrenberg, 1993; Ottenbacher, 1996; Kelly, 2006). As noted by Polio and Gass, it is only through replication that the field will be able to "distinguish the spurious from the real" (1997: 500).

Many different activities and exercises are possible to help students understand why replication studies need to be conducted. For example, students could read one of the many articles that discuss the importance of replication studies (e.g., Valdman, 1993; Beck, 1994; Polio and Gass, 1997; Fahs et al., 2003, on nursing; Macaulay, 2003; Kelly, 2006, on biology; *Language Teaching* Review Panel, 2008, on SLA) and, as a class, discuss the various reasons why the authors advocate more replication research. By examining articles from many different fields, students can begin to understand the importance of replication research to all scientific disciplines.

Another potentially useful activity to help students grasp the importance of replication in SLA would be to examine an oft-cited but in some respects problematic study, such as Johnson and Newport (1989) (which has been used as support by many for a critical period in language acquisition, but has also had its statistical analyses and results questioned). After examining the original study, students can read one or more replications of this study, such as Birdsong and Molis (2001). A discussion of the conflicting findings can help students better understand why the findings of a single study cannot be accepted as "the truth."

A particularly useful illustration of this point can be found in a series of papers published in the *Journal of Economic and Social Measurement* (Breusch and Gray, 2006; Chapman and Gray, 2006; McCullough, 2006). Although the details of the research (on the foregone earnings of Australian mothers) would be of little use to linguistics graduate students, the commentary on replication provided by the editor of the journal, the replicating team of researchers, and the original team of researchers clearly illustrates not only the dangers of accepting the findings of a single study, but also how replication research can be viewed as a positive and cooperative venture that ultimately helps a field reach a better understanding of core issues.

Through readings and activities such as these, students can begin to understand that replication is neither the work of bullies nor mediocrists, but rather the backbone of any field calling itself a science. Cultivating this sense of appreciation at the graduate level can also help ensure that future researchers will value this type of research. As Schneider notes, "unless there is some shared appreciation for the importance of replication, the mechanisms for ensuring the replication of research are probably not worth pursuing" (2004: 1472).

2 Developing replication-related skills

In addition to fostering an appreciation of replications, we also need to help students develop the skills needed to conduct this type of research. Above and beyond instruction on research design, this includes helping students learn to read critically, choose studies worth replicating, and write up their replications in a manner consistent with the norms of the discipline.

2.1 Reading critically

Graduate students need to be able to critically evaluate existing research in order to decide which studies to replicate and also how to design those replications. Critical reading is a skill that takes time and practice to develop: Although no article is beyond criticism, beginning graduate students often lack confidence in their ability to identify a study's limitations. Students may also be under the impression that peer-reviewed publications cannot (or should not) be criticized. However, students need to appreciate that "all studies have weaknesses or otherwise make compromises" (*Language Teaching* Review Panel, 2008: 6). Guided critical reading activities can sensitize students to some of these common limitations, including small sample sizes, non-representative populations, lack of a true control group, confounded variables, self-report bias, and short duration of treatment.

One of the activities that I use to help students identify these types of limitations is to have them read a fictional[1] and very flawed study (on the effect of caffeine on L2 fluency: see below). This paper has numerous problems (e.g., insufficient literature review, confounds, inappropriate methodology, misused and misinterpreted statistics, and unwarranted conclusions about the importance of Red Bull for SLA). Although it is unlikely that any published study will be as flawed as the one presented below, reading and discussing this study can give students practice asking the kinds of questions that will help them read authentic studies critically.

Red Bull and L2 pronunciation: A partial replication of Guiora et al. (1980)

It has been well established that the intake of various substances can positively affect the imbiber's performance, memory, and accuracy. For example, Hollingworth (1912) found that ingesting caffeine positively impacted the speed and quality of typewriting. In his study, the participant ingested either a placebo or a caffeine pill and kept a record of both her typewriting speed and the number of errors. This continued for approximately one month. Based on his participant's performance, Hollingworth (1912) concluded that caffeine increased the speed of typewriting and reduced the number of errors.

Conflicting findings, however, have been reported. For example, Flory and Gilbert (1943) investigated the effect of benzedrine sulphate and caffeine on reading rate, reading comprehension, and "thinking ability." One hundred and twenty-nine college students were assigned to one of three groups: benzedrine sulphate, caffeine citrate, or a sugar pill. The participants were not informed which pill they received and were told that the pill contained some kind of drug. Various tests were administered to the participants, including a reading comprehension test and a vocabulary test. Although no statistical tests were employed, the researchers concluded that no group was superior to any other in terms of their performance.

In a study more directly related to SLA, Guiora et al. looked at the effect of administering different dosages of Valium on the ability of university students to pronounce an unfamiliar language, Thai. The participants in the treatment group were told that they would receive Valium, while those in the control group were tested separately and "were unaware of the use of Valium in the experiment" (1980: 355). Due to circumstances beyond the researchers' control, one of the testers had to be replaced midway through the experiment. Analyzing the results, the researchers found that although there was no significant main effect for group condition on the pronunciation of Thai, there was a significant interaction effect between group and drug condition. Guiora et al. explained that "a subject's score is significantly influenced by the individual who does the testing and that this susceptibility to influence becomes more powerful as Valium dosage increases" (1980: 356).

While this study has made important contributions to the field's understanding of the effect of Valium on the pronunciation of a second language, little is known about the effect of other imbibed substances on L2 pronunciation. As previous research (e.g., Hollingworth, 1912) has found a positive effect for caffeine on language-related tasks, the purpose of the current study is to replicate Guiora et al.'s (1980) study using one of the most caffeinated drinks in existence, Red Bull, instead of Valium.

Research question

Is there a positive effect for Red Bull on the pronunciation of Spanish as a second language by native speakers of English?

Participants

Twenty university students studying at a conservatory in Southern California were recruited to participate in the study. On the background questionnaire students indicated that they had little to no knowledge of Spanish. Only three participants had studied the language for more than three years, and only four participants had study-abroad experience in a Spanish-speaking country.

Procedure

The study employed a controlled / post-test design to investigate the effects of Red Bull on Spanish pronunciation. Half of the students were assigned to the treatment group. These students were informed that they would drink a caffeinated beverage and then would listen to a short clip of a native speaker (NS) of Spanish producing a sentence. Students were to repeat the sentence to the best of their ability. The students were audio-recorded. The recordings were assessed by a panel ($n=2$) of native speakers of Spanish, who rated the speech on a scale of 1 to 5 (5 being "completely native-like" and 1 being "completely unintelligible.") These students were recorded in the morning.

Later on in the day, the experiment was administered to the second group of students (the control group). These students were informed that they would drink a glass of water and then mimic a sentence produced by a NS of Spanish. As with the treatment group, these students were audio-recorded and then assessed by a NS panel of judges.

Results

The mean for the treatment group was 2.5 whereas the mean for the control group was 2.3. A dependent samples t-test indicated that the difference in means was statistically significant, $t(9) = -13.416$, $p = 0$. This proves that ingesting Red Bull leads to significantly better performance on L2 pronunciation than drinking water.

Conclusions

Researchers and practitioners alike have long sought to determine how to help L2 learners increase their accuracy with L2 pronunciation. Guiroa et al. (1980) provided solid evidence that administering Valium to subjects can help with their pronunciation. Their finding was replicated in the present study. Based on these results, we can confidently conclude that giving students Red Bull before class will help them greater approximate native-like pronunciation.

References

Flory, C. and Gilbert, J. (1943). The effects of benzedrine sulphate and caffeine citrate on the efficiency of college students, *Journal of Applied Psychology*, **27**, 121–34.

Guiora, A., Acton, W., Erard, R. and Strickland, F. (1980). The effects of benzodiazepine (Valium) on permeability of language ego boundaries, *Language Learning*, **30**, 351–63.

Hollingworth, H. (1912). The influence of caffeine on the speech and quality of performance in typewriting, *Psychological Review*, **19**, 66–73.

After reading the study, students can be asked to discuss questions such as the following to help them identify the study's limitations (Mackey and Gass, 2005; Meltzoff, 2006; Porte, 2010):

1   *Is the background to the problem adequately described?* The Red Bull study presents information on two early studies on caffeine,

but no recent empirical work in this area is addressed and it is unclear why the author is focusing on the relationship between caffeine and L2 Spanish pronunciation.

2 *Are the research questions unambiguous and supported by the literature review?* It is unclear what constitutes a "positive effect" (better intonation or pronunciation of individual sounds?), and the literature review does not lead to an understanding of how the research question is related to the field's current interests or, alternatively, how it addresses the foundations of any particular theory.

3 *Is sufficient information presented about the participants, how they were selected, and how they were assigned to groups?* Judging from the description, at least seven out of the 20 participants had background knowledge of Spanish, but the extent of this knowledge is not described. The methods by which participants were selected and placed into groups were also not adequately explained (e.g., it is not clear whether the participants volunteered to participate and whether they were randomly assigned to groups).

4 *Have the data collection procedures been adequately described?* Little information is given about the data collection procedures, including what exactly the participants were asked to repeat and why a single sentence was employed. Details on the scale used to assess the students were not provided, and it is unclear whether the raters for the experimental group were the same as those for the control group.

5 *What information about the reliability and validity of the measurement measures is presented?* No information is presented about either interrater reliability (the extent to which the judges agreed with each other on their ratings), the training of the judges to use the assessment scale, and the validity of either the test or the scale.

6 *Was the research design appropriate for addressing the research questions?* The use of a control group and a post-test is appropriate; however, a pre-test is also needed to determine whether the two groups differed significantly with respect to their initial Spanish pronunciation abilities. Without this information, it is impossible to determine whether the treatment was responsible for the purported differences or whether there were significant differences between the two groups at the beginning.

7 *Are there any confounds?* This study is riddled with confounds, including the background of the participants (music students may be better at mimicking sounds and intonation than those without musical training), environmental conditions (Spanish is widely spoken in Southern California, and it is not clear how much Spanish the participants were exposed to), and the students'

Spanish knowledge (some had up to three years of Spanish instruction and four had study-abroad experience in a Spanish-speaking country). In addition, the two groups (control and experimental) were tested at two different times of the day (morning and evening respectively), so it is not clear how much the purported differences between groups were due to the treatment.

8 *Were the appropriate statistical tests carried out? Were the results interpreted correctly?* The wrong statistical test was chosen in the Red Bull study. To compare the means of two groups, an independent (not paired) samples t-test should be used. It is also not clear whether the data were normally distributed (if not, the author should have used the nonparametric equivalent of the independent samples t-test, the Mann-Whitney U-test). The results were also not interpreted correctly – even if the correct statistical test had been employed, a significant finding does not "prove" that a causal relationship exists between the treatment and observed outcomes.

Addressing questions such as these, students can work in small groups to identify the study's weaknesses and, with the instructor's guidance, create a checklist detailing the characteristics of a well-designed and executed study. Later on, students can use this checklist to examine actual published studies and work together to identify the strengths and weaknesses of those studies. This critical analysis can serve as a basis for deciding on potential replication strategies (see this volume, chapters by Porte and by Mackey). For example, if the original study is deemed methodologically sound and the aim is to confirm the original findings (especially if those findings have been used to support theories in the field), an exact replication may be chosen. If there is a question as to whether the results would be generalizable to a different population (e.g., lower proficiency students instead of higher proficiency), setting (e.g., classroom vs. laboratory), or modality (written vs. oral), an approximate replication may be the best choice. Similarly, if there is a question as to whether the same results would be obtained using a different methodology (e.g., observation instead of self-report), then a conceptual replication can be used.

Students can also engage in more independent activities. For example, one activity I use with my students is an "article critique assignment"; here, students choose an article on their own, related to their own interests in language acquisition, and provide a three- to four-page summary and critique of the article. Students do this on a regular basis throughout the semester, receive feedback on their efforts, and also discuss their critiques – and their ideas for replications – in small groups. The students' idea generation can be aided by providing examples of different types of replications in the field of SLA. For example, students can read replications where the participant pool was changed (e.g., Bigelow et al.'s [2006] approximate replication of Philp [2003], using illiterate rather than literate learners), a different context was investigated (e.g., Loewen and Erlam's [2006] approximate replication of Ellis et al. [2006], using a computer-mediated as opposed to a face-to-face context), or where multiple changes were made (e.g., Allen's [2000] conceptual replication of VanPatten and Cadierno [1993], using a different target language, production task, and sample pool). These examples may serve as a source of inspiration for students, allowing them to gain a better understanding of both how and why replications are conducted.

2.2 Choosing a study to replicate

Once students understand why replications are important and have gained some experience identifying study limitations, they need to develop an understanding of the guidelines for choosing studies to replicate (see Mackey, Chapter 1, this volume). Addressing the following questions (from Abbuhl, 2009; in press) in class can be useful toward that end:

1 *Is the original research question in the study you have read still relevant to the concerns and issues of the field?*
Replications are needed of studies that are relevant to the field's current interests and controversies (Kelly, 2006; Kugler et al., 2006; *Language Teaching* Review Panel, 2008). Examining how many times a study has been cited (e.g., through the Web of Science or Google Scholar) and searching through current textbooks, state-of-the-art review articles, and individual peer-reviewed journals in the field can help students identify topics that are relevant to the field's current controversies and debates. Similarly, studying state-of-the-art reviews might reveal the need for replications of past studies that may have been assimilated into the literature and served as foundations for theories of SLA but are perceived not to have been sufficiently replicated to warrant such confidence in the validity and generalizability of their results (see Porte's Concluding remarks, this volume). This was the motivation, for example, of one well-known replication (Birdsong and Molis, 2001), which sought to test the generalizability of an oft-cited study for a critical period in SLA, Johnson and Newport (1989).

2   *What are the strengths and weaknesses of the original study?*
As illustrated in the questions above and detailed in Porte (2010)
and Meltzoff (2006), students can be directed to consider whether
there are any threats to the internal validity of the study, such as
confounds, small samples, practice effects, maturation effects, or
lack of a control group. Questions concerning the external validity
of the study can also be raised, such as whether the sample is representative of the larger population and whether the testing conditions allow the results to be generalized to other settings. Ultimately,
these questions should serve as a starting point for deciding how
to examine alternative explanations for results and for improving
research designs – and thus for determining how (and whether) to
replicate a particular study. In a replication, the researcher can seek
to address the limitations of the original study (while preserving its
strengths) in order to put the original researcher's conclusions to
the test (Porte, 2010).

3   *Have researchers called for replications of certain studies?*
Whereas independent analysis of original studies can help students identify candidates for replication, there are a number of
other published resources that may assist students in this process.
For example, meta-analyses and review articles (e.g., Norris and
Ortega, 2000; Ferris, 2004; Plonsky, this volume) may provide
suggestions on specific studies needing replication. Meta-analyses
may also provide information about effect sizes in a particular
area. Small effect sizes may be due in part to weaknesses in the
original studies; replication studies may be able to address these
weaknesses and thus contribute to the field (*Language Teaching*
Review Panel, 2008). Suggestions for replications may also
be found in the concluding sections of original studies, where
authors commonly discuss the limitations of their research. This
commentary can help students generate ideas for replicating the
study so as to address those limitations.

4   *Is conducting a replication of a particular study feasible?*
Conducting a replication is only feasible when detailed information on the participants, materials, and procedures of the original
study is published or readily available. For example, the replication researcher should have information on the demographic
background of the participants, the data-elicitation instruments,
the data-coding procedure and the experimental protocol (Polio
and Gass, 1997). When such information is not recoverable, either
from the methods section, the appendices, or from digital databases (e.g., the supplementary materials available at the Web site

for the journals *Applied Linguistics* or *Language Teaching*), then the replication researcher should contact the original author(s) directly for more information. Establishing contact with the original researcher(s) at the very beginning of the research process can also be useful: Not only can the replication researcher obtain more details on the original study (and ask questions whenever they arise), but he or she can also receive comments and suggestions from the original researcher(s). Ultimately, this can assist the research process and allow the replication researcher to present a more informed and insightful comparison of the original and replication studies. *Language Teaching* also invites the original study's author to comment on the outcomes of the replication.

2.3 *Writing up replications*

Teachers can also assist graduate students by covering how to write up replication research (see Brown, Chapter 7, this volume). To this end, a genre approach to writing instruction can be useful. One of the central tenets of genre-based writing instruction is that the conventions of a particular genre need to be made explicit to students (e.g., Hyland, 2007). A genre-based approach to writing instruction involves a range of activities to help sensitize students to the organizational and rhetorical characteristics of the genre at hand. These typically include discussing the context, modeling and deconstructing the text, joint construction of the text, independent construction, and linking the target genre to related texts.

In building the context, the class can discuss the purpose of the genre and the relation between the writer and the audience. In modeling and deconstructing the text, the teacher can provide students with examples of exemplary replications (e.g., both Eckerth and Rott, this volume) as well as replications that are poorly executed and written (e.g., the Red Bull study above) to help students clearly understand the conventions of this particular genre. The teacher, using the guidelines presented in Brown (Chapter 7, this volume), can discuss the typical patterns of organization, the lexico-grammatical characteristics, and the authors' strategies for motivating their replications. Joint construction of the text can take the form of collaborative writing activities between teachers and students, perhaps using the teachers' data, while in the independent construction stage, students can submit multiple drafts of their work and receive feedback from both peers and instructors. Finally, in the linking stage, classes can discuss how replications differ from and are similar to related genres.

3 Opportunities and incentives

Ultimately, it is not enough simply to teach students about replications and hope that they will conduct them on their own. As noted in Ortega (2009), there are many obstacles to conducting replication research, including (but not limited to) the lack of prestige associated with this type of research, and also logistical complications (such as the difficulty of obtaining sufficient information about the original study in order to replicate it). For this reason, both opportunities and incentives are needed to help students carry out this type of research.

In terms of opportunities, we can encourage replications by granting students access to the data and materials of original studies, such as those the teacher him or herself has conducted. Students can use these materials and data to conduct replications independently (for example, for a class assignment), in small groups (for a class project) or even with the teacher as part of a research assistantship. In this way, students not only have the access they need to the details of the original study, but also become sensitized to the importance of data sharing and the idea of research as a shared community endeavor. The field is increasingly emphasizing the importance of data sharing (see, for example, the Linguistics Society of America's resolution on data sharing at www.earlham.edu/~peters/fos/2010/01/linguistics-society-debates-data.html, as well as recent efforts to create digital databases, including the *Spanish Learner Language Oral Corpus* [Mitchell et al., 2008] and the *Instruments for Research into Second Languages* [Marsden and Mackey, 2010]).

Such data sharing can be greatly facilitated by recent developments in technology. For example, a number of free and low-cost resources are available to both individuals and schools wishing to create digital databases. These range from password-protected Web pages to the use of databases specially designed for researchers (e.g., the Dataverse Network Project at http://thedata.org/home). Data can be anonymized and agreements can be put in place that require users, for example, to credit the original researcher and not to use the data or materials in any way prohibited by law or standards of ethical conduct (Schneider, 2004).

An additional measure would be to require individual students or teams to conduct replications in their research methodology courses, or to conduct at least one replication study during their masters or doctoral program (in whatever course they choose) (Fitzpatrick, Chapter 6, this volume). Departments could also formally list replication studies as one of the types of research they would accept for comprehensives or thesis work, thus bringing to the students' attention the fact that such work is valued. In this way, replication studies are not shunted to the curb, but rather made an integral part of the students' education.

In terms of incentives, students can be encouraged to conduct replications if we create a department climate that values this kind of research alongside other types of research. Faculty could do "brown bag" talks on replication research that they are conducting so as to familiarize students with the replication research process. Alternatively, they could discuss their own original research and provide ideas or suggestions on how it could be replicated. If we as faculty value replications, and convey the importance of this work, students will also begin to value it.

Additional incentives could take the form of showcasing outstanding student replications. For example, our department holds a yearly "poster session" outside the department to allow students to showcase (and show off) their research. Faculty can encourage replication research in these showcasings, or even devote an entire poster session to replication work. Additionally, students should be encouraged to submit their replication studies to university-level local and national conferences. By helping students become aware of these conferences, encouraging them to submit proposals, and perhaps even covering conference proposal-writing strategies in our methodology classes, we can help students present their work to a wider audience.

Hopefully, by taking the time to address replication research in our classes and by giving students the skills, opportunities, and incentives they need to produce replication studies, we are helping ensure that the next generation of researchers does not view replication research as signs of "intellectual mediocrity" or "a bullying spirit," but rather as a type of research that must be valued alongside original research. I hasten to add that the goal is not just to have students and only students do replication – as Fahs et al. mention, "strategies to promote replication by relying only on students to produce that body of work devalues the principle of replication" (2003: 69) – but to help ensure that future researchers value replication research throughout their careers.

Notes

1   This study is the author's invention and is being used solely for educational purposes. No offence is intended to any of the researchers whose work is mentioned.

References

Abbuhl, R. (2009). Practical methods of integrating replications into linguistic graduate programs. Paper presented at the invited colloquium Encouraging replication research in the field of AL and SLA, Graeme Porte convener. The American Association for Applied Linguistics Annual Conference, Denver, CO, 23 March.

Abbuhl, R. (in press). Why, when and how to replicate research, in Mackey, A. (ed.), *Research Methodologies in Second Language Acquisition*, Oxford, MA: Blackwell.

Allen, L. (2000). Form–meaning connections and the French causative: An experiment in processing instruction, *Studies in Second Language Acquisition*, **22**, 69–84.

Amir, Y. and Sharon, I. (1990). Replication research: A "must" for the scientific advancement of psychology, *Journal of Social Behavior and Personality*, **5**, 51–69.

Beck, C. (1994). Replication strategies for nursing research, *IMAGE: Journal of Nursing Scholarship*, **26**, 191–4.

Bigelow, M., Delmas, R., Hansen, K. and Tarone, E. (2006). Literacy and the processing of oral recasts in SLA, *TESOL Quarterly*, **40**, 665–89.

Birdsong, D. and Molis, M. (2001). On the evidence for maturational constraints in second-language acquisition, *Journal of Memory and Language*, **44**, 235–49.

Breusch, T. and Gray, E. (2006). Replicating a study of mothers' forgone earnings in Australia, *Journal of Economic and Social Measurement*, **31**, 107–25.

Chapman, B. and Gray, M. (2006). Response to Breusch and Gray, *Journal of Economic and Social Measurement*, **31**, 127–38.

Connelly, C. (1986). Replication research in nursing, *International Journal of Nursing Studies*, **23**, 71–7.

Easley, R., Madden, C. and Dunn, M. (2000). Conducting marketing science: The role of replication in the research process, *Journal of Business Research*, **48**, 83–92.

Ellis, R., Loewen, S. and Erlam, R. (2006). Implicit and explicit corrective feedback and the acquisition of L2 grammar, *Studies in Second Language Acquisition*, **28**, 339–68.

Fahs, P., Morgan, L. and Kalman, M. (2003). Call for replication, *Journal of Nursing Scholarship*, **35**, 67–71.

Ferris, D. (2004). The "grammar correction" debate in L2 writing: Where are we, and where do we go from here? (and what do we do in the meantime …?), *Journal of Second Language Writing*, **13**, 40–62.

Gardner, R. (1985). *Social Psychology and Second Language Learning: The Role of Attitudes and Motivation*, London: Edward Arnold.

Hubbard, R. and Armstrong, J. (1994). Replications and extensions in marketing: Rarely published but quite contrary, *International Journal of Research in Marketing*, **11**, 233–48.

Hyland, K. (2007). Genre pedagogy: Language, literacy and L2 writing instruction, *Journal of Second Language Writing*, **16**, 148–64.

Johnson, J. and Newport, E. (1989). Critical period effects in second language learning: The influence of maturational state on the acquisition of English as a second language, *Cognitive Psychology*, **21**, 60–99.

Kane, E. (1984). Why journal editors should encourage the replication of applied econometric research, *Quarterly Journal of Business and Economics*, **23**, 3–8.

Kelly, C. (2006). Replicating empirical research in behavioral ecology: How and why it should be done but rarely ever is, *The Quarterly Review of Biology*, **81**, 221–36.

Kugler, C., Fischer, S. and Russell, C. (2006). Preparing a replication study, *Progress in Transplantation*, **16**, 15–16.

Language Teaching Review Panel (2008). Replication studies in language learning and teaching: Questions and answers, *Language Teaching*, **41**, 1–14.

Lindsay, R. and Ehrenberg, A. (1993). The design of replicated studies, *The American Statistician*, **47**, 217–28.

Loewen, S. and Erlam, R. (2006). Corrective feedback in the chatroom: An experimental study, *Computer Assisted Language Learning*, **19**, 1–14.

Long, M. (1993). Assessment strategies for second language acquisition theories, *Applied Linguistics*, **14**, 225–49.

Macaulay, R. (2003). Repeat after me: The value of replication, *International Journal of English Studies*, **3**, 77–92.

Mackey, A. and Gass, S. (2005). *Second Language Research: Methodology and Design*, Mahwah, NJ: Lawrence Erlbaum Associates.

Marsden, E. and Mackey, A. (2010). *Research Grant. Instruments for Research into Second Language Learning: The Establishment of a Digital Repository*, Economics and Social Research Council (ESRC), UK. www.iris-database.org

McCullough, B. (2006). Replication section: Introduction, *Journal of Economic and Social Measurement*, **31**, 103–5.

Meltzoff, J. (2006). *Critical Thinking about Research: Psychology and Related Fields*, Washington, DC: American Psychological Association.

Mitchell, R., Domínguez, L., Arche, M., Myles, F. and Marsden, E. (2008). SPLOCC: A new database for Spanish second language acquisition research, *EUROSLA Yearbook*, **8**, 287–304.

Muma, J. (1993). The need for replication, *Journal of Speech and Hearing Research*, **36**, 927–30.

Norris, J. and Ortega, L. (2000). Effectiveness of L2 instruction: A research synthesis and quantitative meta-analysis, *Language Learning*, **50**, 417–528.

Ortega, L. (2009). A sociology of replication and replicability in applied linguistics. Paper presented at the invited colloquium Encouraging replication research in the field of AL and SLA, Graeme Porte convener. The American Association for Applied Linguistics Annual Conference, Denver, CO, 23 March.

Ottenbacher, K. (1996). The power of replications and replications of power, *The American Statistician*, 50, 271–5.

Philp, J. (2003). Constraints on noticing the gap: Non-native speakers' noticing of recasts in NS-NNS interaction, *Studies in Second Language Acquisition*, 25, 99–126.

Polio, C. and Gass, S. (1997). Replication and reporting: A commentary, *Studies in Second Language Acquisition*, 19, 499–508.

Porte, G. (2010). *Appraising Research in Second Language Learning: A Practical Approach to Critical Analysis of Quantitative Research* (2nd edn.), Amsterdam/Philadelphia: John Benjamins.

Schmidt, S. (2009). Shall we really do it again? The powerful concept of replication is neglected in the social sciences, *Review of General Psychology*, 13, 90–100.

Schneider, B. (2004). Building a scientific community: The need for replication, *Teachers College Record*, 106, 1471–83.

Valdman, A. (1993). Replication study (editorial introduction), *Studies in Second Language Acquisition*, 15, 505.

VanPatten, B. and Cadierno, T. (1993). Explicit instruction and input processing, *Studies in Second Language Acquisition*, 15, 225–43.

6 Conducting replication studies: Lessons from a graduate program

Tess Fitzpatrick

This chapter examines the process of selecting, designing, implementing, and interpreting replication studies from the perspective of the novice, or apprentice, researcher. It focuses on observations and insights from students of a postgraduate research program which includes replication work as an integral component. In order to contextualize these observations, I begin by describing the structure of that program, and explaining the rationale for including replication study as a fundamental element of it. The degree to which research students' responses map onto this rationale is then explored, and specific critical issues which might affect or determine the value of the replication event are identified. Finally, I build on the observations and insights presented in the chapter to offer a set of advisory guidelines for the successful integration of replication work into a graduate research program.

1 Context: The Swansea program

The postgraduate research program in applied linguistics at Swansea University, as designed by Paul Meara in 1990, is more structured in its approach than most UK-based programs of its kind, and there are, broadly, two reasons for this. The first consideration is that it is primarily a distance-learning program, designed specifically for students who are living and working away from the host university and who are studying for their PhD on a part-time basis. Students on the program are typically working in an academic environment and are seeking to extend their skill and knowledge base in order to progress their careers in that context. As Read and Nation observe, the Swansea program "was designed so that experienced professionals in language teaching could fit doctoral study in with their work commitments, receiving a thorough grounding in research methodology before they undertook their own studies on a variety of innovative topics in the field" (2009: 11). The extended period of study associated with this part-time mode of delivery (typically five to seven years) allows for a more longitudinal, considered, and incremental approach than is often achievable for full-time students on a three-year scheme. However, it also demands that effort, motivation, and momentum be sustained over this protracted period, and the program is designed to facilitate this through clearly defined stages of empirical investigation, supported by a system of regular and formalized exchanges of written work and formative feedback between the student and the supervisory team.

The second consideration which contributes to the structure of the Swansea program is that it focuses on a rather specific area of research. Read and Nation, again commenting on this program, attribute its unique nature to Meara's "vision of what could be achieved through a purpose-built doctoral program specializing in research on vocabulary acquisition" (2009: 11). This focus means that the students themselves can offer a further layer of support to each other: Because they are all working in a specific area of applied linguistics (vocabulary acquisition), most of what any student reads, and most of the studies he or she conducts, will be relevant to their peers. In many cases, students will choose to replicate papers which, being relevant to vocabulary acquisition, are familiar to their peers, or will even replicate work conducted by former students on the network. The result of this is a virtual research network with the potential to offer an academic resource as well as pastoral support from fellow students. The design of the program, and in particular its critical strand (see below), aims to maximize the potential benefits of this feature.

The structure of the program is outlined in Table 6.1. The three phases can be roughly equated to the three years of a standard full-time PhD scheme of study. The experimental studies which constitute the empirical strand of the program are each underpinned by a detailed plan, and at the end of each year that year's study is written up. Both these documents are subjected to the formalized exchanges of feedback and response referred to above. Importantly, it is expected that the studies will be included as chapters in the final thesis, so that each chapter is based on one of these study write-ups. This means that when the student faces the task of writing up the complete thesis, the experimental chapters will already exist in draft form. Interaction between students on the program is formalized through the critical strand of the program. This requires students to review, every month of the academic year, a published paper or book chapter selected by the supervision team for its relevance to the broad field of vocabulary acquisition. In their first years of study, students on the program all review the same paper in any given month, and these critical reviews,

Table 6.1 *PhD program structure*

Phase	Year	Empirical strand	Critical strand	Presentational strand
1	1	1 replication	review 8 papers and 1 book	poster presentation / minor conference
	2	1 experiment	review 8 papers and 1 book	poster presentation / minor conference
2	3	2 experiments	review 8 papers and 1 book	minor / major conference
	4	2 experiments	5 papers and literature review	journal article
3	5	2 experiments	final drafting of the thesis	major conference
	6	final drafting	formal defence of the thesis	major conference

together with comments from the supervision team, are shared around the group so that students can compare their own style of summary and critical response with those of their peers. In later years, students select their own papers for review, in line with their individual literature review. The third strand of the program, the presentational strand, provides the students with a point of contact within the wider research community. Typically, in their first years, students give a presentation at an in-house student conference, or make a poster presentation at a larger event. By their final year they would be expected to have presented their work at an international conference, and to have written (or more usually cowritten with their supervisor) an article for publication in a peer-reviewed journal. These activities inevitably broaden the student's experience of feedback on and defence of their work by exposing them to a body of researchers beyond their immediate supervisory team and student peers.

As can be seen from Table 6.1, the replication study is the first empirical study to be undertaken by the research student. As such, it represents a foundation for subsequent studies in terms of its introduction to rigorous experimental design, precise and accurate implementation of method, and balanced and reasoned interpretation of results. Although occasionally students joining the program with sufficient confidence and experience of empirical research and with a strong research proposal might conduct a pilot study in place of a replication, the majority of students (approximately 80%) complete a replication. In applying for a place on the PhD program, students will have written a proposal which indicates the area of vocabulary acquisition research they are interested in working on. In the first month or so of the program, they are encouraged to read published work in this area and to identify, in close consultation with their supervisor, a relevant study which is potentially replicable. This process of selection and the roles of student and supervisor in the selection process, are discussed later in the chapter. For now, though, Table 6.2 lists some of the studies that have been replicated by students on the program, together with the title, or working title, of the relevant thesis. The majority of the replications listed here were written up as a chapter (usually the first experimental chapter) in the student's final thesis. In the following section, I will examine in more detail some specific reasons for incorporating replication studies into a program of doctoral study, and indeed into the thesis itself. These reasons will be discussed in the light of feedback and comments from students who have worked through the program.

Table 6.2   Sample replication studies, and corresponding theses, from the Swansea Applied Linguistics PhD program

Study replicated	Thesis
Arnaud, P. and Savignon, J. (1997). Rare words, complex lexical units and the advanced learner	McGavigan, P. An exploration of idiom knowledge in non-native speakers of English
Barfield, A. (2009). Exploring productive L2 collocation knowledge	Brown, D. English as a second language productive knowledge and acquisition of collocations (working title)
Bensoussan, M., Sim, D. and Weiss, R. (1984). The effect of dictionary usage on EFL test performance compared with student and teacher attitudes and expectations	Nesi, H. The use and abuse of learners' dictionaries
Fischer, U. (1994). Learning words from context and dictionaries: An experimental comparison	Ronald, J. Second language vocabulary acquisition through dictionary use
Fitzpatrick, T. (2006). Habits and rabbits: Word associations and the L2 lexicon	Racine, J. Investigating the L2 mental lexicon using word association data (working title)
Folse, K. (2006). The effect of type of written exercise on L2 vocabulary retention.	Abboud, O. Word association structures in an L2 (working title)
Gitsaki, C. (1999). *Second Language Lexical Acquisition: A Study of the Development of Collocational Knowledge*	Barfield, A. An exploration of second language collocation knowledge and development

Table 6.2 (continued)

Study replicated	Thesis
Kruse, H., Pankhurst, J. and Sharwood-Smith, M. (1987). A multiple word association probe in second language acquisition research	Munby, I. Development of a multiple response word association test
Laufer, B. and Nation, P. (1995). Vocabulary size and use: Lexical richness in L2 written production	Bell, H. Using frequency lists to assess L2 texts
Linnarud, M. (1986). *Lexis in Composition: A Performance Analysis of Swedish Learners' Written English*	Kenworthy, R. Lexical choices as an indicator of text quality in ESL writers
Malvern, D. and Richards, B. J. (2002). Investigating accommodation in language proficiency interviews using a new measure of lexical diversity	Li, H. Measuring and assessing L2 English spoken vocabulary: Insights from Chinese candidates
Meara, P. M. (1992). Network structures and vocabulary acquisition in a foreign language	Schur, E. An exploration of the structural properties of L2 vocabulary networks
Meara, P. M. and Fitzpatrick, T. (2000). Lex30: an improved method of assessing productive vocabulary in an L2	Clenton, J. Investigating the construct of productive vocabulary knowledge with Lex30
Miller, G. A., and Gildea, P. M. (1985). How to misread a dictionary	Horst, M. Text encounters of the frequent kind: Learning L2 vocabulary through reading
Milton, J. (2006). Language lite: Learning French vocabulary in school	Orosz, A. EFL vocabulary teaching in Hungary (working title)
Nikolova, O. (2002). Effects of students' participation in authoring of multimedia materials on student acquisition of vocabulary	Konstantakis, N. Compiling a list of business vocabulary for English learners
Verspoor, M. and Lowie, W. (2003). Making sense of polysemous words	Maby, M. Polysemy and depth of knowledge (working title)
Wilks, C. and Meara, P. M. (2002). Untangling word webs: Graph theory and the notion of density in second language work association networks	Mochizuki, M. Measures of lexical depth in L2
Wolter, B. (2001). Comparing the L1 and L2 mental lexicon: A depth of individual word knowledge model	Higginbotham, G. L2 vocabulary and word associations (working title)

2 Meara's rationale for using replications

In 1994, in a review of Johnson's *Approaches to Research in Second Language Learning* (1992), Meara set out a detailed argument for using replication studies in research training. He is enthusiastic about the way Johnson addresses the complex nature of language learning and the rather unwieldy factors which influence "the way research is organized at a strategic level" (1994: 275). Johnson's coverage of research methods and their applications, though, leads Meara to reflect on his own approach to research training, which is quite different from that presented in Johnson's book. Rather than teaching his students a set of technical skills and analytical techniques in preparation for their research activities, and then asking them to apply these to the design, implementation, and interpretation of an original piece of research, Meara trains his students through replication work. This, he argues, is advantageous in terms of experimental design and implementation, analytic framework, and reporting the study. It also encourages close and critical reading of the original paper. As noted above, this approach has underpinned the design of the research program Meara founded twenty years ago, which positions a replication study at the foundation of students' independent research experience, so that "the students immediately get their teeth into some real research work, but their task is made relatively easy because they are following a model" (1994: 276).

The following sections explore Meara's rationale for using replication studies in this way, and juxtapose this with comments and feedback (in italic script) from students who have undergone this training program. Students and graduates of the Swansea program provided the data in reply to an e-mail asking for responses to a set of questions relating to their replication study (see Appendix). The e-mail explained that this data would be used, anonymously, in a paper on "Integrating replication work into a PhD programme," which would be presented at the AAAL (American Association for Applied Linguistics) colloquium. The questions were sent to the 28 students currently on the program and to 13 graduates of the program, with the covering e-mail. The data in the following sections is from the 13 current students and the six ex-students who responded in full to the questions. Informants were coded by number, with numbers allocated according to approximate date of graduation (or predicted graduation date).

3 Experiment design

It is common for students starting out on a research degree to propose impractically ambitious research projects which overestimate the number of research questions that can be addressed, the amount of data it is possible to gather, and so on. Correspondingly, the degree of precision and planning necessary in the design stages of empirical research are typically underestimated. Replicating a study which has been published in a peer-reviewed journal or academic volume, and using this as a model means, in Meara's view, that students "no longer produce half-baked designs which generate intractable data. They should be able to adopt the methodology employed by the model, perhaps using the materials the model used, and copy the method of analysis" (1994: 276).

It is perhaps important to note at this point that practical constraints will almost certainly restrict the potential for exact replication. This is often impossible to achieve even in large and well-resourced research projects; a lone research student is likely to find him/herself unable to match the original participant group in any number of variables, including first language, proficiency level, gender, and age, so an exact replication is an unrealistic target. In any case, exact replications are limited in their objectives, focusing on the internal and external validity of the original study, in a way which might not be helpful or relevant to many research aims. The replication studies undertaken by students on the Swansea program are therefore, by necessity, approximate replications. Indeed, they may even push the boundaries of this definition, given that one formal definition of approximate replications is that they change one – and only one – key variable in order to allow for adequate comparison between the study undertaken and that replicated (*Language Teaching* Review Panel, 2008). Students recognize this, commenting, for example, that *"it is hard to 'replicate' a study completely. In other words, it is difficult to control all the variables included in the original study, e.g. participants and testing administration"* (9). Because the primary function of the replication exercise here is as a training tool, this is not overly problematic, but it does draw students' attention to two issues. Firstly, as illustrated in the following two quotations, some students reflecting on their replication study from the distance of several years' research experience, become aware that "replication" has rather a narrow formal definition, which their study perhaps did not meet: *"A thing I have wondered about is the definition of 'replication.' Doing the experiment I've described was definitely a useful step in the development of a program of PhD research, but since I changed the experiment, was it really a replication? ... Does this matter? ... In retrospect, what I did was a xxx-inspired study, not really a replication"* (2). *"Since conducting the replication, I have been advised that in fact the experiment I had intended to replicate was not a replication in the real sense as I had altered some of the parameters of the original test*" (7). The second issue students recognize, and one which we will return to, is that the original paper sometimes lacks certain methodological details, so that the researcher is obliged to approximate experimental design: "*due to the restriction of word limit of a paper, the methodology section in the original article is not all always in great detail*" (9).

In general, though, the research students report that the process of following a predetermined experimental design is helpful for two reasons. Firstly, it means that they can conduct an experiment the design of which they can trust to work. Several students report that this enabled them to gain confidence in their own research skills: "*I ... learned to deal with my own limited self-confidence*" (4); "*I gained confidence*" (1). Secondly, it prompts a realization that good, precise experimental design is not only crucial to the success of any study – it is also immensely time-consuming and usually far from straightforward. The two boxes below present students' reflections in these two areas: confidence in research design and realization of the complexities of planning.

Confidence in the research design

I learned how to set up an experiment but didn't have to work out the experimental design from scratch. (1)

It's good to begin with a replication because you don't have to think about a number of important things which you need to consider when developing an original experiment ... you can focus on data gathering and processing skills without the additional burden or constraints of dealing with important aspects of test design. (13)

Doing a replication gets you into the nitty-gritty of research quickly. But because you are following someone else, a fair number of the decisions have already been made for you, which makes it that much more approachable. (19)

Someone else has done the pre-thinking and your main concern is to do the same with some extra critical thinking. (4)

I think the replication gives grad students some hands-on experience at experimental design, before they go off and design their own experiments. It may help to illuminate some of the potential pitfalls in doing empirical research before actually stumbling into them. (18)

I never did an experiment before with this amount of detail and I could make use of the original to help guide my replication study. (12)

Realization of the complexities of planning

[I gained a] realization of the work involved, and problems to encounter. (6)

It made me begin to be aware that designing a simple but "good" research study was a much more complicated process than I had thought. (5)

[I learned] that the experiments require a tremendous amount of background knowledge in order to justify procedure and conclusions and ... I am still learning from that first replication (such as the need to justify every single step of an experiment). (10)

Replicating others' experiments is helpful in understanding the importance of a sound research design to a good experiment; and acknowledging the kind of problems that I may encounter and that may be avoided in my own experiments. (9)

In terms of following an established experimental design, then, the students' comments seem to reflect one of Meara's main objectives: They can launch into real empirical work at a relatively early stage in their research careers, using the scaffold of a tested methodological framework.

4 Experiment implementation

The implementation of experiment design is guided by the original study, which provides information about what kind of data to collect and, usually, about the materials which are to be used, the profiles of participants and experimental procedure. As suggested above, though, this information is sometimes lacking in detail, making it necessary for the research student to make an educated guess about materials to be used, instructions to give, treatment of data, and so on. There are many examples of this, but a typical instance would be a statement in the original study "proficiency was measured by means of a cloze test," with no further detail about that test. In order to conduct any kind of replication the researcher must design what he or she hopes will be an equivalent test, and make decisions about text selection, length of text, number and frequency of gaps, and so on. The point here is that although it is clearly beneficial, as the previous section confirms, to work from an established design framework, this does not necessarily preclude the research student from having to make certain decisions about design detail.

From the perspective of most students, certainly, the main challenge of the replication study lies in the collection and analysis of data. Meara intends that this should be the case, and that by removing from students the burden of having to design, in detail, an experiment which will appropriately address a set of research questions, the replication process will allow them to focus on carrying out the experimental activity: "the problems that do remain are organizational ones: how do I arrange to interview 50 people? What is the most efficient way of collecting my data? Can I use the equipment properly? And so on" (Meara, 1994: 276). Again, the feedback from students who have completed a replication study bear out his intention: "*I understood more about the practical aspects of running an experiment of this kind, such as organizing students to be tested and inputting and classifying data*" (15).

As mentioned above, Meara's justification for using replication studies as a training tool was made in response to the approach to research training presented by Johnson (1992). For Meara, Johnson's treatment of various research methods is "lucid, thoughtful and interesting" (1994: 275), but nevertheless encourages an overly simplistic two-step approach to research training: First, the students are taught about a selection of research methods, then they put these into practice in their own research projects. Meara argues for a more developmental attitude, with the acquisition of research skills necessarily being an iterative, incremental process: "it's more an attitude of mind, something that takes a very long time to grow ..." (1994: 276). Doing a replication study supports the experiential nature of this process, and includes another important dimension. Although the students are inheriting the research questions and design framework from the author(s) of the original study, they have collected the data in the replication study themselves. This gives students a sense of ownership of and responsibility for their research – after all, they have almost certainly had direct contact with the study participants – which motivates and engages them in a way that simply doesn't happen when working with training data: "they can spend time learning to use the method of analysis with data they have an investment in, rather than with abstract examples" (Meara, 1994: 276). This engagement with the data collected is evident in research students' comments such as: "*[the replication study] set me up for data collection, analysis, methodology, etc. and also taught me that subjects come up with things that you never even dreamed of*" (3).

From the students' comments it is clear that the process of implementing the research design forces them to focus on specific procedural details. As can be seen in the comments in the box opposite, these often arise due to the nature of the experiment itself, but they can also reflect particular weaknesses in the individual's research skill set, and give an early indication of areas for self-development.

Focus on procedural details

I feel I gained in terms of what it's like to collect data and work with it. I remember that the analysis involved rating students' sentences for evidence of understanding the target words. I had to set up the data properly and train another person to do the rating. Of course, we didn't always agree. So it was definitely a learning experience. (2)

In terms of specific things I've learned, there are a lot of practical things: (i) my university's processes re obtaining data from students; (ii) organizing files (physical and computer) and record keeping; (iii) using SPSS [Statistical Package for the Social Sciences]. (19)

I think I've gained a much better appreciation of the types of issues you have to think about, the way you have to think ahead and try to anticipate things that may arise. (19)

Through the implementation of the study design, the research student is made aware of the disciplined nature of good empirical research and, importantly, is alerted to potential stresspoints, both in aspects of the experimental process and in his/her own individual approach to this sort of work.

5 Critical reading

A training element of the replication study which is emphasized much more strongly in the graduate student feedback than by Meara, is its effect on the way students read research work (see also Abbuhl's approach to critical reading training, Chapter 5, this volume). In this sense their replication work augments the critical skills which students develop through the monthly review tasks. Whereas students receive formative feedback from supervision staff on the monthly tasks, though, the replication process sees skills develop experientially. Students report that the process of planning and carrying out the replication obliges them to read the original paper in greater detail, and to engage with it more closely, than papers they would read ordinarily as part of their research: "*The second (lesson learned from doing a replication) was a really close reading of a text*" (4). In the case of more complex papers, this was especially noticeable: "*I could easily understand the strengths and weaknesses of this particular study (which for someone fairly new to the field was quite a difficult paper to get to grips with) by replicating it*" (15). Reading a paper in order to replicate it seems to have drawn students' attention to the details of the study in a way which they have not experienced before: "*I learned how to examine papers in real detail, which is essential (although of course no-one has time to do it all the time)"* (4); *"I began to dissect articles with a very critical eye and began to appreciate the intricacies rather than the bigger pictures"* (10). As has already been mentioned, some students were frustrated to find that details they needed in order to produce a robust replication experiment were missing from the published work. The comment noted above, that *"the methodology section in the original article is not all always in great detail"* (9), reflects this, as does this more skeptical interpretation of omitted detail: *"I realized that a lot of things went unreported in published articles – researchers tend to gloss over aspects of their studies that don't quite go to plan, but which could make important differences to the outcome"* (1).

In fact, as can be seen from the comments in the box below, a critical – and in some cases downright negative – approach to published work emerged strongly from the experience of reading for replication.

Critical approach to published work

Doing the replication and doing the monthly critiques of studies together did change the way I read published research: I realized how much really poor stuff manages to get published. (3)

It made me pay more attention to detail. (8)

I now look more critically at the statistics where as I used to skim over bits I wasn't sure about in the hope that it would make sense by the time I got to the concluding paragraph. (15)

A replication study is certain to raise a point that each experiment may have its limit. It helps me to learn to be more critical when I study other experiments. (9)

When I read published work, I can see how small details (such as number and type of subjects, testing methodology, and scoring systems) may have affected the results and conclusions. You can see how questionable practices easily morph into standard experimental procedures, and how results-based conclusions feed assumptions and expectations which end up as theory. This colors the way you read other published work. (13)

[How did the replication study change the way I read published research?] – it made me increasingly skeptical and downright incredulous at times. (5)

In addition to the obvious training in critical reading of published work, the replication study has two other notable reading-related benefits. The first is related to the careful selection of the study for replication (an issue which will be discussed in more detail below).

One graduate student comments that *"when the replication is a well-chosen study, the bibliography included in the paper also points to the range of studies that should be included in the first-year reading list"* (9). The replication study often provides a direction for students' subsequent experimental work, and in cases like this the bibliography of the original study offers a springboard into the relevant literature.

A second reading-related benefit is included in Meara's rationale for replications. Having gathered, processed, and analyzed their data, students on the Swansea program are required to write up their replication study. For many students this write-up will eventually be redrafted into the text of the first experimental chapter of the thesis. Meara suggests that the students can use the format of the original paper as a model to guide this write-up process: "the model also acts as a sort of template for writing up the work afterwards: if the original was good enough to be accepted by a reputable journal, then it will probably be well structured and logically put together, and [that] will help the students produce their own coherent account of the research they have done" (Meara, 1994: 276). Students will also, of course, be aware of any issues provoking criticism or skepticism which have arisen during their own reading of the original paper, and will attempt to address these in the way they write up their replication study.

6 Problematic aspects of replication studies for graduate students

So far this chapter has focused on the beneficial aspects of including replication studies in a graduate research program, both from the view of the supervisor or trainer (represented here in the most part through Meara's words), and from the perspective of the students themselves. While students' comments about their experiences of working on the replication study were indeed very positive in general, there were, perhaps inevitably, some more negative elements of feedback which should also be reported and considered. These fell into three broad areas: concerns about creativity, concerns about qualities of the original study, and concerns about the fit of the replication with the trajectory of the PhD work.

The first of these possibly originates from the expectations students bring to their graduate research status. The topic area of the dissertation they will have completed at Master's level may have been constrained by supervisor interests or data resources and they may be eager to start work on an area of study which they feel more personal engagement with. On the other hand, many students arrive on a graduate program inspired and motivated by the findings of their

Master's dissertation, and are keen to pursue, immediately, research questions which have emerged from that work. Research proposals from prospective PhD students are often ambitious and innovative, and there is the danger that a disciplined research plan is perceived as constraining, or dampening, that energy: "*by providing the experience of following an 'established' research plan, students may lose the opportunity to 'think outside the box' and explore unique ideas and research designs. In the end, perhaps truly 'unique' research may prove impractical to follow through on, but the freely generated ideas at those early stages may still be useful and innovative at some point later on*" (18). This is echoed in the following comment referring to the practice of obliging research students to conduct a replication experiment in the first year of their program: "*maybe it limits the imagination – we learn 'so this is how it's done.' A kind of clean slate start might produce more creative or innovative research*" (6).

The second area of concern relates to characteristics of published studies which students perceive to be problematic in the replication context. When studies are subjected to the test of being replicated, they often prove not to be straightforward models of good practice and transparent process, challenging Meara's claim that "(the students') task is made relatively easy because they are following a model" (1994: 276). A graduate from the Swansea program, who is now a PhD supervisor in her own right, comments that "*I've found it extremely difficult to persuade my own PhD students to replicate someone else's work. This is usually because they feel that the available studies that are sufficiently simple to replicate are either badly designed or do not address the right research questions*" (1). There are three important messages here. Firstly, there is an implication that students do not recognize the value of replication studies in the wider research world (not only as a training tool); this view is not confined to research students (see Mackey, Chapter 1, this volume), and is one which this volume attempts to address. Secondly, there is the perception that a study must be simple to be replicable. One can see the sense in this: The more complex the data collections, the more resource implications, the more intricate the analysis, the more difficult the study may be to replicate. It could be argued, however, that it is not the complexity of the study, but the transparency and detail with which it is written up, that is most crucial to replicability. The third message here is about the perceived relevance of the study: "*the available studies ... do not address the right research questions*" (1). Presumably the "right research questions" are those which an individual student is interested in pursuing, and this issue relates directly to the final concern.

The final concern, and one which was expressed by several students, is to do with the relevance of the replication study to the rest of the student's PhD work: "*The problem is not doing the replication study, but how that replication work dovetails with other elements of the program and your own processes of research development in those initial stages*" (5). For most students who raised this as an issue, the selection of the study for replication was crucial. Comments related to this are in the box below. While these are far outnumbered by comments from students who consider their (or in many cases their supervisor's) choice of study to be appropriate and relevant (14 of the 19 respondents reported this to be the case), there are enough of the more negative comments to highlight this as a factor crucial to the value to the student of the replication experience.

Concerns about the choice of study for replication

In retrospect, I think deciding on a study to replicate should be inseparable from deciding on a PhD topic. (16)

It gave me a false impression that "this is how it's done." Also, it sent me down a path that is kind of doomed to failure – after three studies I came to realize that! (6)

If I have any regrets about the choice it is that (the original) paper was very much about collocations but my interest is in formulaic language more broadly. So I am now trying to work out how to pursue my interest while building on the work I've already done. (19)

It was the wrong choice on a number of counts: It was a huge one-shot study, with a massive data collection and sample ... So, it wrong-footed me in a number of ways. (5)

[I gained from the experience, but] my feelings may have been different if I had replicated a study that in the end had nothing to do with the eventual direction of my doctorate. (3)

7 The value of including replication studies in a graduate program

The students and former students consulted for the purposes of this chapter overwhelmingly report that they feel they have benefited from the experience of completing a replication experiment. An interesting caveat to this is that many of them admit that while they were actually conducting the experiment, they did not appreciate its value, and some felt frustrated or bewildered as to the worth of this sort of study at the time. The comments in the box below reflect both these viewpoints, with references to the latter underlined. The majority of students consulted (11 of the 19 respondents) reported that they had presented their replication study as a conference paper, conference poster, or journal paper. Research productivity continues on graduation from the program, too; the graduates cited in this chapter have, to date, an average of 10 major research outputs each (Google Scholar), with an average of 42 citations for their most-cited item. Read and Nation note that "the Swansea program has an impressive roll of graduates who are not only challenging inquisitors of other people's research, but also, in many cases, productive researchers in their own right" (2009: 3).

Replication studies as a valuable training exercise (especially with hindsight)

I think the model of doing a number of experiments including the replication early on is very useful. (2)

You feel at first that you're doing something mechanically, and wonder why you are doing it. But when you get into it you realize you are actually gaining from the entire experience. (3)

I now believe the replication was a very useful approach to raise awareness of the various methodological problems that can appear when conducting a replication. (7)

I know that the experience of doing research myself meant that I saw so much I wouldn't have otherwise noticed. In my work with grad students now, I am entirely convinced that doing research is crucial to understanding research. Since one doesn't quite know what to do at the outset (at least I didn't), I am sure that doing guided research in the form of a replication is very useful in this regard. (2)

I can certainly confirm its advantages. I see it as some kind of pushed research output: guided and controlled. It equips students with some necessary skills for conducting research and writing research reports, and ... confidence to apply research skills, since the task is definitely success-oriented! (16)

I feel that students ought to be constantly reminded that they might not feel the benefits at the time of the replication and that this is normal – gains are likely to be made as time progresses and as other experiments are done; the structure of the Swansea PhD helps in this respect because the students on the program know that there are more experiments to come – the replication plays an essential part in this process because of the fact that it provides a number of different springboards for the remainder of the program, such as: the practice of conducting experiments; the statistics; writing up, to name but a few. (10)

8 An advisory guide

In the final section of this chapter, the experience of graduate students from the Swansea program is used to inform an advisory guide to supervisors or students considering the inclusion of a replication study in their PhD work. This is not intended to be prescriptive, comprehensive, or inflexible, but rather to draw on some of the more persistent or insightful comments from students in order to suggest issues to be considered at the various stages of the replication process.

Preparation for replication

- The research student should brainstorm possible research directions and broad research questions, and discuss these with the supervisor.
- The research student, in consultation with the supervisor, should search the literature to find papers which come close to matching these directions and questions.
- The supervisor should guide the student's choice of an appropriate paper for replication, taking into consideration:
  - Is there enough methodological detail in the paper?
  - Does the student researcher have access to, and training in the use of, any necessary experiment resources?
  - Does the student researcher have the necessary skills (e.g., proficiency in a particular language) to conduct this experiment and analyse the data?
- The research student should then undertake a detailed review of the selected paper in preparation for the replication.

Planning the replication experiment

- The supervisor should ensure that the student is aware of the details of the experimental study, so that he or she is equipped to plan the replication carefully.
- The research student should produce an experiment plan, including details of target participants, materials, and procedures.
- The supervisor should check that the student has thought through every aspect of the experiment procedure, including what the researcher and the participants will be doing/saying/writing at all times of the experimental procedure.
- Where appropriate, the experiment procedure should be trialed on a single participant, or a small group.
- The research student should keep a diary record of all decisions made (and their justifications) and all activities related to the experiment.

After the replication experiment

- The supervisor should ensure that the student is aware of the relationship between this study and the general theme of the PhD thesis, and of how the write-up of the study can be turned into a chapter in the thesis.

- The student should write a draft experiment report as soon as possible after completion of the study.
- The supervisor should provide detailed feedback on the draft, in preparation for its development into a thesis chapter.
- The student should be encouraged to present or publish the replication study, and to recognize it as a valuable piece of research in its own right.

9 Conclusion

Wray, describing the Swansea PhD program, notes that "[it] turns out balanced researchers, with a broad and mature understanding of their field of inquiry and of the processes by which interesting research questions can be robustly investigated" (2009: xvii). This is certainly in part testament to Meara's belief in the value of the replication study as a training process for the novice researcher. In their first phase of post-graduate research, students are offered a scaffolded research experience through which they develop an awareness of the complexities of design, implementation, and reporting of experimental work, and a critical approach to the research literature. Students on this part-time program then have a further five years to explore and resolve questions which emerge from the replication experience, allowing many of them to develop a mature and thorough research perspective and to become "challenging inquisitors" (Read and Nation, 2009: 3) in their field.

Appendix: Questions used to elicit student feedback

1   Which study did you replicate?
2   How did you select that study for replication?
3   In retrospect, was the study you chose an appropriate one? Why / why not?
4   Have you presented a report of your replication experiment, either in a published paper, or as a conference paper?
5   What do you feel that you learned, or gained, from doing a replication study in the first year of your PhD?
6   Are there any disadvantages to doing a replication study in the first year of your PhD?
7   Did the replication study change the way in which you read published research? If so, how?

8 In what ways did the replication study influence the subsequent direction of your PhD?
9 Do you have any other comments about integrating replication work into a PhD program?

Acknowledgements

I am grateful to those students and graduates of the Swansea PhD program whose comments and feedback are reported in this chapter.

References

Arnaud, P. and Savignon, J. (1997). Rare words, complex lexical units and the advanced learner, in Coady, J. and Huckin, T. (eds.), *Second Language Vocabulary Acquisition: A Rationale for Pedagogy*, Cambridge: Cambridge University Press, pp. 157–73.

Barfield, A. (2009). Exploring productive L2 collocation knowledge, in Fitzpatrick, T. and Barfield, A. (eds.), *Lexical Processing in Second Language Learners*, Bristol: Multilingual Matters, pp. 95–110.

Bensoussan, M., Sim, D. and Weiss, R. (1984). The effect of dictionary usage on EFL test performance compared with student and teacher attitudes and expectations, *Reading in a Foreign Language*, 2, 2, 262–76.

Fischer, U. (1994). Learning words from context and dictionaries: An experimental comparison, *Applied Psycholinguistics*, 15, 551–74.

Fitzpatrick, T. (2006). Habits and rabbits: Word associations and the L2 lexicon, *EUROSLA Yearbook* 6, 121–45.

Folse, K. (2006). The effect of type of written exercise on L2 vocabulary retention, *TESOL Quarterly*, 40, 273–93.

Gitsaki, C. (1999). *Second Language Lexical Acquisition: A Study of the Development of Collocational Knowledge*, San Francisco, CA: International Scholars Publications.

Johnson, D. (1992). *Approaches to Research in Second Language Learning*, London: Longman.

Kruse, H., Pankhurst, J. and Sharwood-Smith, M. (1987). A multiple word association probe in second language acquisition research, *Studies in Second Language Acquisition*, 9, 2, 141–54.

Language Teaching Review Panel (2008). Replication studies in language learning and teaching: Questions and answers, *Language Teaching*, 41, 1, 1–14.

Laufer, B. and Nation, P. (1995). Vocabulary size and use: Lexical richness in L2 written production, *Applied Linguistics*, 16, 3, 307–22.

Linnarud, M. (1986). *Lexis in Composition: A Performance Analysis of Swedish Learners' Written English*, Malmö, Sweden: Liber Förlag.

Malvern, D. and Richards, B. J. (2002). Investigating accommodation in language proficiency interviews using a new measure of lexical diversity, *Language Testing*, 19, 85–104.

Meara, P. (1992). Network structures and vocabulary acquisition in a foreign language, in Arnaud, P. and Bejoint, H. (eds.), *Vocabulary and Applied Linguistics*, London: MacMillan, pp. 62–72.

Meara, P. (1994). Review of Johnson, D., "Approaches to Research in Second Language Learning," *Language and Education*, 8, 4, 275–77.

Meara, P. and Fitzpatrick, T. (2000). Lex30: An improved method of assessing productive vocabulary in an L2, *System*, 28, 19–30.

Miller, G. A. and Gildea, P. M. (1985). How to misread a dictionary, *AILA Bulletin* 1995, 13–26.

Milton, J. (2006). Language lite: Learning French vocabulary in school, *Journal of French Language Studies*, 16, 2, 187–205.

Nikolova, O. (2002). Effects of students' participation in authoring of multimedia materials on student acquisition of vocabulary, *Language Learning and Technology*, 6, 1, 100–22.

Read, J. and Nation, P. (2009). Introduction: Meara's contribution to research in L2 lexical processing, in Fitzpatrick, T. and Barfield, A. (eds.), *Lexical Processing in Second Language Learners*, Bristol: Multilingual Matters, pp. 1–12.

Verspoor, M. and Lowie, W. (2003). Making sense of polysemous words, *Language Learning*, 53, 3, 547–86.

Wilks, C. and Meara, P. M. (2002). Untangling word webs: Graph theory and the notion of density in second language work association networks, *Second Language Research*, 18, 4, 303–24.

Wolter, B. (2001). Comparing the L1 and L2 mental lexicon: A depth of individual word knowledge model, *Studies in Second Language Acquisition*, 23, 41–69.

Wray, A. (2009). Preface to Fitzpatrick, T. and Barfield, A. (eds.), *Lexical Processing in Second Language Learners*, Bristol: Multilingual Matters, pp. xi–xvii.

PART III

REPLICATION STUDIES IN PRACTICE

7 *Writing up a replication report*

James Dean Brown

Replications are studies that repeat previous studies. They can be exact, approximate, or conceptual replications (see Porte's Introduction, this volume), and they can occur in quantitative, qualitative, and mixed methods research. In order to be inclusive of all of these possible types of replications, I will start out using the frame of reference of a quantitative exact replication study, which leads to the strictest, narrowest, and most clearly defined type of replication report. However, throughout the chapter, I will consider all three types of replication studies in all three types of research, particularly with regard to how they are similar and different.

The purpose of this chapter is both to foster interest in doing replication studies and critically reading such studies, and also to suggest suitable ways of writing up such research. To those ends, I will describe ways that replication reports can be written up for publication by addressing five questions:

1 What can be included in any research paper?
2 What kinds of information from the original study can be included in the replication report?
3 How do these kinds of information from the original study differ depending on the kind of research being used (quantitative, qualitative, or mixed methods)?
4 How do these kinds of information from the original study differ depending on the kind of replication report (exact, approximate, or conceptual)?
5 What issues should the author of the replication report be aware of when reporting the replication findings?

I will address each of these questions in terms of replication studies in general, then apply the same framework to an example replication report (Eckerth, 2009; reprinted in Chapter 8, this volume).

1 Replication reports in general

1.1 *What can be included in any research paper?*

Various types of research require reports that include different types of information, which can in turn be organized in a variety of ways. These types of information and organizational patterns vary along a continuum (Brown, 2004). The strictest form of organization is used primarily on the quantitative end of the continuum, and relatively flexible configurations are used at the qualitative end of the continuum. However, one common structure for research reports includes five main sections: introduction, method, results, discussion, and conclusions.

Various publications provide detailed submission guidelines for the types of information that should be included in each of the five sections (e.g., Brown, 1988, Chapter 5; Chapelle and Duff, 2003: 159–61; and APA, 2010a: 21–59). Overall, the structure of headings and subheadings for a quantitative study in L2 studies will tend to look like those shown in the first column of Table 7.1. Types of research other than quantitative tend to use the five main report sections, but often differ considerably in subsections and in the details under each heading.

1.2 *What kinds of information from the original study can be included in the replication report?*

As mentioned above, I will begin by discussing the kinds of information typically included in an exact replication of a quantitative study. Exact replications are often organized as shown in the first column of Table 7.1, so I will use those headings and subheadings to organize this discussion.

The *Introduction* to almost any research report will move from the general issues to the specific issues that are of interest in the study. In a replication report, this section explains where the original study (and any other replications) fit into the field. The point is to situate the specific replication study being reported. All of this can be achieved under several subheadings: (a) Introduction to the problem, (b) Importance of the problem, (c) Relevant scholarship, and (d) Statement of the purpose. The *Introduction to the problem* subsection provides brief historical and theoretical background, while funneling from the general issues to the specific area of focus. This subsection also describes the original study in terms of how it approached the problem, framed the research questions, and reported the research.

Table 7.1 *Typical structure of an exact replication report (including the types of information that should be included from the original study)*

Report sections *Subsections*	Exact replication
Introduction	General to specific – sets up the replication study by situating the original study and any other replications in the field/literature.
Introduction to the problem	Sets the theoretical and historical background, funneling from general to the specific area of focus; then describes the original study in terms of how it approached the problem, framed the research question(s), and reported the research (i.e., the characteristics that made the study clear enough to replicate).
Importance of the problem	Provides theoretical background and initial indication(s) of why the topic was and remains important; explains the importance of the original research question(s) and their contribution to the knowledge of the field.
Relevant scholarship	Gives a historical overview of initial experimental work in the general area, zeroing in on the specific topic and the need for more specific work in particular contexts; shows how the existing literature still supports the relevance of the topic.
Statement of the purpose	Shows the need for and aims of the replication study and how it supports the results of the original study, either by clarifying issues raised in the original study or by extending its generalizability; any additions or changes to the original study are justified based on current theories, other replications, or related work; research questions/hypotheses are provided and their relationships to the original research questions/hypotheses clarified.
Method	The *Method* section focuses on the replication study itself using traditional subheadings like *Participants*, *Materials*, and *Procedures*; should provide sufficient detail to permit comparisons with the original study; such comparisons should continually be facilitated through appropriate references to the original study, while explaining similarities and differences so readers can understand why something did or did not change in the replication method and judge for themselves the appropriateness of those decisions.
Participants	Describes at least the participants, sampling procedures, sample size, power, and precision, including similarities and differences between the original and replication studies.

Table 7.1 (Continued)

Report sections *subsections*	Exact replication
Materials	Describes any tests, questionnaires, interview schedules, rating/coding strategies, etc., in terms of what they look like, their reliability, their validity, etc.; including similarities and differences between the original and replication studies.
Procedures	Describes the research design, experimental manipulations, interventions, etc., including similarities and differences between the original and replication studies.
Results	Provides a technical report of statistics and data analyses; where necessary, the original study is described and its outcomes discussed in sufficient detail to understand similarities and differences; in addition to traditional statistical results, includes effect sizes, both alpha and power interpretations, and confidence intervals.
Discussion	Provides direct answers to the research questions and how those answers relate to the original study.
Conclusion	Brings study full circle, interpreting the results in terms of the original study and the general research on the topic – looking both backward and forward in time.
Limitations	Considers any problems the researcher encountered in sample size, measurement reliability, participant cooperation, design flaws, etc.
Implications	Reviews the degree to which the replication study achieved its original goal(s) and provided empirical support for the results of the original study, either by clarifying issues raised by the original study or extending its generalizability; discusses in some detail any new evidence that surfaced in the replication study in terms of similarities and/or differences with the original study; accounts for differences, leading to the suggestions in the next section; revisits the degree to which any extensions or modifications of the original study were justified (based on the original study, on the current knowledge on the topic, as well as on what happened in the replication study itself).
Suggestions for future research	Lists ideas for future research and replications in some detail, especially based on what was learned in the original study, other previous research, and the present replication.

The *Importance of the problem* subsection provides additional theoretical background and initial indications of why the topic was originally interesting and still remains important. This subsection may also explain the importance of the original research questions and their perceived contribution to the field. The *Relevant scholarship* or literature review subsection includes a historical overview of initial experimental work in the general area, zeroing in on the specific topic(s) involved by explaining the need for more specific work in particular contexts and showing how the existing literature still supports the relevance and importance of the topic. The *Statement of the purpose* explains the need for and aims of the replication report and how it furthers the results of the original study (either by clarifying issues raised in the original study or by extending its generalizability). It justifies any additions or changes to the original study (based on current theories or related work) and then lists the research questions or hypotheses for the replication study. This subsection may clarify the relationships between the original research questions/hypotheses and those in the replication study.

The *Method* section focuses on the replication report itself and provides sufficient details to allow for pertinent comparisons with the original study. In the process, similarities and differences between the replication and original studies may be presented with the goal of helping readers understand what and why aspects of the original study methodology were changed, so they can judge for themselves whether those decisions were appropriate. Separate subsections also describe at least: (a) the participants, (b) materials, and (c) procedures. The *Participants* subsection describes all participants, including students, teachers, interviewers, raters, and so forth, in terms of their characteristics, as well as sampling procedures, sample size, power, and precision. Naturally, similarities and differences in participants or sampling between the original and replication studies are clarified and justified. The *Materials* subsection includes the characteristics of any tests, questionnaires, interview schedules, rating/coding schemes, and so forth, especially what the materials look like (appended if possible and space permits), as well as relevant issues of reliability and validity. Again, the similarities and any differences in the materials used in the original and replication studies are discussed here. The *Procedures* subsection lays out the steps followed in the research design, experimental manipulations, interventions, and so forth. And yes, the similarities and any differences in the procedures of the original and replication studies are explained. Note that, because of the comparative nature of the replication venture, this back-and-forth process of continually comparing the original and replication studies should probably occur at many points in the replication report. Such comparisons can help readers react critically at those many points in the report and begin to form an opinion about the quality of the replication study itself while they are reading along, instead of just waiting until the end of the paper.

The *Results* section typically provides a technical report of the statistical results and the data analyses that underlay them. This section is often written to help readers understand the technical tables and graphs by explaining what to look for. Where necessary, the report describes the original study, and its results are discussed with enough detail for readers to understand the similarities and differences in results. It is particularly important in replications of quantitative studies that, in addition to traditional statistical results, results for effect sizes, both alpha and power interpretations, and confidence intervals be presented, as appropriate. Traditionally, researchers in our field present and focus only on statistical significance by reporting and examining the *p* values associated with whatever statistical tests are being used in a study (i.e., what I am calling alpha interpretations; see also the discussion of *p* values in Nassaji, Chapter 3, this volume). Adding effect size, power, and confidence interval statistics and interpretations expands the information available to both the researcher and reader in terms of the relative importance of the finding(s) (effect size), the degree to which the study design was adequate for conducting the statistical tests (power), and the ranges of error around whatever statistics are involved (confidence intervals).

Discussion and *Conclusion* sections are used in different ways by various authors, but I find it helpful if the *Discussion* section provides direct answers to the research questions and how those answers relate to the original study. Many readers in our field will be grateful if the technical results in the *Results* section are explained here in nontechnical, lay terms that help readers understand the answers to the research questions. The report may also include comparisons of these answers to the answers found in the original study.

The *Conclusion* section brings the study full circle by interpreting the results in light of results that have previously been found (in the original study and the general research on the topic). Such interpretations typically look both backward and forward in time in three subsections: (a) *Limitations*, (b) *Implications*, and (c) *Suggestions for future research*. The *Limitations* subsection typically considers any problems that the researcher encountered with sample size, measurement reliability, participant cooperation, design flaws, and so forth, and how they may have affected the results and interpretations in the replication study. The *Implications* subsection typically reviews the degree to which the replication study achieved its original goal(s) and provided empirical support for the results of the original study, either by clarifying issues raised in the original study or by extending its generalizability. This subsection also discusses in some detail any new evidence that surfaced in the replication study in terms of similarities and differences with the original study. In addition, any extensions or modifications of the original study should be examined to determine the degree to which they were justified based on the original study, on the current knowledge on the topic or on the results of the replication study itself. Finally, a subsection called *Suggestions for future research* may be particularly important in replication research because the original and replication studies may be the first in a series of related studies or one of an already-established series of such replications. This subsection typically provides a detailed list of ideas for future research and replications based on what was learned in the original study, in previous replications, elsewhere in the literature and/or in the present replication.

In the best of all possible worlds, all of the information listed above for the replication and original studies would be included in all replication reports. However, the page length requirements of some journals make that difficult (see Porte's Introduction, this volume). As a result, replication reports must be written very clearly, succinctly, and tightly. The *Language Teaching* Review Panel put it this way:

> Given the usual space limitations in journals, researchers carrying out replications may be best advised to focus on describing what changes they have made or how their studies differ in terms of methodology or participant population, while providing other details in footnotes and appendices. The results of the original study should also be compared to those of the replication in the discussion section, focusing on how and why they are similar or different.
>
> (*Language Teaching* Review Panel, 2008: 8)

Polio and Gass discuss the possibility of providing "details in footnotes and appendices" (1997: 506) and suggest that online space be provided for such detailed information. Whatever the solution, it is probable that replication studies will need more space than other types of studies.

1.3 How do these kinds of information from the original study differ depending on the kind of research being used (quantitative, qualitative, and mixed methods)?

Recall that the guidelines in the previous section were for a *quantitative* exact replication. In this section, I will explore how replication studies tend to vary in terms of the *kinds* of information supplied for quantitative, qualitative, and mixed methods research replications.

Table 7.2   *Standards for judging quantitative, qualitative, and mixed methods research reports and replications*

General research standards	Quantitative	Qualitative
consistency	reliability	dependability
fidelity	validity	credibility
verifiability	replicability	confirmability
meaningfulness	generalizability	transferability

Brown (2004) showed how any research project can be viewed as falling at different points on an overall qualitative–quantitative continuum (see also Newman and Benz, 1998) for a number of research dimensions. At one end of the qualitative–quantitative continuum, one will find *quantitative research* which tends to be based on the following dimensions: quantitative data, experimental, statistical, hypothesis testing, deductive, controlled, highly intervening, highly selective, variable operationalizing, cross-sectional, large sample, and etic. In contrast, the *qualitative research* end of the continuum tends to be based on these dimensions: qualitative data, nonexperimental, interpretive, hypothesis-forming, inductive, natural, nonintervening, nonselective, variable defining, longitudinal, small sample, and emic. *Mixed Methods Research* (MMR) "should strategically combine qualitative and quantitative methods, approaches, and concepts in a way that produces complementary strengths and non-overlapping weaknesses" (Johnson et al., 2007: 127).

Clearly, with research methods that vary so widely along such a large number of dimensions, the types of information that are supplied in the reports of these sorts of research will also vary considerably. In very general terms, as shown on the left side of Table 7.2, all researchers are concerned with the degree to which their data, results, interpretations, and conclusions have consistency (i.e., are stable across times, places, data sets, etc.), fidelity (i.e., are faithfully and accurately represented), verifiability (i.e., are supportable), and meaningfulness (i.e., are more generally applicable and consequential). This means that researchers and readers have generally agreed that research should have those characteristics, but the ways researchers deal with these issues vary depending on the type of research.

Quantitative research reports usually deal with those four issues by focusing on the concepts of reliability, validity, replicability, and generalizability (see the second column of Table 7.2). In more detail, researchers will usually examine the reliability of their instruments (e.g., their questionnaires, tests, interviews, etc.) and how they are applied (e.g., scoring, rating, coding, etc.), but they will also consider the reliability of the overall study (i.e., the likelihood that the results will occur again if the same research methods and design are used). Researchers enhance reliability by carefully constructing, piloting, and validating their instruments, and they improve overall study reliability by carefully planning and carrying out their research.

Quantitative researchers are also concerned about two types of validity: internal and external validity (Campbell and Stanley, 1963). The internal validity of a research project can be enhanced by controlling for issues like history, maturation, testing, instrumentation, statistical regression, selection bias, experimental mortality, and selection-maturation interaction. External validity will be enhanced by controlling reactivity effects of testing, interaction of selection biases and treatment(s), reactivity effects of experimental arrangements, and multiple-treatment interference. (For definitions of these concepts, see Campbell and Stanley, 1963; Brown, 1988: 29–42.)

Replicability in quantitative research refers to the need for researchers to provide sufficiently clear and detailed information in the research report so that anyone who might want to do the research again in a new context could do so. Indeed, Thompson (1994) argues that the very existence of probability (*p*) values is inspired by the desire to empirically evaluate the replicability of statistical research. Thompson is clearly at odds with Nassaji, who argues about the relevance of *p* values to replicability (Chapter 3, this volume). I tend to agree more with Thompson on this point, but only for those studies where *p* values are part of the underlying logic of the design and analysis.

Generalizability is the degree to which the results of a study based on a particular sample (i.e., a carefully selected subset of people, words, trees, etc.) can reasonably be said to represent a population (i.e., all the people, words, trees, etc., of interest). Generalizability can be enhanced by clearly defining the population and using sound sampling techniques to create a sample that adequately represents the population (for more on sampling, see Brown, in press). (For more on these quantitative research concepts, see Brown, 1988, 2004, 2011; Hatch and Lazaraton, 1991; Scholfield, 1995; or Baayen, 2008.)

Qualitative researcher reports tend to focus on the concepts of dependability, credibility, confirmability, and transferability (see third column of Table 7.2). These categories (originally suggested by Lincoln and Guba, 1985) are commonly, though not universally, accepted. (For alternative ways of looking at these issues, see Sale and Brazil, 2004; Bryman et al., 2008; and Leech et al., 2010; for more on the qualitative research concepts discussed in this subsection, see Davis, 1992, 1995, or Brown, 2001, 2004.)

In more detail, dependability refers to the degree to which observations are consistent, as well as the effects of changing conditions in whatever is being studied. Strategies often used to enhance the dependability include overlapping methods (i.e., using multiple data-gathering procedures to check the consistency of results), stepwise replications (i.e., gathering data at different times to check the consistency of results), and inquiry audits (consulting with a qualified additional researcher to check the consistency of various aspects of the study).

Credibility is concerned with the fidelity of identifying and describing whatever is being studied as the observations and results are viewed by the various parties involved. Strategies often used to enhance credibility include prolonged engagement, persistent observation, triangulation, peer debriefing, negative case analysis, referential analysis (i.e., archiving a portion of the data before analysis, and later checking the conclusions of the analysis against those archived data), and member checking (i.e., asking the stakeholders in a study to consider and give feedback on the conclusions of the study).

Confirmability deals with the degree to which the data in a study can be verified. Strategies that are often used to enhance confirmability include showing transcripts, establishing audit trails and keeping careful data records.

Transferability deals with the meaningfulness and applicability of the results of a study to other contexts. The strategy typically used to enhance transferability is thick description (i.e., providing sufficiently detailed information for readers to decide if the results of the study apply to their contexts).

Triangulation is a concept that permeates the literature on qualitative research methods. According to Brown (2001: 227–9), "triangulation involves studying data from multiple perspectives." Principled use of triangulation seems to be crucial for enhancing the dependability and credibility of qualitative research.

In recent years, MMR has suddenly arrived as a new research paradigm. One could argue that MMR reports should focus on concepts like interpretive rigor (after Leech et al., 2010: 20); legitimation (after Onwuegbuzie and Johnson, 2006: 57); and inference transferability (after Teddlie and Tashakkori, 2009: 311–12) as MMR variants for dealing with consistency, fidelity, and meaningfulness. However, the standards for judging the quality of MMR are still evolving (for excellent discussions, see Leech et al., 2010, and Onwuegbuzie and Johnson, 2006). Until all of this shakes out in the MMR literature, the best course for people in our field may be to heed the conclusion of Bryman et al.: "The findings relating to mixed methods research point to a preference for using a combination of quantitative and qualitative research criteria and for employing different criteria for the quantitative and the qualitative components" (2008: 261). Such a stance means that authors of replication studies should carefully consider whether the research they are replicating is purely quantitative, predominantly quantitative, balanced mixed methods, predominantly qualitative or purely qualitative. The author of the replication study will then need to decide on the appropriate balance of qualitative, mixed method, or quantitative standards and techniques to apply in the replication.

1.4 How do these kinds of information from the original study differ depending on the kind of replication report (exact, approximate, or conceptual)?

Generally, the report of an *exact replication* will refer to the original study more often and provide more information about that original study than will an *approximate replication*, which will in turn reference the original study more often than will a *conceptual replication* report.

In more detail, exact replication "involves duplicating a previous methodologically sound study exactly in order to confirm the original findings" (Porte, Introduction, this volume). As Polio and Gass point out, "To attempt a virtual [read *exact*] replication, a great deal of information on a study is needed" (1997: 502). As a result, it is crucial that: (a) the original study provided adequate details so the replication study can be as exact as possible, and (b) the exact replication report makes comparisons and contrasts with the original study at all important points in the research. The types of information provided for an exact replication will vary depending on whether the study is quantitative, qualitative, or mixed method research. However, in general, the amount of information reported about the original study in an exact replication is bound to be relatively large compared to approximate or conceptual replications.

Approximate replication "involves repeating the original study exactly in most respects, but changing nonmajor variables (in a way that allows for comparability between the original and replication studies)" (Porte, Introduction, this volume). Thus, an approximate replication report should provide evidence about how the different approaches produced similar or different results, along with an explanation of why the similarities and differences occurred and how the different approach furthered the knowledge of the field (*Language Teaching* Review Panel, 2008). Again, the types of information that will be provided for an approximate replication will vary depending on whether it is quantitative, qualitative, or mixed method research. However, generally, the quantity of information reported about the original study in an approximate replication will tend to be less than that in an exact replication but more than in a conceptual replication.

Conceptual replication "begin[s] with a similar problem statement as the original study but employ[s] a new research design to verify the original findings" (Porte, Introduction, p. 8). Or as Polio and Gass put it, " ... to attempt a conceptual replication, one needs only to consider the claims of the research and how one might want to make changes to the original study to see if the claims hold up in a new situation. In principle, a conceptual replication may require less information" (1997: 502). And yes, finally, the types of information that will be provided for a conceptual replication will vary depending on whether the study is quantitative, qualitative, or mixed methods. However, the quantity of information reported about the original study in a conceptual replication will generally be the least of all the replication types.

1.5 *What issues should the author of the replication report be aware of when reporting the replication findings?*

Audience is an important issue for the author of a replication report just as it is for any author. Will the readers be the same as those who read the original report? Will they tend to be researchers? Or is the replication report meant to help language teachers understand and interpret both the original and replication studies? Naturally, audiences vary between language researchers and teachers, or combine members of various groups, and matching the level and content of any article to all possible readers is probably never feasible. Nonetheless, authors of replication reports should think about their audience, especially in terms of the readership targets of the journal where the study is going to be published. In doing so, they can assume a great deal of knowledge common to an audience made up entirely of researchers, but can make no such assumption if the audience is made up of teachers, or is a mixed audience. Indeed, a teacher or mixed audience may tend to need more information about how to interpret various statistical or qualitative terminology, concepts, and procedures.

Collegiality is another issue that must be considered. The one element of the audience that is particularly important is the author of the original study. Whether the observations and comparisons that the replication report makes about the original study are positive or negative is not the issue. The issue is that the author of the replication report should not frame those observations and comparisons in a hurtful way; they should instead be framed in a professional and respectful way. After all, the original study was published, presumably in a respected journal, and was good enough to inspire the replication author to invest considerable time and effort in replicating it.

Clearly, certain lines should never be crossed with colleagues. What exactly these lines might be, I cannot say, but most professionals will recognize them when they see them. For example, one blind review that I received recently informed me that "this author shouldn't be doing research." That was hurtful, certainly disrespectful, and totally unnecessary. Avoiding such thoughtless comments is easy. Just follow the golden rule of doing unto others as you would have them do unto you.

Contacting the author of the original article to get feedback on the replication study and its conclusions would also be a collegial approach. The reactions of the original author could be summarized and discussed in the Discussion and/or Conclusions sections of the replication, or the original author could be offered a chance to write a reaction that would be published alongside the replication report (see Eckerth, Chapter 8, this volume). Either strategy would promote collegiality and foster ongoing debate on the issues involved.

Ethics is another important issue in social sciences research (for a book-length overview, see Kimmel, 1988; for examples of ethical research standards, see APA, 2010b). Some of the most important ethical and professional responsibilities (adapted liberally here to include replication research from Brown, 2004: 497–98), categorized in four categories, follow:

Participant issues:
1 Avoid abusing the participants in a replication study in any way, including at least abuses of their persons, time, or effort; obtain the participants' informed consent.
2 Avoid abusing any colleagues by collecting replication data from their students without their permission or by using too much of their precious class time.
3 Reward the cooperation and efforts of all participants and colleagues in a replication study, at least by giving them feedback on what happened in the study.

Analysis responsibilities:
4   Guard against consciously or subconsciously modifying data or interpretations in the original or replication studies to make them support personal views and prejudices.
5   Select the appropriate replication and research types for the purposes of the original and replication research projects.
6   Select the most appropriate interaction of standards possible for the purposes of the original and replication research projects.

Concerns for the audience:
7   Explain the original and replication research studies clearly so they can be understood by the readers.
8   Organize the report using traditional sections, headings, and other conventions to make it easier for the readers to follow not only the replication report but also the original study.
9   Interpret the original and replication studies carefully while guarding against any temptation to misinterpret the original study's results, or overinterpret or overgeneralize the replication study's results.

Concerns for the original author:
10 Frame any criticisms of the original author (positive or negative) in professional and respectful ways.
11 Do not cross the lines of professional respect (do unto others as you would have them do unto you).
12 Contact the original author (seek and take into consideration the original author's point of view on your replication).

2 Eckerth (2009, reprinted in this volume, Chapter 8)

In this section, I use the framework laid out above to analyze an example replication report. Eckerth labels his study an "approximate replication" of Foster (1998) (see the first sentence of Abstract or the last sentence of Section 1, p. 204) and "qualitative, transcript-based L2 research" (see last sentence of the Acknowledgments, p. 219). I will approach this approximate qualitative replication report by comparing it with the framework shown in Table 7.1 for an exact quantitative replication report, using the main report sections in that table as subheadings to organize my critique. I should point out that I do not expect this approximate qualitative replication to include all of the material that would normally be found in an exact quantitative replication. Nonetheless, this comparison should provide a good starting point for putting into practice what I have suggested above and thereby evaluating the effectiveness of Eckerth's report presentation.

The material covered under Introduction in Table 7.1 is organized by Eckerth into two sections, 1 Introduction, and 2 The original research study. Overall, these two sections move from the general to the specific. The opening sentence talks about the general shift from the belief in our field that language students learn grammar in order to interact, to the belief that students learn grammar by interacting. By the second section, the author has narrowed the focus to the original Foster (1998) study and, even more specifically, to the research questions that drove that study. Thus, Eckerth has set up the replication report by situating the original study and his replication study in the literature, thereby providing a satisfying segue into the replication study itself.

More specifically, Sections 1 and 2 of the replication report provide a more than adequate *Introduction to the problem*. Section 1 (p. 198) sets the theoretical and historical background, funneling from the general literature to the specific area of focus. Section 2 (p. 204) then describes the original study in terms of how it approached the problem and framed the research question(s). However, in this case the researcher chooses to describe the details of the original study later, in "3 The replication study" (p. 204), where the two studies are contrasted point by point, going back and forth between the replication and original studies.

The *Importance of the problem* and the need for replication are introduced in the last two sentences of Section 1, paragraph 5 on pp. 201–2 by providing initial indications of why the topic remains important to the knowledge of the field and why the replication was needed. *Relevant scholarship* (literature review) is covered throughout Section 1, which not only gives a historical overview of initial experimental work in the area, but also zeros in on the specific topic and the need for more specific replication work.

A clear *Statement of purpose* is provided in Section 1, Paragraphs 5 to 9 on pp. 201–4, which explain the aims of the replication study and how it supports the results of the original study. More specifically, Paragraph 5 explains that inconsistent results in the previous research support the need for replication. Paragraph 6 overtly clarifies that the goal of the replication study is to either confirm or not the results of the original study and "shed more light on the validity of Foster's interpretation of these results" (p. 202). Paragraph 7 expands on the study's goals related to the results, and Paragraph 8 does the same for interpretation. Thus, the report clarifies the aims of the replication study and how it supports the results of the original study, both by clarifying issues raised in the original study and by extending its generalizability.

The first sentence of Paragraph 9 goes on to explain the single major addition made to the original study: "For these reasons, and in terms of data collection, a stimulated recall methodology was added to the present replication study" (p. 203). This addition is justified based on previous research and current thinking. The research questions are then clarified as follows: Section 2 clearly explains the research questions of the original research, and Section 3 states that "The replication study closely followed the research procedures adopted in the original study" (p. 204). All in all, the introductory sections here provide ample information for understanding where the replication study fits into the overall field, especially vis-à-vis the original study.

Like a *Method* section, and heralding the main body of the paper, Section 3, The replication study (p. 204), focuses on the replication study itself, but does not use the traditional subheadings of "Participants," "Materials," and "Procedures." Instead, it has subsections headed: "The participants," "The setting," "The tasks," "Data collection," and "Transcription and coding." Recall that this is an approximate replication because it provides an element or variable that was not present in the original study. This extra element is described here under the "Stimulated recall" heading.

While the organization and headings of Section 3, The replication study, do not line up neatly with the traditional headings, they do make sense for this sort of study for two reasons. First, this structure is the same as that used to organize the original study. Having parallel structures has the great advantage of allowing readers to easily line up and compare the subsections in the replication report with those in the original study. Second, the information that would normally be found in the traditional subsections is found here, but organized differently: for information on *Participants* see 3.1, for *Materials* see 3.3, 3.5, and 3.6, and for *Procedures* see 3.2, 3.4, 3.5, and 3.6.

Section 3 is written with sufficient detail to permit comparisons with the original study at many points. Indeed, such comparisons are made overtly by the author throughout these six subsections, a fact that continually facilitates understanding the similarities and differences between the replication and original studies, with explanations whenever something was changed in the replication method so readers can judge for themselves the appropriateness of the replication researcher's decisions. Here are just a few of the many instances of the replication report referencing the original study:

- In 3.1 The participants – "Whereas the original study was conducted with ESL learners at a municipal college in Great Britain, participants in the replication study were students in an L2 German university course." (pp. 204–5)
- In 3.2 The setting – "In line with the original study, the setting of the classroom was preserved as far as possible. Therefore, all recordings were made during three scheduled lessons. In the case of the replication study, these recordings were part of a more extended sequence of data collection for the purpose of a larger research project ..." (p. 205)
- In 3.3 The tasks – "In Foster's study, the two variables 'task type' (optional vs. required information exchange) and 'participant structure' (small group vs. pair work) were systematically combined, exemplified by four tasks with varying 'task foci' ... The replication study did not vary the participation pattern, but rather had all tasks completed in pairs of learners. Such a departure from the original study has been motivated by two factors." [The author goes on to explain.] (p. 205)
- In 3.4 Data collection – "Thus, while replicating the original data collection procedure, the amount of data transcribed and coded was larger both in terms of number of interacting dyads and amount of interactional time." (p. 208)
- In 3.5 Transcription and coding – "... in order to ensure comparability, the replication study used the same coding procedures as the original investigation." (p. 208)

Thus, the participants in the replication study are described along with the sampling procedures and sample size, again including similarities and differences between the original and replication studies. There was no need to report power or precision statistics because the research was qualitative.

The materials were the three tasks (described in 3.3) and the stimulated recall (in 3.6), which are all presented in great detail along with the similarities and differences between the replication and original studies. The coding strategies are described in equal detail (in 3.5) and are compared to the original study. However, there is no overt discussion of reliability or validity. Given that this is a qualitative replication study, the analogous concepts of dependability and credibility would have been more appropriate here, and it would have been reassuring if the author had explicitly explained how these concepts were enhanced in this replication study. The author could have used and described some of the following techniques to enhance the study: overlapping methods, stepwise replications, and/or inquiry audits for *dependability*; and prolonged engagement, persistent observation, triangulation, peer debriefing, negative case analysis, referential analysis, and/or member checking for *credibility* (all of these techniques are described above in the second half of Section 1.3). Descriptions of how some combination of these techniques was implemented could have been supplied in the Method section under Data collection (p. 207), and then explanations of how these techniques enhanced the study could have been included in the Results, Discussion, or Conclusion sections as appropriate.

In terms of procedures, this replication report describes the research design, experimental manipulations, and interventions very clearly, including similarities and differences between the original and replication studies.

The replication report turns next to Section 4 Results (p. 209), just as shown in Table 7.1. However, Eckerth does something very interesting here by combining what are labeled as separate *Results* and *Discussion* sections in Table 7.1 above. The author not only provides a technical report of the results, but does so in subsections that parallel and answer the research questions exactly: 4.1 Language production, 4.2 Comprehensible input, and 4.3 Modified output. The author saves discussion of how the variables task type (optional vs. required information exchange) and participant structure (group vs. pair work) affect the research questions for his Section 5 Discussion.

Eckerth not only shows how his replication answered each research question but also describes the original study and its outcomes in sufficient detail so the reader can again appreciate the similarities and differences between the replication and original studies. Examples follow:

- First paragraph (general introduction) In Section 4 Results – "However, although Foster (1998: 8) explicitly states her intention to 'observe individual students' classroom performance,' no effort has been made to keep the composition of the groups and dyads constant … In the present study, however, it was generally the same students working together on the different tasks." (p. 209)
- In 4.1 Language production – "Such a result is in conflict with Foster's scores, which show the same ratio for the groups, but the reverse for the dyads. Furthermore, compared across dyads and consistent with Foster's study (1998: 9), the overall amount of language production varies widely." (p. 210)
- In 4.2 Comprehensible input – "Foster's study shows a lot of students not negotiating at all, particularly when working in a group

rather than a dyad (Foster, 1998: 13). Thus, the factor of participation pattern seems to have an impact not only on the amount of language production, but also on the amount of meaning negotiation. When it comes to the impact of task type, in line with Foster's results, negotiation was relatively more frequent in the two referential tasks." (p. 211)

- In 4.3 Modified output – "In relation to the overall amount of language production, the extent of output modification is rather limited, as it is also in Foster's data." ... "As Foster discovered (Foster, 1998: 15), no consistent pattern can be found when comparing tasks with optional as opposed to tasks with required information exchange." ... "Table 8.2 summarizes the overall frequency of meaning negotiation and output modification in Foster's (1998) original and in the replication study." (p. 212)

There are limited statistics in the replication report: Eckerth's Table 8.2 (p. 213) summarizes the frequencies of negotiated input and modified output. Those frequencies are described in the last paragraph of Section 4 Results. However, they are so limited that this replication is still almost entirely qualitative. Hence, the ideas of reporting effect sizes, both alpha and power interpretations, and confidence intervals suggested in Table 7.1 of the present chapter are not necessary or appropriate here.

The choices that researchers throughout the field make about what to include in the *Discussion* and *Conclusion* sections of their research reports are very fluid. The *Discussion* section described in Table 7.1 advocates providing direct answers to the research questions and how those answers relate to the original study, but the replication report has already accomplished all of that in its Results section. However, all of the subtopics that fall under *Conclusion* in Table 7.1 are found in either the Discussion or Conclusion section here. For example, the *Limitations* subsection in Table 7.1 will typically deal with problems like sample size, measurement reliability, participant cooperation, design flaws, and so forth. There are several observations along those lines in Eckerth's report. For example:

- Page 213 (first sentence of second paragraph of Section 5 Discussion) – "The present study did not compare group and dyad settings. However, ..."
- Page 217 (last sentence of Section 5 Discussion) – "As the present study shows that students' task perceptions can influence their task performance, such an account of learners' interpretations of their own task work and interactional behavior could have helped with the appraisal of the investigation's ecological validity."

- Acknowledgments – the traditional "Needless to say that all remaining shortcomings are my own responsibility."

Implications are discussed throughout Section 5 Discussion and 6 Conclusion as well. Section 5 Discussion begins with the following sentence: "As the main purpose of a replication study is to better understand the results, outcomes, and implications of the replicated study, it will be helpful to summarize Foster's (1998: 17ff.) findings briefly" (p. 213). The replication goes on to provide just such a brief summary. The discussion then continues alternating back and forth between the replication and original studies while addressing the degree to which the task type (optional vs. required information exchange) and participant structure (group vs. pair work) variables affect each other and the research questions. The discussion considers the degree to which the replication study achieved its initial goals and provided support for the results of the original study by clarifying issues raised in that study. This section also discusses new findings that surfaced in the replication study in terms of similarities and differences with the original study. For example, the author summarizes a key new finding as follows:

> In the present study, combined and related evidence from task completion and stimulated recall data (see e-supplement, Transcripts 12–15) exemplifies how students may deal with communication problems during task-work in the L2 classroom. Task-based learner–learner interaction appears not just as the verbal equivalent of a cognitive language-learning activity; it is at the same time a communicative event and a social process that is mediated by socio-affective variables (p. 215).

In Transcripts 13 and 15 as well as the associated text (see e-supplement) and in Section 6 Conclusion, the author discusses and revisits how the main modification of the original study was justified based on what happened in the replication study itself, saying at the beginning of the very last paragraph that "Combining a stimulated recall methodology with an analysis of task performance, the present study tried to show in what way learners' task perceptions can influence their task-based interactions." In addition, at various points throughout Section 5 Discussion and 6 Conclusion, the author of the replication brings the study full circle, by interpreting the results in terms of the original study and the general research on the topic. For example, on page 216 in 5 Discussion, the author raises the following question: "In what way, then, do the results from this replication and other work on meaning negotiation in the L2 classroom (Foster, 1998; Slimani-Rolls, 2005) relate to the findings of Gass et al.'s (2005) carefully designed comparative study?"

Eckerth has chosen to make few suggestions for future research. On page 218, he does point forward to further research or the need for additional replication when he starts the sentence with "If supported by further research, ..." In addition, the author calls for more research in a general way when he writes, "However, as the empirical base of these and related findings is still limited, all conclusions have to be provisional in nature. Finally, they call for more classroom-based interventionist studies ... " (in the last paragraph of the paper).

Having gone step by step through the replication study to analyze the degree to which adequate information was provided, I have only two issues left to consider: (a) the degree to which the type of research was correctly and effectively implemented, and (b) the degree to which the replication report addressed an appropriate audience, showed collegiality, and adhered to ethical behavior.

In terms of *Type of research*, it was not until Section 6 Conclusion that the author overtly mentions "qualitative analyses" (first sentence of the second paragraph), and not until the last sentence of the Acknowledgments that he labels his replication as "qualitative, transcript-based L2 research." While transferability as it pertains to the transferability of laboratory findings to classroom situations comes up six times, none of the common considerations in qualitative research of dependability, credibility, confirmability, and transferability are mentioned at all in terms of how they apply to Eckerth's own replication study as qualitative research until the last sentence of the Acknowledgments: "Finally, I would like to thank the editorial board of *Language Teaching*, above all Graeme Porte, for suggesting an e-supplement to the printed paper. I believe that providing additional space for the publication of relevant data can significantly increase the transparency and thus the credibility of qualitative, transcript based L2 research." Both *transparency* and *credibility* are important concepts in qualitative research, but neither is discussed beyond their mention in the above quotation. While the four qualitative research concepts of dependability, credibility, confirmability, and transferability are not overtly discussed, it seems to me that *dependability* is enhanced by the fact that this replication report can be viewed as a stepwise replication of the original study and by the triangulation that the author uses (e.g., three tasks and stimulated recall); *credibility* is enhanced by the way the descriptions of the materials and coding strategies are so transparent and directly anchored in the literature; *confirmability* is enhanced by the way the replication reveals large chunks of its data in the form of transcripts in the e-supplement that the reader can consult to confirm the author's interpretations; and *transferability* is enhanced by the fact that the description provided in this report is thick enough for the readers to decide for themselves if the results transfer, or are applicable, in their language teaching/learning contexts.

All in all, overt discussion of these four concepts would have made me happier from the perspective of the quantitative and qualitative paradigms within which I work. Like the vast majority of researchers in the world today, I am an unrepentant positivist, which means that I value consistency, fidelity, verifiability, and meaningfulness (see Table 7.2) in all research. As a necessary consequence, I value the analogous qualitative research concepts of dependability, credibility, confirmability, and transferability. Having identified those four characteristics in Eckerth's replication as well as in the Foster paper that it replicates, I feel comfortable with both. However, I have run into a few researchers who adamantly argue that these four characteristics are hopelessly positivist and unnecessary in postmodernist qualitative research. My guess is that such postmodernist research therefore cannot and should not be replicated. Fortunately, many qualitative studies (like the Foster, 1998, and Eckerth, 2009) do exhibit the four characteristics discussed here and therefore can be replicated.

On a different issue, I think the author of the replication report targeted the interests and level of the target *audience* (i.e., readers of *Language Teaching*) rather well. His style and content were clear to me, an outsider to this particular line of research, but also seemed technical and precise enough to be suitable for those researchers/readers who are interested in the particular topic of this replication study.

Equally importantly, Eckerth treated the author of the original article with the respect and with the degree of *collegiality* called for in such a replication. That he succeeded in finding the right tone to be both positively and negatively critical (in the best sense of that word) is evidenced throughout the replication report, but also by the fact that the "Comment from the author of the original study" (p. 219) published directly after the replication report praises and even seems to appreciate the replication study, while not being the least bit defensive.

The author of the replication study makes no direct mention of *ethics*. Perhaps he should have. However, the points I made in the previous two paragraphs show a pattern that leads me to doubt that there is any reason to suspect unethical behavior.

3 Conclusion

This chapter set out to address five questions. In doing so, I tried to show the general types of information that can be included in a replication report and how they can be organized generally in terms of introduction, method, results, discussion, and conclusions. In the process, I discussed in considerable detail the kinds of information that can be included in a replication report (exact, approximate, or conceptual). I tempered these choices in light of how the kinds of information may vary depending on the kind of research involved (quantitative, qualitative, or mixed methods) and the kind of replication study (exact, approximate, or conceptual). I also discussed issues of audience, collegiality, and ethics as they relate to replication reports. All of these issues were then applied to the example of Eckerth's (2009) replication report.

In order to be inclusive of all these possibilities, yet clear, I started out using the frame of reference of exact quantitative replication reports because they tend to be the strictest, narrowest, and most clearly defined type of replication study. I warned that fewer and fewer parts of that quantitative exact framework shown in Table 7.1 might be applicable to approximate or conceptual replications, respectively, and that the framework would probably need to be applied in a different way to qualitative research. Nonetheless, it turned out that the framework in Table 7.1 served rather well when used with a bit of flexibility to approach Eckerth's approximate qualitative replication report. Most of the information I was looking for based on Table 7.1 was present in the example replication report. While the information was not always where I expected to find it, it was nonetheless present and complete. (Readers who like a hands-on approach may find it useful to now apply this same framework to the Rott replication report in Chapter 9 of this book. It is also an approximate replication, but more quantitative in nature.)

By describing ways that replication reports can be written up in preparation for publication, I hope that I have achieved the purpose of this chapter, which was to foster interest not only in doing replication studies but also in critically reading such studies.

References

APA (2010a). *Publication Manual of the American Psychological Association* (6th edn.), Washington, DC: American Psychological Association.

APA (2010b). *Ethical Principles of Psychologists and Code of Conduct*, Washington, DC: American Psychological Association. Retrieved 26 August 2010 from www.apa.org/ethics/code/index.aspx

Baayen, R. H. (2008). *Analyzing Linguistic Data: A Practical Introduction to Statistics Using R*, Cambridge: Cambridge University Press.

Brown, J. D. (1988). *Understanding Research in Second Language Learning: A Teacher's Guide to Statistics and Research Design*, Cambridge: Cambridge University Press.

Brown, J. D. (2001). *Using Surveys in Language Programs*, Cambridge: Cambridge University Press.

Brown, J. D. (2004). Research methods for applied linguistics: Scope, characteristics, and standards, in Davies, A. and Elder, C. (eds.), *The Handbook of Applied Linguistics*, Oxford: Blackwell, pp. 476–500.

Brown, J. D. (2011). Quantitative research in second language studies, in Hinkel, E. (ed.), *Handbook of Research in Second Language Teaching and Learning* (vol. 2), Mahwah, NJ: Lawrence Erlbaum Associates, pp. 190–206.

Brown, J. D. (in press). Sampling, in Chapelle, C. A. (ed.), *The Encyclopedia of Applied Linguistics*, Malden, MA: Wiley-Blackwell.

Bryman, A., Becker, S. and Sempik, J. (2008). Quality criteria for quantitative, qualitative, and mixed methods research: A view from social policy, *International Journal of Social Research Methodology*, **11**, 261–76.

Campbell, D. T. and Stanley, J. C. (1963). *Experimental and Quasi-experimental Designs for Research*, Chicago: Rand McNally.

Chapelle, C. A. and Duff, P. A. (2003). Some guidelines for conducting quantitative and qualitative research in TESOL, *TESOL Quarterly*, **37**, 157–78.

Davis, K. A. (1992). Validity and reliability in qualitative research on second language acquisition and teaching: Another researcher comments … , *TESOL Quarterly*, **26**, 605–8.

Davis, K. A. (1995). Qualitative theory and methods in applied linguistics research, *TESOL Quarterly* **29**, 427–53.

Eckerth, J. (2009). Negotiated interaction in the L2 classroom, *Language Teaching*, **42**, 109–30.

Foster, P. (1998). A classroom perspective on the negotiation of meaning, *Applied Linguistics*, **19**, 1–23.

Gass, S., Mackey, A. and Ross-Feldman, L. (2005). Task-based interactions in classroom and laboratory settings, *Language Learning*, **55**, 575–611.

Hatch, E. and Lazaraton, A. (1991). *The Research Manual: Design and Statistics for Applied Linguistics*, Rowley, MA: Newbury House.

Johnson, R. B., Onwuegbuzie, A. J. and Turner, L. A. (2007). Toward a definition of mixed methods research, *Journal of Mixed Methods Research*, **1**, 112–33.

Kimmel, A. J. (1988). *Ethics and Values in Applied Social Research*, Newbury Park, CA: Sage.

Language Teaching (2009). Call for papers: Replication research studies, *Language Teaching*, **42**, i.

Language Teaching Review Panel (2008). Replication studies in language learning and teaching: Questions and answers, *Language Teaching*, **41**, 1–14.

Leech, N. L., Dellinger, A. B., Brannagan, K. B. and Tanaka, H. (2010). Evaluating mixed research studies: A mixed methods approach, *Journal of Mixed Methods Research*, 4, 17–31.

Lincoln, Y. S. and Guba, E. (1985). *Naturalistic Inquiry*, Beverly Hills, CA: Sage.

Newman, I. and Benz, C. R. (1998). *Qualitative-Quantitative Research Methodology: Exploring the Interactive Continuum*, Carbondale, IL: Southern Illinois University Press.

Onwuegbuzie, A. J. and Johnson, R. B. (2006). The validity issue in mixed research, *Research in the Schools*, 13, 48–63.

Polio, C. and Gass, S. (1997). Replication and reporting: A commentary, *Studies in Second Language Acquisition*, 19, 499–508.

Sale, J. E. and Brazil, K. (2004). A strategy to identify critical appraisal criteria for primary mixed-method studies, *Quality and Quantity*, 38, 351–65.

Scholfield, P. (1995). *Quantifying Language: A Researcher's Guide to Gathering Language Data and Reducing it to Figures*, Clevedon, UK: Multilingual Matters.

Slimani-Rolls, A. (2005). Rethinking task-based language learning: What we can learn from the learners, *Language Teaching Research*, 9, 195–218.

Teddlie, C. and Tashakkori, A. (2009). *The Foundations of Mixed Methods Research: Integrating Quantitative and Qualitative Approaches in the Social and Behavioral Sciences*, Thousand Oaks, CA: Sage.

Thompson, B. (1994). The pivotal role of replication in psychological research: Empirically evaluating the replicability of sample results, *Journal of Personality*, 62, 157–76.

8 Negotiated interaction in the L2 classroom: An approximate replication

Johannes Eckerth[†]

[†]This replication study, first published in the Cambridge University Press journal *Language Teaching* (Vol. 42.1, 109–30), is reprinted here in honor of Dr Eckerth, who was involved in this book project from its inception until his untimely passing in 2009. This paper was published with additional tables and data in an e-supplement on the journal Web page.

Abstract

The present paper reports on an approximate replication of Foster's (1998) study on the negotiation of meaning. Foster investigated the interactional adjustments produced by L2 English learners working on different types of language-learning tasks in a classroom setting. The replication study duplicates the methods of data collection and data analysis of the original study, but alters the target language (L2 German) and adds a stimulated recall methodology. The results of the replication study partially confirm Foster's results, and introduce some further differentiated findings. It is concluded that the original study's concern with the transferability of laboratory findings to classroom settings should be investigated in greater detail.

1 Introduction

[1]* Ever since the basic assumption endorsed in the seminal work of Hatch in the late 1970s that learners learn the structure of a language through interaction rather than learning grammar in order to interact (Hatch, 1978), the relationship between interaction and acquisition has been one of the core issues in second language acquisition (SLA) research. A central claim resulting from this research is that, though interaction may not be strictly necessary, it nevertheless constitutes the primary means by which language learners obtain data for language learning, not only because interaction is how most learners

*Initial paragraphs are numbered to facilitate those following Brown's (Chapter 7) commentary on this text.

receive input, but also because the input obtained through interaction is more conducive to acquisition than input received in other ways. Within SLA research, input obtained via interaction has been conceptualized and researched in terms of "comprehensible input" (Krashen, 1981), "negotiation of meaning" (Long, 1983), and "comprehensible output" (Swain, 1985, 1995, 2005). The interrelatedness of these three notions is concisely articulated in Long's revised version of the Interaction Hypothesis:

> I would like to suggest that negotiation for meaning, and especially negotiation work that triggers interactional adjustments by the NS or more competent interlocutor, facilitates acquisition because it connects input, internal learner capacities, particularly selective attention, and output in productive ways.
>
> (Long, 1996: 451–2)

Given the assumed acquisitional potential of negotiated interaction, the question arises as to how to best create a learning environment in which negotiation of meaning and interactional adjustments can occur. From the middle of the 1980s onward, a large number of studies have been conducted which observe language learners working on specially designed tasks. These "referential communication tasks," as they have been called (see Yule, 1997, and Pica et al., 2006, for an overview of their use in L2 research), have been classified along several task variables (see Pica et al., 1993), such as information distribution (information shared among vs. split between interactants) and information flow between interactants (one-way vs. two-way). Typically, then, such tasks have been investigated as to how they induced L2 production, the negotiation of meaning, and/or the modification of output (see Pica, 1994; Gass, 1997; Gass and Mackey, 2006, 2007; Mackey, 2007, for research overviews).

[2] Although this strand of research is primarily concerned with the cognitive and interactive conditions of language acquisition, such studies on negotiated interaction also claim to be directly or indirectly relevant to SLA and L2 pedagogy. Tasks, although they were developed for research, are claimed to be of immediate applicability as a teaching tool in the L2 classroom (e.g., Long and Porter, 1985; Long and Crookes, 1987; Pica et al., 1996; Pica, 2005; Eckerth, 2006). However, these studies have typically not been conducted in classrooms:

> The bulk of task-based research in SLA has taken place under laboratory conditions rather than in actual classrooms. A question of some interest to SLA researchers interested in the pedagogical application of their research is whether the results they have obtained can be replicated under normal classroom conditions. Task evaluations conducted

by teachers, then, can serve as a way of testing the transferability of research findings.

(Ellis, 1997: 230)

What Ellis stated over ten years ago still reflects the current tendency (see Gass et al., 2005). Given the immense productivity of task-based research – see the research overviews in book length (Ellis, 2003) as well as several edited volumes (Bygate et al., 2001; Leaver and Willis, 2004; Müller-Hartmann and Schocker-von Ditfurth, 2004; Edwards and Willis, 2005; Ellis, 2005; van den Branden, 2006; García Mayo, 2007; van den Branden et al., 2007; Eckerth and Siekmann, 2008; Samuda and Bygate, 2008), and the ever-growing popularity of task-based language pedagogy (see Lee, 2000; Nunan, 2004; Swan, 2005), the question of the transferability of research results to the language classroom is a pressing one. The issue at hand is not the external validity or even the legitimacy of experimental and laboratory L2 research per se (see Hulstijn, 1997, for the possibilities and limitations of experimental SLA research). Rather, the critical question is whether an approach to L2 pedagogy which claims to be firmly founded in, and closely related to, research findings is not at risk of losing some of its credibility, if this research does not attempt to demonstrate its validity in laboratory *and* in classroom settings. One way to do this is to attempt to reproduce the results of a laboratory study in the L2 classroom, an approach chosen by Foster (1998). Another approach is to use the same tasks in both settings and in one and the same investigation, as recently exemplified by Gass et al. (2005). As the Gass et al. (2005) study was in part a reaction to Foster (1998), in the following I shall discuss the latter before focusing in the main part of the paper on the former.

[3] Gass et al. (2005) conducted a comparative same-methodology/different-settings investigation of learners' task-based interaction. Three different tasks were administered in the two settings. The subjects were 74 native speakers of English who were enrolled in third-semester university-level Spanish courses. In one of the three dyadic tasks, information exchange was optional – on the basis of shared information about several universities, pairs of students had to decide which university they would recommend a friend to choose. In the other two tasks, information exchange was obligatory – the tasks involved spotting differences in two similar pictures, one of which was held by each student, and drawing a driving route on a shared map on the basis of different pieces of information held by each of the students in the pair. Intact classes were randomly assigned to either classroom or laboratory settings. Whereas 44 students completed all

three tasks during their regular class time with their regular instructor, 30 students from the other two classes accomplished the tasks in a laboratory setting with a research assistant. Learners' interactions in both settings were audiotaped and coded for negotiation of meaning, language-related episodes, and recasts. The two guiding research questions were: (i) In what way does task-based interaction in the classroom compare to task-based interaction in a laboratory setting? and (ii) How do different tasks influence learners' interactions in both settings? In order to answer these questions, two-factorial repeated-measures analyses of variance (ANOVAs) with the factors "task" and "setting" and the dependent variable "learners' interactions" were conducted. Overall results showed no significant interaction between the setting and task factors, and no significant differences between the two settings. Significant differences, however, were reported between the different tasks in terms of all three measurements, i.e., amount of meaning negotiation, language-related episodes, and recasts. Thus, the authors conclude, although the setting had no influence on the frequency of the three interactional patterns under investigation, the type of task did (Gass et al., 2005: 596–7).

[4] The Gass et al. study was partly motivated by Foster's (1998) claim that her own results "call into question the typicality of previous research into the incidence of negotiation of meaning and the justification therefore for constructing an SLA theory upon it" (Foster, 1998: 19, as cited in Gass et al., 2005: 578). The indirect reference here is to Pica et al. (1989). Foster argues explicitly against the use of inferential statistical analyses of the quantitative results employed in the Pica et al. (1989) study; first because "complex statistical computations obscure what is happening at an individual level" (Foster, 1998: 8), and second because the purpose of her own investigation "was not to test a hypothesis but to observe individual students' classroom performance" (ibid.). Whereas Pica et al. inferred from their results gained in a laboratory setting that negotiation of meaning and output modification were 'alive and well' (Pica et al., 1989: 83), Foster concludes from her own study "that uncoached negotiation for meaning is not 'alive and well' in the classroom, and, given the minute number of syntactically modified utterances, is much too fragile to bear the weight of the SLA theory that researchers like Pica have built upon it" (Foster, 1998: 19).

[5] Given the inconsistent empirical results achieved by Gass et al. (2005) and Foster (1998), the author of the present paper decided to conduct a replication of Foster's (1998) original study. This decision was motivated inter alia by the huge impact of Foster's study in the field. Not only does Foster's 1998 paper rank among the 50 most

frequently read articles that have been published in the refereed journal in question since its first issue in 1980 (see www.applij.oxford-
journals.org), but it has also been frequently cited and discussed in
major books (e.g. Skehan, 1998; Ellis, 2003) and papers (e.g. Gass
et al., 2005; Seedhouse, 2005; Swan, 2005).

[6] The goal of the present replication study was twofold. First, it
was set up to confirm or otherwise the results of Foster's (1998) study.
Second, it attempted to shed more light on the validity of Foster's
interpretation of these results. In particular, the replication sought
to address the question whether it is warranted to consider Foster's
results as a function of the classroom setting in which the data was
collected. It furthermore attempted to explore whether, in so far as
Foster's findings diverge from results achieved in the laboratory, Foster's results evidence a lack of transferability of experimental research
findings. The distinction between the results and the conclusions
derived from those results was informed by the findings of previous
and current research into task-based interaction.

[7] With respect to results, a great number of studies investigating
students' interactions when working on information-gap tasks in a
controlled environment have reported high frequencies of meaning
negotiation. Among them have been studies that included monitored
sessions outside the classroom (Long, 1985; Pica and Doughty, 1987;
Pica et al., 1989, 1991, 1996), special researcher visits to actual
classrooms (Pica, 1991), and breaks during regular class meetings
(Doughty and Pica, 1986). All these studies used different kinds of
information-gap tasks and were conducted at different places with
differing participants by different researchers. Thus, it is noteworthy that all of these studies report similar overall frequencies of
meaning negotiation. These results, then, can be taken to show the
robustness of meaning negotiation based on information-gap tasks
across participants, target languages, and level of L2 proficiency.
Given such a robustness of the interactional pattern across experimental settings, it appears to be highly appropriate to investigate
task-based meaning negotiation under nonexperimental classroom
conditions.

[8] With regard to the interpretation of these results, at least three
issues have to be considered, the first referring to research settings,
and the other two related to research methodology. First, as has been
pointed out by Gass et al. (2005: 579), "claims about research in
classroom contexts require us to decide what is meant by a classroom." Obviously, types of classrooms – status and function of the
L2, intensity, characteristics, goals, purposes of instruction, etc. – can
differ to a large degree, as can different laboratory settings and the

perception of these settings by different learners. In other words, if the participants believe that a certain research is simply part of their teaching program, then it is a classroom happening in the relevant sense. Rather than assuming characteristics of a certain setting, such an assumption should be verified against learners' perceptions of the setting. Second, there is growing empirical evidence that learners' task-based interactional behavior cannot be explained exclusively by the variable "task type." Using transcript-based and individualized post-hoc tests, some studies (Swain and Lapkin, 1995, 1998, 2001; Williams, 2001; Loewen, 2002, 2005; Eckerth, 2008a) have shown how learners exploit learning opportunities beyond the pedagogic focus of the task, thus adapting the task to their individual learning needs and goals. In the same vein, several studies have shown how different learning activities can result from the same task when completed by different learners (Coughlan and Duff, 1994; Gourlay, 2005) and how these learning activities might be contingent on learners' perceptions of the task (Slimani-Rolls, 2005). In light of these findings, task-based research is slowly shifting from the conceptualization of the L2 learner as a mere "task executioner" to a "task interpreter" (Breen, 1987; Ellis, 2003; Mondada and Pekarek Doehler, 2004; Lantolf and Thorne, 2006; Eckerth, 2008b). Third, there is a growing awareness in the field that a straightforward identification of classes of interactional moves on the part of the researcher may or may not conform with the communicative intentions of the interactants. Thus, whereas a speaker's repetition of an interlocutor's previous utterance with rising intonation has typically been labeled "clarification request" (e.g. Long and Porter, 1985; Pica et al., 1989; Pica, 1994; Gass, 1997; Gass et al., 2005), it is not always clear whether the speaker's intention actually had been to clarify a lack of understanding (see Firth and Wagner, 1997; Hauser, 2005).

[9] For these reasons, and in terms of data collection, a stimulated recall methodology was added to the present replication study. On the one hand, it was assumed that this procedure would not interfere with the main data collection instrument, that is, the administration and observation of different tasks in the classroom (see below). On the other hand, it was expected that the triangulation of interactional data with the interactants' accounts of their own performance could help to better understand and interpret the results of Foster's original study. It was hypothesized, for instance, that it was not the difference in setting per se which caused the incongruent results in the studies of Foster (1998) and Gass et al. (2005), but rather the learners' perception of these settings (issue 1 above) as well as differences in research methodology (issues 2 and 3 above). Investigating students' perceptions

of their task work was judged as a suitable means to bridge both interpretative issues, the research setting issue and the research methodology issue. With respect to the latter, it was expected that students'
accounts of their task performance would provide a check of the
researcher's interpretative accuracy. For instance, Foster suggests that
students may perceive the laboratory as a more formal setting, where
the emphasis is rather on accuracy, and thus may apply a "check and
clarify" strategy (Foster, 1998: 19). Accordingly, the replication study
attempts to explore whether students may perceive the classroom as
a more relaxed setting, thus focusing rather on fluency and applying
a "let it pass" strategy (Firth, 1996: 243). Consequently, empirical
evidence supporting such an assumption of differing student perceptions could explain some of the frequency differences in input negotiation and output modification between the two studies. Therefore, the
approximate replication reported in the remainder of this paper closely
duplicates the methods of data collection and data analysis of Foster's
original study, while altering the target language (L2 German).

2 The original research study

Foster's original study was set up to see " 'what the student in the classroom does' with the negotiation of meaning" (Foster, 1998: 5). For this
purpose, lower intermediate ESL learners in an actual classroom were
observed while they were working in small groups and in pairs on different language-learning tasks. The study sought to investigate to what
extent the learners would produce a) talk in general, b) comprehensible input, and c) modified output, and whether the variables "task
type" (optional vs. required information exchange) and "participant
structure" (group vs. pair work) would affect a), b), and c).

3 The replication study

The replication study closely followed the research procedures
adopted in the original study. As will be specified in the following sections, the relevant parameters such as participants (3.1), setting (3.2),
tasks (3.3), data collection procedures (3.4), and data coding (3.5)
were identical or closely comparable to those in the original research,
whereas the stimulated recall methodology (3.6) has been added to
the research design.

3.1 The participants

Whereas the original study was conducted with ESL learners at a
municipal college in Great Britain, participants in the replication

study were students in an L2 German university course. The class met four times a week for approximately three hours a day as compared to three times a week for two hours a day in Foster's study. With the exception of some L1 speakers of various Slavic languages, the students came from similar L1 backgrounds as in the original study (Arabic, French, Korean, Spanish) and from a similar range of ages (20–42 years compared to 17–41 years) with an average age of 23 years (as compared to 21). As in Foster's study, they were of lower intermediate L2 proficiency and had been assigned to the class based on a written test and an interview. Whereas the ESL learners consisted of typical "part-time learners in colleges throughout Britain" (Foster, 1998: 5), the L2 German learners can be characterized as typical college and university applicants in Germany. As in the original study, the class had been running for eight weeks at the time of data collection. Due to erratic attendance, 12 out of the 16 students in the class were observed in this study, most of them female, as was the case in the original study.

3.2 The setting

In line with the original study, the setting of the classroom was preserved as far as possible. Therefore, all recordings were made during three scheduled lessons. In the case of the replication study, these recordings were part of a more extended sequence of data collection for the purpose of a larger research project (see Eckerth, 2008c). At the time of the recordings the students had become fairly accustomed to the presence of the researcher and the recording devices. The researcher had been introduced and occasionally acted as a co-teacher, unlike in Foster's study, where researcher and teacher were identical. As in the original study, on each of the data collection occasions the students were asked to do one task which was presented as part of the normal class routine. They all did the task at the same time and in the same room, as is normal classroom practice.

3.3 The tasks

In Foster's study, the two variables "task type" (optional vs. required information exchange) and "participant structure" (small group vs. pair work) were systematically combined, exemplified by four tasks with varying "task foci" (three linguistically unfocused tasks, one linguistically focused consciousness-raising task). The replication study did not vary the participation pattern, but rather had all tasks completed in pairs of learners. Such a departure from the original study has been motivated by two factors. First, research on the effect of participant structure on task-based interactional behavior is fairly consistent in showing a more balanced distribution of turns and negotiation moves when compared to small groups (e.g., Pica, 1987, 1994; Gass, 1997). Second, a particular interest of the replication study was to investigate Foster's claim that her results were due to the nature of the classroom as opposed to a laboratory setting (Foster, 1989: 19). Thus, the replication study had to be relatable to relevant research that addressed the transferability issue either directly (Gass et al., 2005) or indirectly (Slimani-Rolls, 2005). As both of these studies exclusively employed dyadic tasks, the use of dyadic tasks was felt to enhance the potential of relating the results of the replication study to the current discussion. However, the replica maintained the variation and comparison of "task type" and "task focus" of the original study.

Three tasks were chosen for the replication study, two linguistically unfocused referential tasks and one linguistically focused consciousness-raising task. In contrast to Foster's study, the tasks were not taken from actual textbooks, but had been developed by the researcher. In the case of the grammar-based task, for instance, this decision was guided by the interest of shifting the focus of the task more toward meaning and meaning negotiation, as opposed to a rather mechanical manipulation of L2 forms which is typical of Foster's (1998: 6) grammar-based task. With respect to the two referential communication tasks, one was identical in structure to Foster's "consensus task" and the other was a variation of her "picture difference" task (Foster, 1998: 6). As picture difference tasks had been frequently used in the classroom under investigation, such a variation has been introduced in order to keep students motivated and interested. Thus, as the tasks developed for the purpose of the replication study closely corresponded to Foster's tasks as well as to typical textbook tasks of the respective type, such a procedure was not expected to affect the comparability of the two studies. In order to ensure their authenticity and their face value as judged by the students, the tasks were didactically embedded in the curriculum through extensive discussion with the teacher cooperating in the investigation. Both the researcher and the teacher had the impression that the tasks were perceived by the learners as part of the regular language study program. The tasks recorded for the replica (see Appendices A–C in the electronic supplement) were as follows:

1   Consciousness-raising task "text repair"
    Students were required to work on a written L2 text (e.g., a farewell letter) with missing grammatical information. Completing a text repair task involved inserting items such as articles, reflexive pronouns, or verbal complements, and inflecting pronouns and

verbs appropriately. Students working on this text in pairs had to produce a written version of the text that is grammatically correct, semantically coherent, and pragmatically appropriate. Though this task focuses on specific L2 features (reflexive prepositional verbs), it does not confront learners with isolated, decontextualized linguistic forms, thus allowing them to make use of their own language resources. However, as there is no obligation to exchange information, this task is, like the "grammar-based task" in Foster's (1998: 6) original study, classified as optional information exchange.

2   Assembly task "women"
Students held sets of numbered pictures showing different women. Through the detailed description of a particular woman by one learner, the interlocutor had to identify this woman on his or her own worksheet. When in doubt about the woman's identity, the interlocutor was supposed to inquire about specific features of the person in question. This could only be done by students sharing individually held information and is classified – like the "picture difference" task in Foster's (1998: 6) original study – as required information exchange task.

3   Decision-making task "desert"
Students were provided with one worksheet showing a list of 16 equipment items available for a planned desert trip. They were required to argue for and to agree on a selection of the eight most useful items to be taken on the trip. Once they had reached a consensus on which items to select, they received a further piece of information which set them a new problem to solve. They again had to reach a consensus, which entailed further problems and choices until the task ended. As all the information was available to both students, this task is, as the "consensus" task in Foster's (1998: 6) original study, classified as optional information exchange task.

3.4 Data collection

As in the original study, recordings were made at weekly intervals during scheduled classes. The tasks were all part of the normal lesson plan and were not presented as being in any way "special." In contrast to the original study, an external microphone was connected to the tape recorder, ensuring high sound quality. No tapes had to be discarded from the data analysis due to unintelligible speech, as reported by Foster (1998: 7). This resulted in five recorded dyads per task, in contrast to the three dyads and groups per task in Foster's study. Foster transcribed the first five minutes of three tasks and the first ten minutes of the remaining task, halving the scores from the ten-minute recording to enable comparison. In the replication study, the first ten minutes of each interaction were transcribed and coded for data analysis. Thus, while replicating the original data collection procedure, the amount of data transcribed and coded was larger both in terms of number of interacting dyads and amount of interactional time. The decision to quantitatively alter the original study's data collection procedure was taken in the interest of assembling a larger, that is, more representative corpus (2175 vs. 918 c-units in the original study; see below) as well as reducing potential biases from the recording of untypical "warming-up" sequences (Aston, 1986: 132 as cited in Gass et al., 2005: 580). As in Foster's study, some learners were observed for all three tasks, but, because of erratic attendance, some were not. Table 8.1 shows the composition of learner dyads and their distribution across tasks.

Table 8.1   Recorded learner dyads across tasks

Learner dyad	Consciousness-raising task	Referential tasks	
		optional info-exchange	required info-exchange
Nino and Macit	X	X	X
Esin and Tamuna	X	X	X
Olga and Yusuf	X	X	X
Prerana and Ismail	X		
Sanie and Odeta	X		
Nancy and Ismail		X	X
Sanie and Fatih		X	X

3.5 Transcription and coding

Identical with the original study (Foster, 1998: 7), the "c-unit" was used to measure students' speech production. Foster et al. (2000) have suggested the "A-unit" as better suited for the measurement of spoken language and have, rather atypically, attempted to operationalize the unit in a detailed way. However, in order to ensure comparability, the replication study used the same coding procedures as the original investigation. Thus, all data was counted for c-units, defined as "utterances, for example, words, phrases, and sentences, grammatical and ungrammatical, which provide referential or pragmatic meaning to native speaker (NS)–non-native speaker (NNS) interaction" (Foster, 1998: 8, referring to Pica et al., 1989, and Brock, 1986). Thus, whereas false starts would be excluded from analysis, elliptical constructions, which abound in oral language and are meaningful and pragmatically sufficient, would be counted. Along with the original study, negotiated interaction was coded for clarification requests – a request for further information from an interlocutor about a previous utterance; comprehension checks – the speaker's query of the interlocutor(s) as to whether or not they have understood the previous speaker utterance(s); and confirmation check – the speaker's query as to whether or not the speaker's (expressed) understanding of the interlocutor's meaning is correct (Foster, 1998: 8, referring to definitions from Chaudron, 1988: 45). Also in accordance with the original study and in order to measure modified output, the transcripts were coded using the definitions from Pica et al. (1989: 88) for semantic modification (through synonym, paraphrase, or example); morphological modification (through addition, substitution, or deletion of inflectional morphemes and/or functors); phonological modification; and syntactic modification (through embedding and elaboration in clauses).

3.6 Stimulated recall

For reasons stated earlier in this paper, a stimulated recall methodology was included in the design of the replication study. Data was collected in the form of interviews with pairs of learners who had jointly worked on a task the day before. After class, students were accompanied to the researcher's office, where the purpose of the interview was explained to them. They were assured that the interview would have no effect on their course grades and that all information would be held confidential (see Section 3.6 of the e-supplement for more details).

4 Results

As the purpose of the investigation was to observe task-based language learner performance in an actual L2 classroom rather than to test pre-specified hypotheses, both the original and the replication study left the coded data in the form of simple totals and percentages. However, although Foster (1998: 8) explicitly states her intention to "observe individual students' classroom performance," no effort has been made to keep the composition of the groups and dyads constant. As Foster (1998: 8) claims, this was not possible "without compromising the naturalistic setting of the study." In the present study, however, it was generally the same students working together on the different tasks. This procedure was not a condition of the research project imposed onto the classroom, but rather accorded with the established and common classroom practice of working with one's neighbor. It allowed for a performance comparison across learners as well as across tasks for that subset of students who completed all three tasks.

In line with the structure of Foster's paper, the data will be presented according to the research questions posed earlier: language production (Tables 2 and 3 in the e-supplement, Section 4.1), comprehensible input (Tables 4 and 5 in the e-supplement, Section 4.2), and modified output (Tables 6 and 7 in the e-supplement, Section 4.3). Within each of these three categories, the first table specifies the performance of the dyads, and the second table breaks these figures down as to individual learner performance. Assigning negotiation moves to individual students was not based on the assumption that the initiators of an input-negotiation move or an output-modification move would benefit more (or less) from this move than their interlocutors. Rather than the assumption of unequal benefits in terms of language acquisition, the guiding interest was to see in what way certain tasks varied in stimulating a more or less equal distribution of speech production, negotiation, and modification within dyads.

4.1 Language production

Language production was analyzed as a function of task type and individual student. First, c-units were calculated to measure the amount of language produced by each dyad (Table 2 in the e-supplement). A cross-task comparison reveals clearly less speech production for the referential task with required information exchange as compared to the referential task with optional information exchange. As can be seen in Table 2 in the e-supplement, this does not only hold true in terms of the total of c-units produced by all dyads, but mostly also in terms of individual dyads. Such a result is in conflict with Foster's scores, which show the same ratio for the groups, but the reverse for the dyads. Furthermore, compared across dyads and consistent with Foster's study (1998: 9), the overall amount of language production varies widely. For example, in the consciousness-raising task, the c-units produced by different dyads vary between 171 and 89, and in the referential task with required information exchange, between 171 and 96. A closer look at the performance of different dyads also reveals that in both types of referential tasks it is always the same dyad who talks most (Esin–Tamuna) or least (Nancy–Ismail). Also instructive in this regard is Table 3 in the e-supplement, which reports the individual variation of speech production within the dyads.

In contrast to a small-group constellation, a dyad makes it hard to completely drop out of the verbal interaction. Accordingly, there are no instances when a learner does not produce any or hardly any language, as reported by Foster (1998: 10). However, the individual students in a dyad contribute varying proportions of the amount of language produced by the dyad as a whole. In contrast to the student Yusuf, who produces less than half the amount of language his interlocutor does (49%; Olga and Yusuf, Table 3 in the e-supplement), the distribution of c-units between Nino and Macit or Nancy and Ismail is rather balanced (92% for both dyads; Table 3 in the e-supplement). Again, a comparison across learners is informing. Looking at the dyads which have carried out two or three different tasks clearly shows that if one learner verbally dominates his partner, this learner dominates not only in one, but in all tasks.[1] The final section will consider in what way these results reflect the relationship between particular task features and individual task performers.

4.2 Comprehensible input

Negotiation of meaning was measured by calculating the number of negotiation moves (confirmation checks, clarification requests, comprehension checks; examples are provided in the e-supplement, Section 4.2, Transcripts 1–3) across tasks and dyads. Table 4 in the e-supplement shows both the total number of negotiation moves and their percentages when compared to the number of c-units produced by a dyad. As a whole, the corpus includes 123 negotiation moves with all the students producing at least a few negotiation moves. Foster's study shows a lot of students not negotiating at all, particularly when working in a group rather than a dyad (Foster, 1998: 13). Thus, the factor of participation pattern seems to have an impact not only on the amount of language production but also on the amount of meaning negotiation. When it comes to the impact of task type, in line with Foster's results, negotiation was relatively more frequent in the two referential tasks. Negotiation was also the most frequent in the task that required information exchange. This applies both to the average percentages of all dyads as it does for the single dyads. This picture changes somewhat when looking at the relative distribution of negotiation moves within the dyads (Table 5 in the e-supplement).

Although one might assume that the split distribution of information among both learners would result in a mutual responsibility for information exchange and therefore in a balanced share of meaning negotiation, this is not the case. When comparing the ratio of negotiation moves produced by the two learners of a dyad, the two tasks with shared information distribution and optional information exchange produce higher average percentages (44% and 28%, Table 5 in the e-supplement). However, a comparison across learners reveals that if learners dominate their interlocutors in terms of negotiation moves, they do this not only in one task, but in all tasks. This finding is consistent with the pattern of verbal dominance with regard to the distribution of language production within dyads (Table 3 in the e-supplement).

4.3 Modified output

Modified output, that is, utterances which were semantically, morphologically, syntactically, or phonologically altered in response to a negotiation move, were calculated across tasks and dyads (see the e-supplement, Section 4.3, Transcripts 4–7). Table 6 in the e-supplement shows both the absolute and relative number of negotiation moves produced by a dyad.

In relation to the overall amount of language production, the extent of output modification is rather limited, as it is also in Foster's data. A total of 123 negotiation moves (Table 4 in the e-supplement) is followed by an output modification in 32 cases. As Foster discovered (Foster, 1998: 15), no consistent pattern can be found when comparing tasks with optional as opposed to tasks with required information exchange. More revealing is the comparison across learners. Almost half of all output modifications are produced by one dyad, Esin and Tamuna. Furthermore, relating output modification to input negotiation, the students in this dyad are also found to be the most active input negotiators (Table 4 in the e-supplement). As with language production and input negotiation, modified output has also been measured with respect to the relative distribution of output modifications within the dyads (see Table 7 in the e-supplement)

The dyad-internal distribution of modified output (Table 7 in the e-supplement) is consistent with the distribution of negotiation moves (Table 5 in the e-supplement) in two ways. First, a comparison across tasks shows again the two tasks with optional information exchange to produce a more balanced distribution of output modification. Second, a comparison across learners reveals that if learners dominate their interlocutors in terms of output modification, they do this not only in one task, but in all tasks. Again, this is consistent with the distributional pattern of language production (Table 3 in the e-supplement) and input negotiation (Table 5 in the e-supplement) within dyads. Table 8.2 summarizes the overall frequency of meaning negotiation and output modification in Foster's (1998) original and in the replication study.

Table 8.2   Absolute and relative overall frequency of negotiated input and modified output

Study	Total speech production, c-units	Negotiated input moves	Modified output moves	Ratio c-units: neg. input	Ratio neg. input: mod. output
		n	n	%	%
Foster	918	87	20	9.5	23
Eckerth	2175	123	32	5.7	26

5 Discussion

As the main purpose of a replication study is to better understand the results, outcomes, and implications of the replicated study, it will be helpful to summarize Foster's (1998: 17ff.) findings briefly. First, based on the total scores for groups and dyads in relation to task type, Foster states (i) no recognizable pattern relating task type to language production; (ii) the most consistent occurrence of meaning negotiation during pair work on tasks with required information exchange; and (iii) the most frequent occurrence of output modification when working in a dyad setting independent of task type. Second, based on the individual scores, Foster reports that (i) the amount of meaning negotiation and output modification per student was rather low; and (ii) the range of scores between individual students was extremely wide. Third, she explains these results with reference to (i) the potentially painstaking, frustrating, and face-threatening nature of extensive negotiation and modification, resulting in a "pretend and hope" rather than in a "check and clarify" strategy; (ii) the classroom environment as opposed to a laboratory setting with its tightly designed information-gap tasks; and (iii) she calls for tasks which do allow and encourage the reflection and negotiation of form, rather than absorbing learners' cognitive resources by the need to exchange information most efficiently.

The present study did not compare group and dyad settings. However, in comparison to Foster's study, it found a more consistent distribution of language production (Foster: Table 2 and 3 in the e-supplement) and a more consistent occurrence of meaning negotiation (Foster: Table 4, page 12, Tables 4 and 5 in the e-supplement). This outcome indirectly supports the assumption that a dyadic setting is more conducive to a balanced distribution of both speech and negotiation. In a pair, as opposed to a small group, it is much harder for a single student to retreat or to drop out of the communication.

Neither the original nor the replication study could confirm the overriding effect of task type (required vs. optional information exchange) on the amount of language production and meaning negotiation established by former studies (e.g., Pica and Doughty, 1985; Doughty and Pica, 1986). Foster explains her results as a consequence of the learners' adaptation of the tasks, resulting in a strategy that "could reduce some information exchange tasks to a format whereby the side holding the information need only answer 'yes' or 'no' to the informed guesses of the other side" (Foster, 1998: 11). With regard to dyadic task completion, such task adaptation strategies are unequivocally confirmed by the findings of the replication study (see Transcript 11 in the e-supplement).

The evidence of task adaptation points to the necessity of investigating individual learners' actual task-based interactions more closely. "Across the data as a whole," Foster (1998: 18) summarizes her results, "the range in individual scores is so wide, and the lack of participation by so many students is so striking as to make any statistics based on group totals very misleading." With respect to the dyadic tasks, this outcome is consistent with the results of the present replication study. It was consistently the same dyad (Esin and Tamuna) who talked most (Table 2 in the e-supplement), negotiated most (Table 4 in the e-supplement), and modified most (Table 6 in the e-supplement), rather independently of task type. Furthermore, the replication study allowed not only for the comparison of dyads, but also for the comparison of individual students across tasks. The present study shows that if one learner dominated one dyadic exchange with respect to one of the three investigated parameters – language production, negotiation of input, modification of output – s/he would dominate all exchanges with respect to this very parameter (Tables 3, 5, and 7 in the e-supplement). Moreover, there is a strong tendency for the learner who verbally dominates with respect to one parameter, to dominate with respect to all three parameters (Tables 3, 5, and 7 in the e-supplement).

Variation of meaning negotiation across dyads and individual learners is also reported by Slimani-Rolls (2005). While 60% of the negotiation sequences in her study come from only 25% of the learners, another 25% of the learners do not contribute at all (ibid.: 202). Gass et al. (2005), however, do not show asymmetrical distributional patterns of meaning negotiation across dyads (ibid.: 598).[2] Neither variation of meaning negotiation between single learners and dyads nor variation between settings is confirmed by the results reported by Gass et al. (2005). The question of individual variance and the related question of transferability of experimental research

findings to classroom settings therefore deserve more extended discussion. It may well be the case that the consistency of Gass et al.'s
results across individuals, across dyads, and across settings is a function of the characteristics of the settings investigated, and the research
methodology, that is the instruments of measurement used.

As has been mentioned earlier, Foster (1998) accounts for her main
results – comparatively low frequency of interactional adjustments combined with marked variation across subjects – by referring to the very
nature of task-based learner–learner interaction in the classroom, as
opposed to task work in the laboratory. She considers that task-based
learner–learner interaction in a classroom might be seen by the students
as a rather informal activity taking place in the sheltered intimacy of
a pair or a group, and with the focus on practicing the language and
maintaining the smooth flow of conversation rather than on accuracy,
self-monitoring, and learning. Thus, if students regard pair work as
a "light-hearted and informal part of class, rather than a pedagogical
activity specifically designed to promote SLA," Foster (p. 19) claims,
"we cannot be surprised if they are relaxed enough about communication problems to let them pass, thereby missing opportunities to
gain comprehensible input and to create modified output." However,
Foster provides no specific evidence to support her claim that it was
the classroom environment which stimulated the learners in her study
"to let them [communication problems] pass." In the present study,
combined and related evidence from task completion and stimulated
recall data (see e-supplement, Transcripts 12–15) exemplifies how students may deal with communication problems during task work in
the L2 classroom. Task-based learner-learner interaction appears not
just as the verbal equivalent of a cognitive language-learning activity;
it is at the same time a communicative event and a social process that
is mediated by socio-affective variables. At times, learners might even
decide to "react to social motives at the expense of their own pedagogical advancement, to preserve their social relationships" (Slimani-Rolls,
2005: 208). As research has shown, comprehension can take place without much input processing (Ellis, 1994: 92). Top–down processing of
existing linguistic knowledge (Faerch and Kasper, 1986; Ellis, 1994),
guessing from the linguistic context (Frantzen, 2003), guessing based
on knowledge of social appropriateness (Hymes, 1972), pretending
comprehension and hoping for more clues from the ongoing conversation (Hawkins, 1985; Firth, 1996) are all strategies that contribute
to the understanding of one's interlocutors' utterances. Rather than
following a "the more the merrier" principle (Aston, 1986; Allwright
and Bailey, 1991: 145), students' moderate use of requests for clarification and confirmation or checks of one's interlocutor's comprehension

appear to reflect the social nature of the "interactional architecture" (Seedhouse, 2004) of the L2 classroom.

In what way, then, do the results from this replication and other work on meaning negotiation in the L2 classroom (Foster, 1998; Slimani-Rolls, 2005) relate to the findings of Gass et al.'s (2005) carefully designed comparative study? As mentioned earlier in this paper, results of the ANOVAs showed no significant differences between the two settings. However, significant differences were reported between the different tasks in terms of all three measurements, that is, amount of meaning negotiation, language-related episodes, and recasts. Thus, the authors conclude that whereas the setting did not have any influence on the frequency of the three interactional patterns under investigation, the type of task had (Gass et al., 2005: 596–7).

As Gass et al. (2005) used different measures (absolute frequency counts rather than relative to the amount of speech production), it is hard to directly compare their quantitative results with the outcomes of Foster's original study and the present replication study. However, this is hardly a satisfying answer. After all, if, as Gass et al. (2005) convincingly demonstrate, participants do the same thing whether working in the classroom or in the laboratory, then why care about the students' perceptions, interpretations, and motivations? One possible answer could be that we indeed do not have to care if we could know for sure that they were doing the same thing. In other words, what may be coded and counted as the same interactional pattern on a discourse level might turn out to reflect quite different cognitive operations and discourse functions.

Since the comparison of task-based interaction in an actual classroom versus a laboratory setting is at the very center of the Gass et al. (2005) study, the authors take great care to describe the conditions under which the data has been collected (ibid.: 583–4). However, while the reported data collection procedures clearly contribute to the internal validity of the study, they might at the same time threaten its external, or, more precisely, ecological validity.[3] "Ecological validity," as Bronfenbrenner (1979: 29) defines the term, "refers to the extent to which the environment experienced by the subjects in a scientific investigation has the properties it is supposed or assumed to have by the investigator." To what degree this has been the case in the Gass et al. (2005) study, however, is hard to assess. For one thing, it is rather surprising that all three tasks, which were different in detail but similar in design, were administered in uninterrupted succession and without any variation of the social pattern in class, that is, dyadic learner–learner interaction. For another, the reader is further surprised to learn that these three-task sessions hardly varied in length, both in the classroom and the laboratory setting, with all of them lasting between 50 and 55 minutes. Based on the study reported in this paper, and on abundant episodic evidence from language teachers, it is hard to imagine that all learners accomplished all three tasks in nearly the same time. One wonders, then, how exactly the teacher in the classroom setting was "keeping the students on task where necessary" (Gass et al., 2005: 584), and how much interference was required to do so. Therefore, while the classroom may have looked like a classroom, it may not have been perceived as such by the students. As the present study shows that students' task perceptions can influence their task performance, such an account of learners' interpretations of their own task work and interactional behavior could have helped with the appraisal of the investigation's ecological validity.[4]

6 Conclusion

Growing empirical evidence demonstrates that tasks of the kind commonly used in SLA research "are not just performed but rather are interpreted, resulting in activity that is 'constructed' by the participants in accordance with their particular motives and goals" (Ellis, 2003: 187). Using transcript-based and individualized post-hoc tests, some studies show in what ways learners exploit tasks beyond the pedagogical focus of the task, thus adapting the task to their individual learning needs and goals (see Swain and Lapkin, 1995, 1998, 2001; Williams, 2001; Nabei and Swain, 2002; Loewen, 2002, 2005; Adams, 2007; Eckerth, 2008a). Moreover, studies such as Kumaravadivelu (1991), Coughlan and Duff (1994), Gourlay (2005), and Harris (2005) have revealed different activities emerging from the same task when completed by different learners. Thus, what has been called the "permeability of tasks" (Mondada and Pekarek Doehler, 2004: 512) or their "interactional reconfiguration" (ibid.: 510) points to two major challenges in task-based research.

First, there seem to be good reasons for bringing together qualitative analyses of contextualized task-based interactions with quantifications of isolated linguistic units. Rather than perpetuating unproductive "paradigm wars" (Edge and Richards, 1998: 335), such a multi-methodological perspective seeks to connect different approaches in order "to link, but not reduce, one perspective to another" (Wertsch, 1998, as cited in Ellis and Larsen-Freeman, 2006: 578). Such an integrated approach might be one way to inform us about potential gaps between "intended" and "actual" pedagogy

(Seedhouse, 2005) and to improve the content validity of our research constructs. If supported by further research, evidence of learners' task adaptation, I suggest, does not question the validity of inter-actional adjustments and its significance for SLA (see Gass, 2003; Doughty, 2004; Pica et al., 2006; Gass and Mackey, 2006, 2007; Mackey, 2007). It also does *"not* prevent tasks and their range of influence from being researchable at the level of *probable* outcomes," as Skehan and Foster suggest (1999: 117; my emphasis). However, they conclude, this does not imply that "task characteristics might have a *deterministic* impact on performance" (ibid.; my emphasis).

Second, studies on task adaptation sketch a picture of the language learner as an intentional and reflective practitioner as well as a social agent, rather than a data processor with purely cognitively defined "data needs" (Pica, 1998: 11). Unfortunately, there are still rather few accounts of how learners perceive tasks and how they position themselves within a task. Apart from the work that has been done within a sociocultural approach to language learning (Roebuck, 2000; Lantolf and Thorne, 2006), an integration of the learners' perceptions and perspectives has been attempted (e.g. Nakahama et al., 2001; Mackey, 2002, 2006; Nabei and Swain, 2002; Swain and Lapkin, 2002; Lindgren, 2002; Adams, 2003; Egi, 2004; Ewald, 2004; Carpenter et al., 2006; Polio, 2006; Roehr, 2006; Watanabe and Swain, 2007; Tavakoli et al., 2009) and should be pursued in psycholinguistically oriented SLA.

Combining a stimulated recall methodology with an analysis of task performance, the present study tried to show in what way learners' task perceptions can influence their task-based interactions. This study also attempted to contribute to our understanding of task-based L2 classroom learning as being perceived by the learners as a cognitive activity, a communicative event, and a social process. However, as the empirical base of these and related findings is still limited, all conclusions have to be provisional in nature. Finally, they call for more classroom-based interventionist studies (Brumfit and Mitchell, 1990: 12). Such investigations require not only a sound understanding of research methods but also a thorough knowledge of the learning–teaching environment in which any interventions and research instruments are introduced. Only then will we arrive at research designs which do not result in "disrupting the class or compromising the data" (Foster, 1998: 21).

Acknowledgments

I would like to thank Willis Edmondson and Tucker Childs as well as the anonymous reviewers for their insightful suggestions and feedback on an earlier version of this paper. Needless to say that all remaining shortcomings are my own responsibility. Finally, I would like to thank the editorial board of *Language Teaching*, above all Graeme Porte, for suggesting an e-supplement to the printed paper. I believe that providing additional space for the publication of relevant data can significantly increase the transparency and thus the credibility of qualitative, transcript-based L2 research.

Comment from the author of the original study

I often thought that I would replicate my 1998 study, having been told on so many occasions that my results were the random outcome of poor data gathering. It was my first foray into classroom research and I was dealing with recording in a very noisy place with equipment that appears antediluvian now. I was not surprised that the pervasive background noise (a normal feature of communicative classrooms) made some of my recordings unusable, but I was never convinced that somewhere in all that untranscribable chatter were the missing negotiations of meaning. If, ten years later, I were doing that replication, the recording equipment would be completely different, but the authentic classroom setting I was so keen to preserve would be the same. A learner in a classroom is aware that a task with a partner is as much a social interaction as a pedagogic exercise, and crystalline clarity is neither a necessary nor desirable goal.

As in my study, the participants in this replication are in their scheduled class, and they are doing nothing other than normal class work. Apart from using only dyads (which makes sense given the way groups allow participants to remain silent), the procedures and analyses are all very similar. And gratifyingly, as summarized in Table 8.2 here, the numbers come out rather similar also. More importantly, the author has improved on my study. He has been able to get considerably more data than I did, and this strengthens his conclusions. He has also added a stimulated recall procedure which demonstrates what I was only guessing at, that learners will put up with partial understanding in order to keep the task interaction moving forward. This paper lays out together the transcript evidence and the recall evidence in a neat demonstration of how learners will smooth over the bumps rather than make explicit their lack of complete understanding.

In seeking an explanation for the results in Gass et al. (2005), which show no difference in the incidence of negotiation of meaning in classroom or laboratory settings, the author very plausibly suggests that their classroom setting might not have appeared much like a classroom to the participants, who had to do three tasks in seamless progression. But the way to test properly the effect of setting on L2 performances is to use a within-participants design comparing task interaction in an environment that very clearly is a classroom and one that very clearly is not, and this has not been done. For me, though, it is not so much whether negotiations of meaning happen in one setting or another, or in one task type or another; rather it is whether their overwhelmingly lexical nature makes them as valuable as is claimed.

Dr Pauline Foster
Reader in Applied Linguistics, St Mary's University College

Notes

1   "Verbal domination" has been operationalized purely quantitatively as producing a higher amount of the linguistic unit under investigation (c-units, input negotiation moves, output modification moves) than one's interlocutor.
2   As Gass et al. (2005) report variance between single dyads only in the case of meaning negotiation (in one out of the three tasks used), and although being of vital interest in current interaction research, language-related episodes (Swain and Lapkin, 1998; Williams, 2001; Eckerth, 2008a) and recasts (Loewen and Philip, 2006; Long, 2007) will not be considered in this paper.
3   Far from discrediting experimental research, it is generally acknowledged in SLA research that studies implemented under controlled conditions lack the ecological validity that research during actual class time can offer (DeKeyser, 2003; Doughty, 2003).
4   Further support for the assumption of the influence of the environment on subjects' interactional behavior comes from research such as Oliver (2000) and Nicholas et al. (2001) on negotiation and feedback in actual classrooms as compared to laboratory settings. Nicholas et al. (2001: 749), for example, conclude that "recasts appear to provide more useful input to learners in the laboratory setting than in the classroom setting." However, both the study conducted by Oliver (2000) and the research reviewed by Nicholas et al. (2001) include classroom settings that consisted of teacher-fronted lessons as opposed to task-based pair work in the laboratory settings. Therefore, it is hard to know whether the differing interactional patterns were due to the different settings, the different tasks, or both.

References

Adams, R. (2003). L2 output, noticing, and reformulations: Implications for IL development, *Language Teaching Research*, 7, 3, 347–76.
Adams, R. (2007). Do second language learners benefit from interacting with each other?, in Mackey, A. (ed.), *Conversational Interaction in Second Language Acquisition*, Oxford: Oxford University Press, pp. 29–51.

Allwright, D. and Bailey, K. (1991). *Focus on the Language Classroom*, Cambridge: Cambridge University Press.

Aston, G. (1986). Trouble-shooting in interaction with learners: The more the merrier?, *Applied Linguistics*, 7, 2, 128–43.

Breen, M. (1987). Learner contributions to task design, in Candlin, C. and Murphy, D. (eds.), *Language Learning Tasks*, Englewood Cliffs, NJ: Prentice Hall International, pp. 23–46.

Brock, C. (1986). The effect of referential questions on ESL classroom discourse, *TESOL Quarterly*, 20, 1, 47–58.

Bronfenbrenner, U. (1979). *The Ecology of Human Development*, Cambridge, MA: Harvard University Press.

Brumfit, C. and Mitchell, R. (1990). The language classroom as a focus of research, in Brumfit, C. and Mitchell, R. (eds.), *Research in the Language Classroom*, London: Modern English Publications, pp. 3–15.

Bygate, M., Skehan, P. and Swain, M. (eds.) (2001). *Researching Pedagogic Tasks: Second Language Learning, Teaching and Testing*, London: Longman.

Carpenter, H., Jeon, K., MacGregor, D. and Mackey, A. (2006). Learners' interpretation of recasts, *Studies in Second Language Acquisition*, 28, 2, 209–36.

Chaudron, C. (1988). *Second Language Classrooms*, Cambridge: Cambridge University Press.

Coughlan, P. and Duff, P. (1994). Same task, different activities: Analysis of SLA task from an activity theory perspective, in Lantolf, J. and Appel, G. (eds.), *Vygotskian Approaches to Second Language Research*, Norwood, NJ: Ablex, pp. 173–93.

DeKeyser, R. (2003). Implicit and explicit learning, in Doughty, C. and Long, M. (eds.), *The Handbook of Second Language Acquisition*, Oxford: Blackwell, pp. 313–48.

Doughty, C. (2003). Instructed SLA: Conditions, compensation and enhancement, in Doughty, C. and Long, M. (eds.), *The Handbook of Second Language Acquisition*, Oxford: Blackwell, pp. 256–310.

Doughty, C. (2004). Effects of instruction on learning a second language: A critique of instructed SLA research, in VanPatten, B., Williams, J., Rott, S., and Overstreet, M. (eds.), *Form–Meaning Connections in Second Language Acquisition*, Mahwah, NJ: Lawrence Erlbaum Associates, pp. 181–202.

Doughty, C. and Long, M. (eds.) (2003). *The Handbook of Second Language Acquisition*, Oxford: Blackwell.

Doughty, C. and Pica, T. (1986). "Information gap" tasks: Do they facilitate second language acquisition?, *TESOL Quarterly*, 20, 2, 305–25.

Eckerth, J. (2006). Three theses on the pedagogical relevance of second language acquisition research, *Dil Dergisi Turkish Language Journal*, 130, 1, 18–36.

Eckerth, J. (2008a). Investigating consciousness-raising tasks: Pedagogically-targeted and non-targeted learning gains, *International Journal of Applied Linguistics*, 18, 2, 119–45.

Eckerth, J. (2008b). Task-based language learning and teaching – old wine in new bottles?, in Eckerth, J. and Siekmann, S. (eds.), *Research on*

Task-Based Language Learning and Teaching: Theoretical, Methodological and Pedagogical Perspectives, New York: Peter Lang, pp. 13–46.

Eckerth, J. (2008c). Task-based learner–learner interaction: Investigating learning opportunities, learning processes, and learning outcomes, in Eckerth, J. and Siekmann, S. (eds.), *Research on Task-Based Language Learning and Teaching: Theoretical, Methodological and Pedagogical Perspectives*, New York: Peter Lang, pp. 89–118.

Eckerth, J. and Siekmann, S. (eds.) (2008). *Research on Task-based Language Learning and Teaching: Theoretical, Methodological and Pedagogical Perspectives*, New York: Peter Lang.

Edge, J. and Richards, K. (1998). May I see your warrants, please?: Justifying outcomes in qualitative research, *Applied Linguistics*, **19**, 3, 334–56.

Edwards, C. and Willis, J. (eds.) (2005). *Teachers Exploring Tasks in English Language Teaching*, Houndmills: Palgrave MacMillan.

Egi, T. (2004). Verbal reports, noticing, and SLA research, *Language Awareness*, **13**, 4, 243–64.

Ellis, R. (1994). A theory of instructed second language acquisition, in Ellis, N. (ed.), *Implicit and Explicit Learning of Languages*, London: Academic Press, pp. 79–114.

Ellis, R. (1997). *SLA Research and Language Teaching*, Oxford: Oxford University Press.

Ellis, R. (2003). *Task-based Language Learning and Teaching*, Oxford: Oxford University Press.

Ellis, R. (ed.) (2005). *Planning and Task Performance in a Second Language*, Amsterdam: John Benjamins.

Ellis, N. and Larsen-Freeman, D. (2006). Language emergence: Implications for Applied Linguistics, *Applied Linguistics*, **27**, 4, 558–89.

Ewald, J. (2004). A classroom forum on small group work: L2 learners see, and change, themselves, *Language Awareness*, **13**, 3, 163–79.

Faerch, C. and Kasper, G. (1986). The role of comprehension in second-language learning, *Applied Linguistics*, **7**, 3, 184–99.

Firth, A. (1996). The discursive accomplishment of normality. On "Lingua Franca" English and conversation analysis, *Journal of Pragmatics*, **26**, 2, 237–60.

Firth, A. and Wagner, J. (1997). On discourse, communication, and (some) fundamental concepts in SLA, *The Modern Language Journal*, **81**, 3, 285–300.

Foster, P. (1998). A classroom perspective on the negotiation of meaning, *Applied Linguistics*, **19**, 1, 1–23.

Foster, P., Tonkyn, A. and Wigglesworth, G. (2000). Measuring spoken language: A unit for all reasons, *Applied Linguistics*, **21**, 3, 354–75.

Frantzen, D. (2003). Factors affecting how second language Spanish students derive meaning from context, *The Modern Language Journal*, **87**, 2, 168–99.

García Mayo, M. (ed.) (2007). *Investigating Tasks in Formal Language Learning*, Clevedon: Multilingual Matters.

Gass, S. (1997). *Input, Interaction, and the Second Language Learner,* Mahwah, NJ: Lawrence Erlbaum Associates.

Gass, S. (2003). Input and interaction, in Doughty, C. and Long, M. (eds.), *The Handbook of Second Language Acquisition,* Oxford: Blackwell, pp. 224–55.

Gass, S. and Mackey, A. (2006). Input, interaction and output: An overview, *AILA Review,* **19,** 3–17.

Gass, S. and Mackey, A. (2007). Input, interaction and output in second language acquisition, in VanPatten, B. and Williams, J. (eds.), *Theories of Second Language Acquisition,* Mahwah, NJ: Lawrence Erlbaum Associates, pp. 175–99.

Gass, S., Mackey, A. and Ross-Feldman, L. (2005). Task-based interactions in classroom and laboratory settings, *Language Learning,* **55,** 4, 575–611.

Gass, S. and Madden, C. (eds.) (1985). *Input in Second Language Acquisition,* Rowley, MA: Newbury House.

Gourlay, L. (2005). Directions and indirect action: Learner adaptation of a classroom task, *ELT Journal,* **59,** 3, 209–16.

Harris, K. (2005). Same activity, different focus, *Focus on Basics,* **8,** 1, 7–10.

Hatch, E. (1978). Discourse analysis and second language acquisition, in Hatch, E. (ed.), *Second Language Acquisition,* Rowley, MA: Newbury House, pp. 401–35.

Hauser, E. (2005). Coding "corrective recasts": The maintenance of meaning and more fundamental problems, *Applied Linguistics,* **26,** 3, 293–316.

Hawkins, B. (1985). Is an "appropriate response" always so appropriate?, in Gass, S. and Madden, C. (eds.), *Input in Second Language Acquisition,* Rowley, MA: Newbury House, pp. 162–78.

Hulstijn, J. (1997). Second language acquisition research in the laboratory: Possibilities and limitations, *Studies in Second Language Acquisition,* **19,** 2, 131–43.

Hymes, D. (1972). Models of the interaction of language and social life, in Gumperz, J. and Hymes, D. (eds.), *Directions in Sociolinguistics: The Ethnography of Communication,* New York: Holt, Rinehart and Winston, pp. 35–71.

Krashen, S. (1981). *Second Language Acquisition and Second Language Learning,* Oxford: Pergamon.

Kumaravadivelu, B. (1991). Language-learning tasks: Teacher intention and learner interpretation, *ELT Journal,* **45,** 2, 98–107.

Lantolf, J. and Thorne, S. (2006). *Sociocultural Theory and the Genesis of Second Language Development,* Oxford: Oxford University Press.

Leaver, B. and Willis, J. (eds.) (2004). *Task-based Instruction in Foreign Language Education,* Washington, DC: Georgetown University Press.

Lee, J. (2000). *Tasks and Communication in Language Classrooms,* Boston, MA: McGraw-Hill.

Lindgren, E. (2002). The effect of stimulated recall on 14-year-olds' L1 Swedish and EFL writing and revision, *Language Teaching Research,* **6,** 3, 267–8.

Loewen, S. (2002). The Occurrence and Effectiveness of Incidental Focus on Form in Meaning-focused ESL Lessons. Unpublished doctoral thesis, University of Auckland.

Loewen, S. (2005). Incidental focus on form and second language learning, *Studies in Second Language Acquisition*, **27**, 3, 361–86.

Loewen, S. and Philip, J. (2006). Recasts in the adult English L2 classroom: Characteristics, explicitness, and effectiveness, *The Modern Language Journal*, **90**, 4, 536–56.

Long, M. (1983). Native-speaker/non-native speaker conversation and the negotiation of comprehensible input, *Applied Linguistics*, **4**, 2, 126–41.

Long, M. (1985). Input and second language acquisition theory, in Gass, S. and Madden, C. (eds.), *Input in Second Language Acquisition*, Rowley, MA: Newbury House, pp. 377–93.

Long, M. (1988). Instructed interlanguage development, in Beebe, L. (ed.), *Issues in Second Language Acquisition: Multiple Perspectives*, Rowley, MA: Newbury House, pp. 115–41.

Long, M. (1996). The role of the linguistic environment in second language acquisition, in Ritchie, W. and Bhatia, T. (eds.), *Handbook of Second Language Acquisition*, San Diego, CA: Academic Press, pp. 413–68.

Long, M. (2007). Recasts: The story so far, in Long, M. (ed.), *Problems in SLA*, Mahwah, NJ: Lawrence Erlbaum Associates, pp. 75–116.

Long, M. and Crookes, G. (1987). Intervention points in second language classroom processes, in Das, B. (ed.), *Patterns of Classroom Interaction*, Singapore: SEAMEO Regional Language Centre, pp. 137–52.

Long, M. and Porter, P. (1985). Group work, interlanguage talk, and second language acquisition, *TESOL Quarterly*, **19**, 2, 207–28.

Mackey, A. (2002). Beyond production: Learners' perceptions about interactional processes, *International Journal of Educational Research*, **37**, 3/4, 379–94.

Mackey, A. (2006). Epilogue. From introspections, brain scans, and memory tests to the role of social context: Advancing research on interaction and learning, *Studies in Second Language Acquisition*, **28**, 2, 369–79.

Mackey, A. (2007). Interaction as practice, in DeKeyser, R. (ed.), *Practice in a Second Language*, Cambridge: Cambridge University Press, pp. 85–110.

Mondada, L. and Pekarek Doehler, S. (2004). Second language acquisition as situated practice: Task accomplishment in the French second language classroom, *The Modern Language Journal*, **88**, 4, 501–18.

Müller-Hartmann, A. and Schocker-von Ditfurth, M. (eds.) (2004). *Task-Based Language Learning and Teaching*, Tübingen: Narr.

Nabei, T. and Swain, M. (2002). Learner awareness of recasts in classroom interaction: A case study of an adult EFL student's second language learning, *Language Awareness*, **11**, 1, 43–63.

Nakahama, Y., Tyler, A. and van Lier, L. (2001). Negotiation of meaning in conversational and information gap activities: A comparative discourse analysis, *TESOL Quarterly*, **35**, 3, 377–405.

Nicholas, H., Lightbown, P. and Spada, N. (2001). Recasts as feedback to language learners, *Language Learning*, **51**, 4, 719–58.

Nunan, D. (2004). *Task-based Language Teaching*, Cambridge: Cambridge University Press.

Oliver, R. (2000). Age differences in negotiation and feedback in classroom and pairwork, *Language Learning*, **50**, 1, 119–51.

Pica, T. (1987). Second language acquisition, social interaction, and the classroom, *Applied Linguistics*, **8**, 1, 3–21.

Pica, T. (1991). Classroom interaction, participation, and negotiation: Redefining relationships, *System*, **19**, 4, 437–52.

Pica, T. (1994). Research on negotiation: What does it reveal about learning conditions, processes, outcomes?, *Language Learning*, **44**, 3, 493–527.

Pica, T. (1998). Second language learning through interaction: Multiple perspectives, in Regan, V. (ed.), *Contemporary Approaches to Second Language Acquisition in Social Context*, Dublin: University College Dublin Press, pp. 9–31.

Pica, T. (2005). Classroom learning, teaching, and research: A task-based perspective, *The Modern Language Journal*, **89**, 3, 339–52.

Pica, T. and Doughty, C. (1985). The role of group work in classroom second language acquisition, *Studies in Second Language Acquisition*, **7**, 2, 233–48.

Pica, T. and Doughty, C. (1987). The impact of interaction on comprehension, *TESOL Quarterly*, **21**, 4, 737–58.

Pica, T., Holliday, L., Lewis, N., Berducci, D. and Newman, J. (1991). Language learning through interaction: What role does gender play?, *Studies in Second Language Acquisition*, **13**, 3, 343–76.

Pica, T., Holliday, L., Lewis, N. and Morgenthaler, L. (1989). Comprehensible output as an outcome of linguistic demands on the learner, *Studies in Second Language Acquisition*, **11**, 1, 63–90.

Pica, T., Kanagy, R. and Falodun, J. (1993). Choosing and using communication tools for second language instruction, in Crookes, G. and Gass, S. (eds.), *Tasks and Language Learning: Integrating Theory and Practice*, Clevedon: Multilingual Matters, pp. 9–34.

Pica, T., Kang, H. and Sauro, S. (2006). Information gap tasks: Their multiple roles and contributions to interaction research methodology, *Studies in Second Language Acquisition*, **28**, 2, 301–38.

Pica, T., Lincoln-Porter, F., Paninios, D. and Linnell, J. (1996). Language learners' interaction: How does it address the input, output and feedback needs of L2 learners?, *TESOL Quarterly*, **30**, 1, 59–84.

Polio, C., Gass, S. and Chapin, L. (2006). Using stimulated recall to investigate native speaker perceptions in native–nonnative speaker interaction, *Studies in Second Language Acquisition*, **28**, 2, 237–67.

Roebuck, R. (2000). Subjects speak out: How learners position themselves in a psycholinguistic task, in Lantolf, J. (ed.), *Sociocultural Theory and Second Language Learning*, Oxford: Oxford University Press, pp. 79–95.

Roehr, K. (2006). Metalinguistic knowledge in L2 performance: A verbal protocol analysis, *Language Awareness*, **15**, 3, 180–98.

Samuda, V. and Bygate, M. (2008). *Tasks in Second Language Learning*, Houndsmill: Palgrave Macmillan.

Seedhouse, P. (2004). *The Interactional Architecture of the Language Classroom: A Conversation Analysis Perspective*, Malden, MA: Blackwell.

Seedhouse, P. (2005). "Task" as a research construct, *Language Learning*, 55, 3, 533–70.

Skehan, P. (1998). *A Cognitive Approach to Language Learning*, Oxford: Oxford University Press.

Skehan, P. and Foster, P. (1999). The influence of task structure and processing conditions on narrative retellings, *Language Learning*, 49, 1, 93–120.

Slimani-Rolls, A. (2005). Rethinking task-based language learning: What we can learn from the learners, *Language Teaching Research*, 9, 2, 195–218.

Swain, M. (1985). Communicative competence: Some roles of comprehensible input and comprehensible output in its development, in Gass, S. and Madden, C. (eds.), *Input in Second Language Acquisition*, Rowley, MA: Newbury House, pp. 235–53.

Swain, M. (1995). Three functions of output in second language learning, in Cook, G. and Seidlhofer, B. (eds.), *Principle and Practice in Applied Linguistics*, Oxford: Oxford University Press, pp. 125–44.

Swain, M. (2005). The output hypothesis: Theory and research, in Hinkel, E. (ed.), *Handbook of Research in Second Language Teaching and Learning*, Mahwah, NJ: Lawrence Erlbaum, pp. 471–83.

Swain, M. and Lapkin, S. (1995). Problems in output and the cognitive processes they generate: A step towards second language learning, *Applied Linguistics*, 16, 3, 371–91.

Swain, M. and Lapkin, S. (1998). Interaction and second language learning: Two adolescent French immersion students working together, *The Modern Language Journal*, 82, 3, 320–37.

Swain, M. and Lapkin, S. (2001). Focus on form through collaborative dialogue: Exploring task effects, in Bygate, M., Skehan, P. and Swain, M. (eds.), *Researching Pedagogic Tasks: Second Language Learning, Teaching and Testing*, London: Longman, pp. 99–118.

Swain, M. and Lapkin, S. (2002). Talking it through: Two French immersion learners' responses to reformulation, *International Journal of Educational Research*, 37, 3/4, 285–304.

Swan, M. (2005). Legislation by hypothesis: The case of task-based instruction, *Applied Linguistics*, 26, 3, 376–401.

Tavakoli, P. (2009). Investigating task difficulty: Learners' and teachers' perceptions, *International Journal of Applied Linguistics*, 19, 1, 1–25.

van den Branden, K. (ed.) (2006). *Task-based Language Education: From Theory to Practice*, Cambridge: Cambridge University Press.

van den Branden, K., van Gorp, K. and Verhelst, M. (eds.) (2007). *Tasks in Action: Task-based Language Education from a Classroom-based Perspective*, Newcastle: Cambridge Scholars Publishing.

Watanabe, Y. and Swain, M. (2007). Effects of proficiency differences and patterns of pair interaction on second language learning: Collaborative dialogue between adult ESL learners, *Language Teaching Research*, **11**, 2, 121–42.

Wertsch, J. (1998). *Mind as Action*, Oxford: Oxford University Press.

Williams, J. (2001). The effectiveness of spontaneous attention to form, *System*, **29**, 3, 325–40.

Yule, G. (1997). *Referential Communication Tasks*, Mahwah, NJ: Lawrence Erlbaum Associates.

9 The effect of task-induced involvement on L2 vocabulary acquisition: An approximate replication of Hulstijn and Laufer (2001)

Susanne Rott

Abstract

This study reports on an approximate replication of Hulstijn and Laufer (2001). The current investigation sought to further explore the predictive power of the Involvement Load Index (ILI) to classify and manipulate the effectiveness of vocabulary-learning tasks. Hulstijn and Laufer investigated whether vocabulary retention is contingent on the amount of task-induced involvement by operationalizing involvement with the varying degree of motivational and cognitive dimensions: need, search, and evaluation. Comparing a reading plus gloss, reading plus fill-in, and an essay-writing task, the current investigation duplicates the treatment conditions, methods of data collection, and data analysis of the original study. It altered the target language (L2 German) and the language level (intermediate learners). It also expanded on measures used in the original study by including a word knowledge measure (productive knowledge), a fill-in choice analysis, and a text comprehension measure (L1 recall). The results of the replication study only partially confirm the Involvement Load Hypothesis. Findings suggest that the ILI may not successfully determine the effectiveness of lexical interventions during contextualized tasks, if learners' processing strategies during the task cannot be accurately predicted or controlled. This may be particularly the case for more obtrusive interventions where the focus on words competes for processing resources with the content-focused task. In addition, the effectiveness of lexical interventions should be assessed in the context of their performance on the content-focused task.

1 Introduction

Advanced lexical capacity is marked by L2 users' breadth (size of the lexicon) and depth (knowledge of word aspects) of the mental lexicon. Besides a word's basic meaning, orthography, pronunciation, and word class, advanced users' interlanguage provides evidence for the command of a word's pragmalinguistic functions, its meaning in conventionalized and metaphorical expressions, and its collocations (e.g., Nation, 2001; Schmitt and Carter, 2004). This means, for example, that L2 users have a choice of words to capture their ideas precisely. This choice requires the awareness of conceptual boundaries of words (e.g., *hat, cap, hood*), the ability to distinguish between polysemous meanings of individual words (e.g., the meaning of *break*: he broke his leg; who broke [announced] the news?; he broke [failed to keep] his promise; he broke [improved] yet another record), and the ability to differentiate between homonyms (e.g., a *file*: used to put papers in, or a tool). Likewise, advanced L2 users need to be able to retrieve conventionalized multi-word units from their mental lexicon instead of word-for-word L1 translations (e.g., ride a bike vs. drive a bike [L1 translation of German *Rad fahren*]). Nevertheless, numerous qualitative analyses of L2 users' oral and written language revealed that even advanced learners' knowledge of conventionalized expressions lags behind the overall knowledge of vocabulary (Bahns and Eldaw, 1993). Consequently, learners overuse expressions they know (e.g., Cowie and Howarth, 1996; Granger, 1998; Cobb, 2003) and the ones that serve similar functions in the learners' L1 (Granger, 1998; Nesselhauf, 2003). Even though the ultimate goal is not to sound like a monolingual native speaker when learning another language, the ability to function effectively in the target language environment strongly depends on the above outlined lexical abilities. Consequently, the longstanding educationally relevant question has been how to most effectively learn vocabulary to reach advanced L2 capacities and to identify task factors that can be manipulated by teachers.

Many L2 researchers agree that at the initial L2 learning stage large quantities of words (between 2,000 and 3,000 word families) can be learned effectively with Focus on FormS (FonFS) exercises where words are treated as the object of study (e.g., Nation, 2001; Laufer 2006), such as the L2 to L1 translation lists found in many textbooks. However, the sheer number of words that need to be learned in order to reach advanced levels renders FonFS learning strategies inefficient beyond the initial stage. To function in an academic setting learners need about 10,000 word families (Hazenberg and Hulstijn,

1996), and to reach a native-like lexicon about 15,000 to 20,000 word families (Nation and Waring, 1997). Further acknowledging the complexity of the mental lexicon, researchers agree that learners cannot develop a functional L2 lexicon by committing isolated words to memory. Rather, they need to encounter words at the discourse level in authentic usage contexts. Naturally, reading provides rich lexical input vital to developing many of the word aspects outlined above. However, studies assessing the default hypothesis of reading as a main source for lexical development (Krashen, 1989) have shown that only a small number of words can be "picked up" during reading (Day et al., 1991; Hulstijn, 1992; Horst et al., 1998; Zahar et al., 2001; Waring and Takaki, 2003; but also Horst, 2005). Laufer (e.g., 2003) has summarized why an uninstructed position to lexical development, such as mass reading, leaves word learning to random chance and may not be the most effective route for lexical development, either. She explains why reading a text for meaning may not trigger processing mechanisms essential for word learning: Noticing (Schmidt, 2001) a new lexical form or a new meaning for an already familiar form is generally considered a prerequisite either for establishing a new form–meaning connection or restructuring an existing one. While focusing on comprehending the content of a text, L2 readers may fail to notice a new word form or meaning, or they may fail to understand the word in its context and thereby fail to retain it. At the same time, learners may not realize that a word's meaning is unfamiliar when encountering polysemes and homonyms of words they already know. Even if L2 readers notice a new word, however, they may not be able to infer the correct word meaning because the context does not provide sufficient clues, the readers do not have the relevant background knowledge, or they do not understand the context well enough and end up inferring an incorrect meaning. Finally, L2 learners may have to encounter words repeatedly in order to learn them (e.g., Horst et al., 1998; Rott, 1999), a requirement which seems unrealistic in an instructed learning environment.

Addressing the shortcomings of an exclusive FonFS or reading-based approach to vocabulary learning, lexical researchers have adopted a Focus on Form (FonF) task paradigm which was originally conceptualized for the learning of grammar (e.g., Long and Robinson, 1998). In FonF tasks, lexical items are tools to complete a content-focused task, such as reading a text and learning about the target culture, or writing an essay to convey ideas. Only briefly and intermittently do learners shift their attention to words they need to comprehend or use to complete the task successfully. The shift of attention to lexical items can be either more obtrusive (e.g., looking up a word in a dictionary) or less obtrusive (e.g., look-ing at an L1 gloss or choosing a word from a given list). It can happen during the reading or writing task or after completing the task (e.g., answering comprehension questions involving the target words). In any case, the words should be relevant to the content of the task.

The majority of lexical intervention studies have been based on reading as a source of input; few have been conducted on oral input or interaction tasks. While some studies compared the effect of the intervention task on word gain with an unenhanced control condition, others compared the effect of different interventions by manipulating the quality and quantity of word processing.

These interventions include the following:

1 Enhancing the noticing and processing of words as well as the assignment of the correct word meaning with L1, L2, multiple choice, and pictorial types of glosses (e.g., Pak, 1986; Davis, 1989; Hulstijn, 1992; Jacobs, 1994; Jacobs et al., 1994; Hulstijn et al., 1996; Watanabe, 1997; Kost et al., 1999; Rott et al., 2002; Yoshii, 2006; Rott, 2007).

2 Increasing the frequency of exposure to new words to foster establishing an initial memory trace and to enhance the filling-in of additional information during subsequent processing (e.g., Brown, 1993; Hulstijn et al., 1996; Rott, 1999, 2007).

3 Training word-inferencing strategies to foster correct mean-ing assignment (e.g., Joe, 1998; Fraser, 1999; Zaki and Ellis, 1999).

4 Providing access to a dictionary, concordance, or other multi-media resources to process form–meaning connections elab-orately and to learn the context-specific meaning of a word (e.g., Luppescu and Day, 1993; Knight, 1994; Chun and Plass, 1996; Hulstijn et al., 1996; Fraser, 1999; Jones and Plass, 2002 [oral input]; Hill and Laufer, 2003; Horst et al., 2005; Peters et al., 2009).

5 Supplying post-reading vocabulary activities to ensure the processing and rehearsal of words (Paribakht and Wesche, 1996; Zimmerman, 1997; Wesche and Paribakht, 2000; Min, 2008; Peters et al., 2009).

6 Using output at the sentence or discourse level to trigger the notic-ing of a lexical gap (Rott et al., 2002; Rott and Williams, 2003), enhance semantic processing (Rott, 2007; Barcroft, 2009), and foster a deeper level of processing and rich associations (Hulstijn and Trompetter, 1998).

7   Encountering interactionally or premodified input to foster noticing and reflection on output (Ellis et al., 1994; Ellis and He, 1999;
de la Fuente, 2002; Smith, 2004).

The central concern of these classroom-based investigations has been
to identify variables that explain why some word interventions in input-
and output-based activities are more effective for long-term word gain
than others. Findings for superior word learning and retention have
generally been explained with a deeper level and elaborative processing,
rich associations of multiple word aspects, or encoding of multiple concept representations (semantic, pictorial, and phonological). Nevertheless, these findings do not provide definitive guidance as to which lexical
interventions are more effective. Likewise, a cohesive account of how to
transfer research results to the language classroom has been missing.

1.1 Introduction to the problem

Summarizing research on cognition and motivation, Laufer and
Hulstijn proposed the construct of task-induced involvement (Table
9.1) to "operationalize general constructs such as noticing, elaboration,
motivation, or need, at the micro level of learning task" (2001: 9). The
motivational-cognitive construct of involvement entails three components: need, search, and evaluation. Each of the three components can
be present or absent when processing a new word. The motivational
component need exists when a word is essential for the successful
completion of a task. Laufer and Hulstijn make a distinction between
moderate (ILI 1) and strong (ILI 2) need depending on whether it is
externally imposed or intrinsically motivated. Search and evaluation
are the two cognitive, information-processing components occurring
when learners attend to form–meaning relationships. Search (ILI 1)
is present when a learner attempts to find the meaning of an L2 word
or the L2 translation of an L1 word. Finally, "*(e)valuation* entails a
comparison of a given word with other words, a specific meaning of
a word with its other meanings, or combining the words in order to
assess whether a word does or does not fit in its context" (Laufer and
Hulstijn, 2001: 14; emphasis in the original). An evaluation is moderate (ILI 1) if it requires assessing differences between words, and strong
(ILI 2) if it "requires making a decision about additional words which
will combine with the new word in an original sentence or text" (2001:
15). Tasks with higher degrees of need (ILI 1 or 2), search (ILI 0 or 1),
and evaluation (ILI 1 or 2) induce a higher involvement load and are
therefore expected to be more effective for word learning than tasks
that induce a lower involvement load.

Table 9.1   *Definition and descriptions of levels of involvement*

Dimension	Definition	ILI	Example Task
Motivational: Need	Perceived need to comprehend or use an L2 word.	Moderate (ILI 1): when imposed by an external agent, such as task or teacher.	• Requirement to use the target word in a sentence • Consulting textual glosses to answer text comprehension questions
		Strong (ILI 2): when imposed by the learner.	• Decision to use a concept without knowing the L2 word for it
Cognitive: Search	The attempt to find the meaning of an unknown L2 word for comprehension or production.	(ILI 1)	• Consulting a dictionary • Asking somebody
Evaluation	Comparing and/or combining the L2 word with other words.	Moderate (ILI 1): when a differentiation between words or between different senses of a word has to be made.	• Fill-in-the-blank task with words provided
		Strong (ILI 2): when a decision needs to be made on how to words combines with other words in contextual use.	• Writing an original sentence or composition after looking up a word in the dictionary

Note: based on Laufer and Hulstijn, 2001: 14–15

1.2 The original study

Hulstijn and Laufer (2001) assessed the predictive power of the Involvement Load Hypothesis on the initial learning and subsequent retention of 10 target words (TW) by advanced adult learners of English as a foreign language in Israel ($n = 128$) and the Netherlands ($n = 97$). They compared three tasks with three different levels of involvement load: reading comprehension with marginal glosses (ILI 1), reading comprehension plus fill-in (ILI 2), and writing a composition incorporating the target words (ILI 3). In both reading conditions learners read a text (621 words) and answered 10 comprehension questions. Time-on-task was regarded as inherent to the task and differed in the following way: Learners who read the text with glosses had 40–45 minutes and learners who read the text and filled in gaps had 50–55 minutes. This included the answering of 10 comprehension questions. For the writing of the essay, learners had 70–80 minutes. Receptive word gain was assessed with an L2 to L1 translation measure immediately after the treatment. Long-term retention was assessed one week later in the Netherlands and two weeks later in Israel. Findings of the Hebrew–English experiment confirmed the predictions of the Involvement Load Hypothesis: The composition group outperformed the fill-in group on both post-tests, and the fill-in group scored significantly higher than the reading group. However, the results of the Dutch–English experiment lent only partial support to the Involvement Load Hypothesis: The composition group outperformed the fill-in and reading groups; the fill-in group did not achieve significantly higher scores than the reading group on either post-test.

1.3 Importance of the problem

The appeal of the Involvement Load Hypothesis for SLA research and language practitioners is apparent. Since the construct of involvement can be operationalized and investigated empirically, the effectiveness of a wide spectrum of lexical interventions can be compared. The resulting task classification could have a direct instructional application and reveal whether a few involving tasks can compensate for the relatively infrequent amount of exposure to new words that is characteristic of a foreign-language-learning environment. Additionally, the construct of involvement allows the classification and comparison of meaningful input and output tasks that have ecological validity in an academic learning setting, such as reading texts and writing essays. Understanding how much word learning can be expected from a content-focused task (FonF task) will be very useful for instructors.

As a result, the construct of involvement load (Laufer and Hulstijn, 2001) and the subsequent empirical study (Hulstijn and Laufer, 2001) have had an important impact on the field. Two replication studies (Laufer, 2003 Experiment 2; Kim, 2008 Experiment 1), and several follow-up studies (Laufer, 2003 Experiment 1; Folse, 2006; Keating, 2008; Kim, 2008 Experiment 2; Pulido, 2009; Walsh, 2009) have been motivated by the prospect of being able to categorize the effectiveness of lexical tasks.

1.4 *Relevant scholarship*

Comparing the reading comprehension and marginal gloss (ILI 1) with the composition writing (ILI 3) condition (Experiment 2), Laufer (2003) replicated the Hulstijn and Laufer study. Results based on the same text and target words and a similar student population (Hebrew–English) as in the original study confirmed the Involvement Load Hypothesis. Likewise, Kim (2008) showed in her replication study (Experiment 1), in which she compared a reading (575 words) comprehension and marginal gloss condition (ILI 1) with a reading comprehension plus fill-in (ILI 2) and composition writing (ILI 3) condition, that the writing condition resulted in the largest word gain followed by the fill-in and the reading condition two weeks after the treatment. She modified the study by comparing the effect for ESL students of two proficiency levels (TOEFL scores of 470–520, and 520 and above), controlled for time-on-task (40 minutes for each group), and used a modified Vocabulary Knowledge Scale measure instead of the L2 to L1 translation task used in the original study. She found no effect for proficiency level.

Further expanding this line of research, Kim (2008: Experiment 2) compared the effectiveness of two output tasks with the same involvement load (ILI 3): writing a composition and writing sentences. The immediate and the delayed post-tests showed no difference in word gain, again confirming the construct of involvement. Similarly, in Experiment 3, Laufer (2003) assessed the effect of three tasks with the same involvement load (ILI 3). She compared word learning by Arabic EFL learners (900 hours of instruction) who either read a text (211 words) for comprehension and looked up unknown words in the dictionary, wrote original sentences with the target words, or completed sentences provided by the researcher with the target words after looking up their meaning in a dictionary. Findings did not corroborate predictions of the Involvement Load Hypothesis. On the immediate post-test, the scores of the reading condition were significantly lower than the other two conditions. On the delayed post-test, the scores of all three groups were significantly different from each other, with the sentence completion condition acquiring most words. However, in a follow-up study (Experiment 1) based on the same materials as in Experiment 2, Laufer (2003) found that word gain was higher in a sentence-writing task (ILI 3) as compared to a reading comprehension plus gloss task (ILI 1). Keating (2008), in turn, also compared the reading comprehension and marginal gloss condition (ILI 1) with a reading and fill-in (ILI 2) and a sentence-writing condition (ILI 3). His modifications were more extensive: He used beginning learners of Spanish, provided a shorter reading passage (299 words and 8 target words), allowed the writing group to review the list of target words for 10 minutes before using each word in a sentence-writing task, and used an additional L1 to L2 production test. His results only partially confirmed the Involvement Load Hypothesis. As in the Hulstijn and Laufer (Dutch–English group) study, his beginning learners gained more receptive knowledge when they engaged in the writing task, whereas they gained a similar number of words after engaging in the reading and fill-in and reading plus gloss condition. The assessment of productive word knowledge confirmed the Involvement Load Hypothesis with highest word gain in the writing condition followed by the reading plus fill-in and the reading plus gloss condition immediately after the treatment. Two weeks later, however, the writing group showed the same amount of productive word gain as the reading plus fill-in group, still outperforming the reading plus gloss group. In addition, Keating performed a statistical analysis to determine the effect of time-on-task. Calculating the words learned per minute on each task, he found that there was no statistically significant difference in word gain between the three tasks. Walsh (2009) sought to gain further insights into the aspect of evaluation. His study exposed two levels (about 897 words or 1,462 words on Nation's 2,000-level word list) of Japanese learners of English to a text (326 words) with 15 target words. Learners either read the text under a fill-in (ILI 2) or a sentence-writing (ILI 3) condition followed by comprehension questions that required the comprehension of the target words. In the sentence-writing condition, target words were underlined and glossed with an L1 translation. Learners were expected to write an original sentence using each target word. Based on an L2 to L1 translation task, results revealed that for lower-level learners there was no task effect. For higher-level learners the sentence-writing task resulted in more word gain than the gap-fill task. Finally, Folse (2006), in his follow-up study, compared the effect of input and output tasks when controlling time. Intermediate to advanced level ESL students received three different treatments:

one five-sentence fill-in task with an alphabetical list of the target words (mini-dictionary), three separate five-sentence fill-in tasks for the same target words, and an original sentence-writing task for the provided target words. Folse controlled for time-on-task assuming that the three five-sentence fill-in tasks took the same amount of time as the writing task. In contrast to the predictions of the Involvement Load Hypothesis, findings showed that using new words to write original sentences (ILI 5; sic) was equally effective as supplying new words in gapped sentences once (ILI 4; sic). Considering the same amount of time used to complete each task, Folse concluded that completing three gapped-sentence activities, and thereby engaging with the words three times, was superior to the sentence-writing task where learners engaged with the words only once.

Further exploring the nature of the involvement load during lexical input processing, Pulido (2009) examined the effect of L2 reader factors, background knowledge and reading proficiency, on word processing and learning. Search, which was operationalized with readers' ability to infer meaning, was found to be more successful when learners had background knowledge about the text content. Successful evaluation of the initial inference, which was measured through time needed to process the target word, depended on the availability of processing resources. She found that only the more proficient readers had the necessary processing resources. Assessing motivation through a questionnaire revealed that the easier it was to infer word meanings, the less time learners spent on evaluating the fit. The multiple-choice word retention measure showed that better readers gained more words than weaker readers, and that learners picked up more words from the familiar topic content. However, as background knowledge and reading ability improved, there was a decline in word retention on the L2 to L1 translation task for the familiar topic reading. Pulido concludes that the "results help to illustrate a negative relationship between ease and success in lexical input processing and retention across a variety of tasks" (2009: 52). Table 9.2 on the following pages summarizes modifications in the replication studies.

1.5 Statement of purpose

Given the inconsistent empirical findings in the original Hulstijn and Laufer (2001) study, the goal of the current approximate replication was to confirm or disconfirm these findings. Whereas Laufer's (2003, Experiment 2) and Kim's (2008, Experiment 1) findings supported the Involvement Load Hypothesis by corroborating results of the Hebrew

Table 9.2 Summary of modifications in replication studies

Study	Type according to *Language Teaching Review Panel* (2008)*	ILI compared	Research question/topic	What was changed	What was added	Confirmed original study and Involvement Load Hypothesis?	Findings of additional measures
Laufer (2003: Experiment 1)	Approximate replication	ILI 1 and ILI 3	Task with higher involvement load will be more effective for vocabulary retention than tasks with lower involvement load	• No comparison with ILI 2 condition task • Sentence-level writing task instead of composition		Yes	
Laufer (2003: Experiment 2)	Exact replication	ILI 1 and ILI 3	Task with higher involvement load will be more effective for vocabulary retention than tasks with lower involvement load	• No comparison with ILI 2 condition task		Yes	

Laufer (2003: Experiment 3)	Constructive replication	Three tasks with ILI 3	Are tasks with the same involvement load equally effective for vocabulary retention?	• Arabic EFL learners • Shorter text • Tasks: reading and look-up of words in dictionary; sentence writing; text with blanks and dictionary look-up	No		
Folse (2006)	Constructive replication	ILI 2 and ILI 3 (author presents different ILI figures: ILI 4 and ILI 5)	Task with higher involvement load will be more effective for vocabulary retention than tasks with lower involvement load	• ESL learners • ILI 2 task: five-sentence fill-in task with list of words provided	No	• Two proficiency levels • Control for time-on-task by completing ILI 2 task three times	• Completing ILI 2 task three times resulted in more word gain than the ILI 3 task

(cont.)

Table 9.2 (continued)

Study	Type according to *Language Teaching* Review Panel (2008)*	ILI compared	Research question/topic	What was changed	What was added	Confirmed original study and Involvement Load Hypothesis?	Findings of additional measures
Kim (2008: Experiment 1)	Approximate replication	ILI 1, ILI 2, ILI 3	Task with higher involvement load will be more effective for vocabulary retention than tasks with lower involvement load	• ESL learners • Text was slightly shorter • Change in word-knowledge measure	• Two proficiency levels • Control for time-on-task	Yes	• No effect for proficiency level
Kim (2008: Experiment 2)	Conceptual replication	Two tasks with ILI 3	Are tasks with the same involvement load equally effective for vocabulary retention?	• ESL learners • No comparison with ILI 1 and ILI 2 tasks	• Sentence-level writing task	Yes	

| Keating (2008) | Conceptual replication | ILI 1, ILI 2, ILI 3 | Task with higher involvement load will be more effective for vocabulary retention than tasks with lower involvement load | • American learners of Spanish as a foreign language • Lower proficiency level • Shorter text • Fewer target words • Sentence-level writing task instead of composition • Time to review target words before writing the sentence | • Additional production test • Time-on-task statistical evaluation | No | • Immediate production test confirmed ILH but the delayed test showed mixed findings • Statistical time-on-task calculation showed all three ILI conditions resulted in the same amount of word gain |

(cont.)

Table 9.2 (continued)

Study	Type according to *Language Teaching Review Panel* (2008)*	ILI compared	Research question/ topic	What was changed	What was added	Confirmed original study and Involvement Load Hypothesis?	Findings of additional measures
Pulido (2009)	Constructive replication	Processing mechanisms involved in the dimension of search and evaluation	What is the impact of proficiency and background knowledge on search and evaluation processes?	• American learners of Spanish as a foreign language • More and less familiar content of reading passage • Nonsense words as target words • Multiple-choice word retention measure	• Inference verification task • TW episodic memory test • Strategy questionnaire		• Familiarity with content aided inferencing • Evaluation requires additional processing resources • Higher proficiency and topic familiarity resulted in more word gain • Ease in input processing is negatively related to retention

Walsh (2009)	Conceptual replication	ILI 2 and ILI 3	Do tasks with strong ILI 3 result in more word retention than tasks with moderate ILI 3 for lower level learners of Japanese?	• Japanese EFL learners • Shorter text • No ILI 1 task • ILI 3 task: Reading with glosses; learners write original sentences with glossed words	• Two proficiency levels	Yes, for advanced learners; no, for lower level learners

* Criteria: Exact: Everything including the subjects is kept the same. Approximate or systematic: One "key variable (such as the learners' proficiency, L1 background or learning context) is changed" (p. 3). Constructive or conceptual: This may involve changing the operationalization of a construct, the study design, or "nonmajor" (p. 3) variable.

group from the original study, subsequent follow-up investigations only found partial support for the Involvement Load Hypothesis corroborating results of the Dutch group. However, modifications made in the set-up of these investigations do not shed any further light on the inconsistent findings of the original study. Studies using sentence-length input and output tasks instead of text comprehension and composition tasks lacked consistency in comparing content-driven FonF tasks (Laufer, 2003; Folse, 2006; Keating, 2008; Kim, 2008). Even though learning words in decontextualized sentence tasks may be a very useful word-learning strategy, its primary goal is to learn words, not to learn about content or express an idea. Although Laufer and Hulstijn (2001) propose that the construct of involvement applies to contextualized lexical intervention and decontextualized word-learning tasks, comparing the effectiveness of the two types of tasks appears theoretically not well motivated. Likewise, some follow-up studies used much shorter texts (Laufer, 2003, Experiment 3; Keating, 2008; Kim, 2008; Walsh, 2009), leading to a higher percentage of unknown words (target words) in relatively short texts.

Additionally, the current study sought to provide further insight into the interpretation of the results of the original study, in particular because Hulstijn and Laufer did not provide any explanation for the differential performance of their participating groups. With respect to the inconclusive results for the fill-in task in the original study, further analyses of the collected data may shed more light on learners' differential performance, and consequently the applicability of the ILI. There are two possible explanations why the Dutch–English group did not retain more words after completing the fill-in task than learners in the gloss-enhanced reading task. One reason may have been that choosing the correct word form from the provided list was very easy and did not require the readers to evaluate the correct choice of meaning. Readers, therefore, may not have processed the form–meaning assignments at a deeper level. As outlined above, Pulido (2009) found in her cognitive analysis for the construct evaluation that easy and successful target word processing was negatively related to retention. Another, quite opposite reason, may have been the readers' inability to choose the correct meaning from the word list that included five distracters. In fact, qualitative analyses on the processing of multiple-choice glosses have shown that learners may not be successful in using context clues to choose and assign the correct meaning of a target word, even if the meaning is provided as one of multiple choices (e.g., Rott and Williams, 2003; Rott, 2005). This may also have been the case with the fill-in task. Limited understanding of the local context may have resulted in spending processing resources on context comprehension and therefore limiting processing resources for evaluating the correct meaning choice. Indeed, scoring the performance on the fill-in task is essential for better understanding the instructional value of this task. Consequently, the current replication study added two additional data analyses: one focusing on the learners' ability to choose and fill in the correct word meaning; another on the relationship between the correct word choice and word learning.

Another issue regarding the interpretation of the results of the original study concerns the possible interaction between the lexical intervention task and text comprehension. As mentioned above, comprehending a text and processing a word for long-term retention may be two distinct processes competing for the same resources. In fact, studies have been inconclusive about whether, and which, lexical interventions foster or interfere with text comprehension. Single glosses aided comprehension as compared to an unenhanced, a multiple-choice gloss (Davis, 1989; Jacobs et al., 1994; Watanabe, 1997), or an appositive condition (Watanabe, 1997). However, other studies did not confirm a positive effect for glosses (e.g., Pak, 1986; Jacobs et al., 1994). Rott et al. (2002) further found a statistically significant increase in text recall for readers who received multiple-choice glosses as well as readers who simultaneously engaged in an output task, compared to the control group. In turn, Rott (2007) found a positive effect when words were glossed four times, but requiring learners to recall the word after it had been glossed affected text comprehension negatively. Taking these inconclusive findings into consideration, the analysis of text comprehension scores may provide further insights into the possible interaction between filling in gaps, text comprehension, and word learning. Even though Hulstijn and Laufer's study participants were asked to answer ten comprehension questions, the authors did not report the scores. Therefore, the current replication analyzed text comprehension scores to determine whether the lexical intervention with a higher involvement load resulted in equal, better, or less comprehension of the text. Instead of using comprehension questions, an L1 recall protocol was used to gain more detailed insights into text comprehension (see Materials section).

Finally, another variable of interest to interpret the results of Hulstijn and Laufer's study concerns the type of word knowledge gained. In most models of L2 vocabulary development, it is assumed that learning a word usually progresses from receptive to productive knowledge (e.g., Meara, 1996; Nation, 2001). Testing receptive word gain, therefore, has generally been considered an indication that the first step of learning a new word has taken place and that subsequent encounters will lead to filling in more word aspects. More recently, researchers have been conducting more detailed analyses, ranging from partial word form learning (e.g., Barcroft and Rott, 2010), to a more refined analysis of receptive and productive word knowledge (Laufer and Goldstein, 2004), to a wide range of word aspects (e.g., Webb, 2005; Pigada and Schmitt, 2006). Moreover, Hulstijn and Laufer emphasize that the Involvement Load Hypothesis does not make predictions about the effect of input and output tasks but that the determining factor of lexical interventions is the level of the ILI. However, determining the effectiveness of tasks for receptive as well as productive word knowledge gain has a strong pedagogical value. Given that the ultimate goal of FonF tasks is to use the content gained from a text and transfer ideas expressed in an essay to another task, the ability to use words productively is crucial. Since the lexical intervention tasks compared in the original study were equal in the level of need (ILI 1) and search (ILI 0) but varied in the level of evaluation (gloss condition = 0, fill-in condition = 1, essay writing = 2), it will be interesting to determine how the absence of evaluation and the different levels of cognitive involvement of evaluation (1 or 2) affect productive word knowledge gain. In order to further strengthen the generalizability of the original study and gain further insight into the effectiveness of the compared tasks (text comprehension and essay writing) on lexical learning, the present replication added a productive word measure assessment as well as a partial word knowledge analysis.

To summarize: The inconsistent findings regarding the validity of the ILI for the fill-in task in the original and the follow-up studies warrant the need for replication. Consequently, the aim of the current replication was twofold: a) to provide further insights into learners' interaction with the reading comprehension and fill-in task by further analyzing the data and b) to further extend the generalizability of the classificatory power of the Involvement Load Hypothesis. Based on theory and research outlined above, the study added the following analyses without modifying the original set-up: The replication analyzed students' ability to choose the correct target word form, assessed the competence to comprehend the text while choosing and filling in words, and determined the effectiveness of tasks at different ILI levels for partial and productive word gain. The original study was modified in terms of the student population (adult learners of German in the United States) and the level of language proficiency (intermediate learners).

1.6 Research questions

1.6.1 ORIGINAL RESEARCH QUESTION

Hulstijn and Laufer (2001) sought to determine whether tasks with a higher involvement load are more effective for receptive word knowledge gain and retention than tasks with a lower involvement load. They hypothesized that the retention scores would be highest for learners completing the writing task with an ILI 3; lower for learners completing the reading plus fill-in task with an ILI 2; and lowest for learners reading the text with glosses with an ILI 1. The current replication study adopted the original research question and the hypothesized outcomes.

1.6.2 ADDITIONAL RESEARCH QUESTIONS

Additional research questions were created to address inconclusive findings of the original study and extend the generalizability of the findings:

2   Are tasks with a higher involvement load more effective for productive (complete and partial) word knowledge gain than tasks with a lower involvement load?
3   Does the ILI level affect the type of word knowledge gain (receptive and productive)?
4   Does a gloss and a fill-in lexical intervention task affect text comprehension? If so, is word learning related to text comprehension?
5   Can L2 learners fill the gap correctly in a reading and fill-in task? If so, is the ability to fill the gap correctly related to word learning and retention?

2 Materials

2.1 Participants

Participants in the original study were advanced EFL learners of English with Dutch and Hebrew as their L1s. As in the original study, participants in the current investigation were adult college-level learners. However, for this replication study the student population as well as the language level were modified in order to determine the applicability of the involvement load classification scheme for intermediate learners of German as a foreign language. The intermediate-level participants were competent completing the three treatments, as both types of treatment tasks, reading a text and writing essays, were part of the regular language curriculum. Nevertheless, intermediate learners' reading and writing abilities generally differ from those of advanced learners. It is safe to assume that participants in the current investigation had less experience reading texts and writing essays than the advanced learners in the original study. Therefore, processing words for learning while at the same time processing text for comprehension or writing a meaningful essay may have placed different demands on intermediate learners' attentional and processing resources. Sixty-nine participants in five intact classes were randomly assigned to the three different treatment conditions. Because 13 students did not complete all parts of the study, only 56 participants' data were used in the final analysis.

2.2 Treatment materials

2.2.1 TARGET WORDS

As in the original study, ten words and expressions which were unfamiliar to the participants were selected as target words: six nouns (*Bereicherung, Rücksicht, Erlebnis, Gepflogenheiten, Bewerbung, Mühe*), three verbs (*sich einstellen, bewältigen, unterbrechen*) and one adjective (*unabhängig*). All target words were part of the main textual propositions and were therefore relevant for text comprehension.

2.2.2 TREATMENT TASKS

In line with the original study, participants received one of three different treatments with different involvement loads.

Task 1 Reading comprehension with marginal glosses. Approximating the original study, participants read an expository text on the topic of study abroad that was 620 words long. Comprehension of the text did not require any specific cultural background information. The ten target words were highlighted in bold print and glossed in the L1 in the margin of the text. Students were instructed to read the text for comprehension and anticipate comprehension questions. Unlike in the original study, however, students did not receive comprehension questions but were asked to recall the content of the passage in their L1. This departure from the original study was motivated by two factors. First, a recall protocol provides more detailed insights into L2 readers' comprehension of textual propositions. Second, testing text comprehension in the L1 does not interfere with students' L2 productive language abilities (Lee, 1986). The time allotted to complete the reading task was shortened from the original study to 15–20 minutes to allow for a more ecologically valid reading experience. Reading a text of this length should take no longer than 15–20 minutes, unless students reread the text several times, or memorize the content. Participants did not have access to the text while recalling the propositions. The task induced moderate need, but neither search nor evaluation, resulting in an ILI of 1.

Task 2 Reading comprehension and fill-in. Participants were given the same text and the same recall protocol as those receiving Task 1. For Task 2, however, the ten target words were deleted from the text, leaving ten gaps of the same size numbered 1–10. The ten target words, along with five words that were thematically related but had not appeared in the text, were printed in random order as a list on a separate page. Target words were presented with their L1 translation, L2 synonyms, and a sample sentence. For example:

die Bewerbung (noun, countable)
Antrag, Kandidatur
Example: *Ich schicke meine Bewerbung an eine Firma.*
English: application

The instructions were to read the text, fill in the ten gaps with words from the provided list, and answer comprehension questions. As was the case for Task 1, students engaged in an L1 recall protocol and the reading time was shortened to 20–25 minutes. Students had five minutes longer to complete this task as compared to the reading plus gloss condition because they had to look at the word list, make a decision on the correct word, and write it into the gap in the text. The task induced a moderate need, no search, and a moderate evaluation, resulting in an ILI of 2.

Task 3 Writing a composition and incorporating the target words. Participants were asked to write a composition in German on the topic of study abroad: Are you interested in studying abroad? Explain why or why not. The instructions were adopted from the original study as follows: "In your [essay], YOU MUST USE THE FOLLOWING TEN WORDS. You may decide yourself in which order you will use them. Explanations of the words and examples of usage are given below" (Hulstijn and Laufer, 2001: 547). The target words were presented in the same way as in the reading and fill-in task (see above). For the writing task the allotted time was also shortened to 35–40 minutes to present a more ecologically valid classroom writing situation for intermediate learners. In terms of involvement load, Task 3 induced a moderate need, no search, and a strong evaluation, resulting in an ILI of 3.

2.2.3 MEASURES AND SCORING

Vocabulary pre-test

Unlike in the original study, unfamiliarity with the target words was assessed with a pre-test two weeks before the study. Participants received a list with the ten target words and 25 distracters and were asked to translate them into English. They were expected to cross out words they did not know at all. In Hulstijn and Laufer's study, students were asked on the post-test itself whether they had been familiar with the target words before the study. In the current investigation a pre-test was used instead to avoid attrition of the participant population due to knowledge of the target words. The target words could have been modified if the pre-test had shown that students were familiar with particular target words. This procedure is commonly used in lexical research and does not have any impact on the study itself.

Receptive word knowledge gain

Replicating the word-learning measure from the original study, participants received a list with the ten target words and were asked to provide an L1 equivalent or explanation. The assessment task took about five minutes. A correct response received one point, an incorrect response no points. A "semantically approximate" response received half a point. There were no semantically approximate responses. Several additional measures were added for the replication study.

Productive word knowledge gain

In an effort to gain more detailed knowledge about the effectiveness of tasks with varying ILI (1, 2, or 3) for lexical development, a productive word knowledge measure was added. To add the productive test after having completed the receptive measure was not ideal but necessary to replicate the original study. Therefore, a distracter task was added. After the participants had completed the receptive measure, the sheets were collected and the class chatted about reading in German. This was done to prevent rehearsal of the L2 target word forms from the receptive test. Students were not aware that a productive test was to follow. After about five minutes, learners were presented with a productive word knowledge measure. The target words were presented in English, and participants were asked to provide an equivalent or an explanation in the L2. Again, five minutes were allotted for the test. A correct response received one point, an incorrect one zero.

An additional score for partial word knowledge was calculated. The theoretical assumption was that learning the spelling of a previously unknown word form is of equal importance to learning the word's conceptual aspect and establishing a connection between the word form and its meaning. Moreover, an initial partial memory trace of a word form, such as a syllable or a couple of letters, can be filled in during subsequent additional exposures (e.g., VanPatten et al., 2004). Likewise, an initial incorrect form–meaning connection, such as a learner recalling the wrong word form *Messer* (knife) when seeing a fork, can be restructured by replacing the meaning knife with the meaning fork during subsequent encounters. Both scenarios, connecting the complete word form to its meaning and establishing the correct form–meaning connection, will require less mental effort than having no memory trace of the word form at all (e.g., Boogards, 2001). Consequently, the partial word knowledge score included credit for words that were produced correctly but for the wrong L1 equivalent. Half a point was awarded for these words because participants had learned the target word form but had not established the form–meaning connection. Additionally, when learners produced 50% or more of the target word letters (see, e.g., Barcroft and Rott, 2010) they received half a point. Partial word gain was scored by two raters. Interrater reliability was 95%.

Type of word knowledge gain

In order to determine whether a treatment task was superior for the development of either receptive or productive word knowledge, receptive and productive word-learning scores were compared for each treatment condition. For this analysis the total of partial and full productive word knowledge was compared to receptive knowledge scores.

Fill-in choice

A score was calculated to determine whether readers were able to choose the correct target word meaning for Task 2. Correct choices received one point, and incorrect, no points.

Text comprehension

Text comprehension was assessed with a recall protocol in English. Participants were asked to recall the content of the text in as much detail as possible. The baseline of the propositional content was established by three bilingual speakers of German and English who completed a recall protocol. The bilingual speakers were instructed to recall the main ideas of the passage. The divergence in four propositions was resolved through discussion, resulting in 23 textual propositions. The participants' recalls were scored by two raters. Interrater reliability was 93%.

3 Results

In order to determine internal reliability of all criterion measures, receptive and productive (full, partial, total), assessed immediately after the treatment and two weeks later, Cronbach's α was calculated for each treatment condition. For all three treatment conditions reliability was high: reading plus gloss condition $\alpha = .84$, reading plus fill-in, $\alpha = .85$, and the writing condition, $\alpha = .89$.

3.1 Receptive word knowledge gain

The first research question focused on confirming or disconfirming Hulstijn and Laufer's (2001) findings. Therefore, the study assessed whether tasks with a higher involvement load lead to more receptive word gain immediately after the reading and writing tasks and two weeks later. Immediate and delayed retention scores of the receptive post-tests are displayed in Table 9.3.

Table 9.3   Number of participants, mean retention receptive scores, and standard deviations in immediate and delayed post-tests

Treatments	N	Immediate Mean (SD)	Delayed Mean (SD)
Reading + gloss	18	2.00 (1.08)	1.39 (0.92)
Reading + fill-in	23	2.13 (0.97)	1.35 (0.78)
Writing	15	3.20 (1.12)	2.20 (1.01)

Note: Maximum points = 10

Histograms and descriptive statistics indicated that the data were skewed. Statistically significant results for the Kolmorgorov-Smirnov test confirmed that student performance in the three treatment conditions at both times of measure was not normally distributed. Therefore, word-learning scores were submitted to a Kruskal-Wallis test with task as the grouping variable (reading, reading and fill-in, writing) and receptive word gain (immediate and delayed) as the test variable. A statistically significant effect was obtained for treatment task on the immediate post-test (H(2) = 10.50, $p < .05$) as well as on the delayed post-test (H(2) = 6.42, $p < .05$). A Mann-Whitney U post-hoc test was conducted to further compare the effect of the three different treatment conditions on receptive word learning. Since three comparisons were conducted, a level of significance was set at $p < .02$. The analyses revealed that immediately after the treatment the writing condition gained statistically significantly more word knowledge than the reading plus gloss condition, $U = 60.50$, $p < .02$, $r = -.49$, and the fill-in condition, $U = 80.00$, $p < .02$, $r = -.47$. But there was no statistically significant difference in word gain between the fill-in and the gloss condition, $U = 189.00$, ns. Results were the same two weeks after the treatment. The writing condition outperformed the reading plus gloss, $U = 82.50$, $p < .02$, $r = -.35$, and the fill-in condition, $U = 98.00$, $p < .02$, $r = -.39$. In turn, differences in findings in the reading plus gloss and the fill-in condition were not statistically significant, $U = 200.00$, ns. Subsequently, as in Hulstijn and Laufer's analysis, the scores of the two reading conditions were combined in one group ($n = 41$) and compared to the writing condition ($n = 15$). The comparison of the immediate and the post-test scores showed that when learners engaged in an essay-writing task, they gained statistically significantly more receptive word knowledge than students who learned words while reading. This was the case immediately after the treatment, $U = 140.50$, $p < .02$, $r = -.43$, and two weeks later, $U = 180.50$, $p < .05$, $r = -.34$. Both effect sizes were medium. These results partially confirmed the hypothesis that a lexical intervention task with a higher ILI will result in more word gain and retention. The writing task with an ILI of 3 yielded more word gain than the reading and gloss (ILI 1) and the reading and fill-in (ILI 2) tasks. However, as with the Dutch group in the original study, similar word gain scores for the reading and gloss (ILI 1) and the reading and fill-in (ILI 2) tasks did not support the Involvement Load Hypothesis.

3.2 Productive word knowledge gain

With research question two, the study sought to develop further insights into the effectiveness of the involvement load categorization and strengthen its generalizability. Therefore, productive word knowledge gain of the lexical intervention tasks with three different ILI were compared. Table 9.4 reports productive word-learning scores for words that were learned fully and scores for words that were learned partially (at least 50% of word forms and words produced completely but for the incorrect L1 target word translation).

Table 9.4 Number of participants, mean retention scores of full and partial productive word knowledge, and standard deviations in immediate and delayed post-tests

Treatments	N	Immediate			Delayed		
		Full Mean (SD)	Partial Mean (SD)	Total Mean (SD)	Full Mean (SD)	Partial Mean (SD)	Total Mean (SD)
Reading + gloss	18	1.28 (1.02)	0.28 (0.43)	1.45 (1.19)	0.72 (0.67)	0.08 (0.19)	0.81 (0.69)
Reading + fill-in	23	1.13 (0.97)	0.61 (0.56)	1.73 (1.04)	0.70 (0.70)	1.02 (0.69)	1.72 (1.02)
Writing	15	2.66 (1.11)	1.67 (0.70)	4.33 (1.36)	2.07 (0.96)	2.03 (0.67)	4.10 (1.23)

Note: maximum points for full word knowledge = 10; maximum points for partial word knowledge = 5.

Histograms and descriptive statistics indicated that the data of the individual measures were skewed. Statistically significant results of the Kolmorgorov-Smirnov test confirmed that production scores in the three treatment conditions at both times of measure were not normally distributed. Productive word-learning scores were submitted to a Kruskal-Wallis test with task as the grouping variable (reading, reading and fill-in, writing) and full and partial productive word gain (immediate and delayed) as the test variable.

With regard to productive word knowledge gain of full word forms, a statistically significant effect was obtained for treatment task in the immediate post-test ($H(2) = 15.15$, $p < .05$) as well as on the delayed post-test ($H(2) = 19.40$, $p < .05$). A Mann-Whitney U post-hoc test was conducted to further compare the effect of the three different treatment conditions. Since three comparisons were conducted, a level of significance was set at $p < .02$. The analysis of the immediate post-test revealed that the writing condition gained statistically significantly more productive word knowledge than the reading and gloss, $U = 51.00$, $p < .02$, $r = -.54$, and the fill-in condition, $U = 54.00$, $p < .02$, $r = -.69$. But there was no statistically significant difference in complete productive word knowledge gain between the fill-in and the gloss condition, $U = 189.50$, ns. The analysis of the delayed post-test revealed similar findings. The writing condition gained statistically significantly more full productive word knowledge than the reading and gloss, $U = 35.50$, $p < .02$, $r = -.65$, and the fill-in condition, $U = 46.00$, p $< .02$, $r = -.64$. But there was no statistically significant difference in full productive word knowledge gain between the fill-in and the gloss condition $U = 201.00$, ns. Subsequently, the scores of the two reading conditions were combined in one group ($n = 41$) and compared to the writing condition ($n = 15$). The analyses showed that after engaging in an essay-writing task learners gained more complete productive word knowledge than during reading. This was the case immediately after the treatment, $U = 105.00$, $p < .02$, $r = -.52$, and two weeks later, $U = 85.50$, $p < .02$, $r = -.59$. Both effect sizes were medium. Complete productive word-learning scores only partially supported the Involvement Load Hypothesis.

The Kruskal-Wallis test for partial productive word knowledge gain showed a statistically significant effect for condition immediately after the treatment ($H(2) = 25.26$, $p < .05$) and two weeks later ($H(2) = 38.53$, $p < .05$). Mann-Whitney U post-hoc tests revealed that partial productive word gain was statistically significantly different for all three treatment conditions immediately after the treatment. The writing condition outperformed the gloss $U = 14.00$, $p < .02$, $r = -.79$, and fill-in, $U = 45.00$, $p < .02$, $r = -.63$, condition, and the fill-in condition outperformed the gloss condition $U = 136.00$, $p < .02$, $r = -.31$. These statistically significant differences held also true on the delayed post-test. The writing condition outperformed the gloss, $U = 15.00$, $p < .02$, $r = -.89$, and fill-in, $U = 49.00$, $p < .02$, $r = -.61$, condition, and the fill-in condition outperformed the gloss condition $U = 31.50$, $p < .02$, $r = -.75$. Effect sizes were medium to large. Partial productive word knowledge gain supported the Involvement Load Hypothesis.

3.3 Type of word knowledge gain

Research question three sought to assess whether the level of ILI of lexical interventions affects the type of word knowledge gain (receptive and productive). Table 9.4 provides means and standard deviations of the total productive word knowledge (full and partial); Table 9.3 provides receptive word knowledge scores.

Wilcoxon's signed rank tests were conducted to compare receptive and productive word learning in the three different treatment conditions (reading and gloss, reading and fill-in, writing) immediately after the treatment. When learners read a text with glosses they gained about the same amount of receptive (20%) and productive (15%) word knowledge, $t = 24$, ns. Similarly, when learners read the text and had to fill in the target words, receptive word gain (21%) was statistically significantly, but only marginally, higher than productive (17%), $t = 46.50$, $p < .05$, $r = -.41$. Yet, when learners engaged in the writing task they gained significantly more productive (43%) than receptive (32%) knowledge $t = 3.00$, $p <. 05$, $r = -.84$.

Analyses of the delayed post-test scores showed that in the gloss condition learners retained more receptive (14%) than productive (8%) word knowledge $t = 15.00$, $p <. 05$, $r = -.51$. In the fill-in condition learners retained about the same amount of receptive (14%) and productive (17%) word knowledge $t = 85.50$, ns., and in the writing condition learners retained more productive (41%) than receptive (22%) word knowledge, $t = 2.00$, $p <. 05$, $r = -.85$. Effect sizes were medium to large.

3.4 The effect of glosses and fill-in tasks on text comprehension

Research question four further explored the effect of the two lexical interventions, glosses or a fill-in task, on text comprehension. Means and standard deviations for the idea units that learners recalled are presented in Table 9.5.

Table 9.5   Mean and standard deviation of idea units recalled in the reading plus gloss and reading plus fill-in conditions

Treatment	N	Idea Units M (SD)
Reading + gloss	18	17.88 (3.03)
Reading +fill-In	23	12.39 (3.11)

Note: Maximum number of idea units = 23

The Mann-Whitney U test compared idea units recalled by learners in the gloss and learners in the fill-in condition. It revealed that learners who read the text enhanced with glosses comprehended statistically significantly more propositions than learners who engaged in a fill-in task during reading, $U = 43.50$, $p < .05$, $r = -.67$.

Additionally, research question four sought to determine whether word learning, receptive and productive, was related to text comprehension. The data analysis showed no statistically significant correlation between word learning and text comprehension for the gloss reading condition. In turn, when learners engaged in the fill-in task text, comprehension was statistically significantly related to full word knowledge gain measures immediately after the treatment, $r = .45$, p (two-tailed) $< .05$. Moreover, text comprehension was related to total (full and partial) productive word knowledge retention measured two weeks after the treatment, $r = .42$, p (two-tailed) $< .05$.

3.5 The ability to fill in gaps correctly

Research question five further explored whether learners were able to choose the correct word meaning to fill in the gap in the reading passage. On average, learners were able to fill in 6.48 (sd. 1.14) words correctly. In addition, their ability to fill in the target words correctly was statistically significantly related to almost all word-learning measures. This was the case immediately after the treatment for the receptive ($r = .65$) and the productive ($r = .49$) measures as well as two weeks later for the delayed receptive ($r = .59$) and productive ($r = .66$) measures. All analyses were based on a two-tailed test with $p < .05$.

4 Summary of results

1   For receptive and productive word knowledge gain, the Involvement Load Hypothesis was partially supported. The writing task with an ILI of 3 led to more receptive and productive word gain than the reading tasks with an ILI of 1 and 2. However, the reading and fill-in task with an ILI of 2 did not lead to more word gain than the reading and gloss task with an ILI of 1.

2   However, partial productive word gain measured immediately after the treatment and two weeks later supported the Involvement Load Hypothesis. Partial word learning was highest for the task with an ILI of 3, followed by the task with an ILI of 2 and lowest for the task with an ILI of 1.

3   The three treatment tasks which varied in the level of evaluation (0, 1, or 2) showed different patterns of type of word knowledge gain. While the essay-writing task with an evaluation level of 2 resulted in more productive than receptive word knowledge gain, the fill-in task with an evaluation level of 1 resulted in about the same amount of receptive and productive word knowledge. In contrast, the gloss task with an evaluation level of 0 led to the same amount of receptive and productive word knowledge immediately after the reading treatment. Productive retention scores were statistically significantly lower two weeks later.

4   Text comprehension was statistically significantly higher for learners in the gloss task with an ILI level of 1 as compared to the fill-in task with an ILI level of 2.

5   Word learning did not correlate with text comprehension when learners encountered the target words as glosses (ILI 1). In turn,

when learners encountered the target words during the fill-in task (ILI 2), productive word knowledge gain was statistically significantly related to text comprehension.

6   In only 65% of the instances were learners able to fill in the correct target word form. This result was statistically significantly related to word learning.

5 Discussion

The main goal of this approximate replication study was to strengthen the generalizability of the ILI. Hulstijn and Laufer (2001) sought to demonstrate that the effectiveness of a word-learning task can be classified according to the degree of motivational and cognitive processing of word dimensions: need, search, and evaluation. In their investigation they compared three word interventions embedded in meaning-focused tasks. They hypothesized that the retention scores in the essay task, which required learners to use the target words, would be highest; that retention scores in the reading task, which required learners to choose the correct word meaning from a list and write it into the gap in the text, would be lower; and that the retention scores in the reading task, which was enhanced with glosses, would be lowest. Based on the learning outcome from two different advanced student populations (Dutch and Hebrew), the hypothesis was confirmed, but only partially. The receptive word-learning scores of the Hebrew group confirmed the predictions of the Involvement Load Hypothesis. By contrast, the receptive word-learning scores of the Dutch group showed highest gains for the essay-writing condition but about the same word gain in both reading conditions.

Findings from the current replication further demonstrated that the involvement load task classification scheme was only partially predictive for receptive lexical development. Intermediate learners of German performed like the Dutch participants in the original study, gaining more words after writing an essay as compared to the two reading conditions. These results further corroborated findings from Keating (2008), which were based on beginning learners of Spanish.

The limited predictive power of the Involvement Load Hypothesis was further substantiated with the additional productive word gain measure added to the replication study. Unlike Keating's (2008) beginning learners, who showed a different pattern for productive than for receptive word gain, current learners exhibited the same pattern: When they engaged in the essay-writing task they retained more productive word knowledge than when they encountered the target words in the fill-in and gloss reading conditions. By contrast, whereas immediate productive scores in Keating's study validated involvement load predictions, the delayed scores did not. In the current study, learners showed superior productive word retention for the writing task as compared to the fill-in and gloss task.

As a result, findings to date strongly support Hulstijn and Laufer's prediction that memory traces are weaker when words are processed at a low level of involvement, such as glosses during reading, than when they are processed with a high level of involvement, such as an essay-writing assignment. This prediction has been validated for advanced (Laufer, 2003; Kim, 2008), intermediate (current investigation; Kim, 2008), as well as beginning learners (Keating, 2008). Additionally, as shown in the current study as well as Keating (2008), the prediction seems to hold not only for receptive but also for productive word knowledge gain.

Nevertheless, the findings of these studies also imply that the predictive power of the involvement load may not be applicable to all tasks or all proficiency levels. In fact, learning outcomes for the reading and fill-in task varied across studies. When learners' attention was directed to choosing a correct word meaning from a list of words to fill in a gap in a text, intermediate learners in the current replication study did not gain the amount of word knowledge anticipated by the involvement load construct. This finding corroborated results from previous investigations with beginning learners (Keating, 2008; Walsh, 2009) as well as advanced learners from the original study (Dutch group). While most studies (original study; this replication; Walsh, 2009) found that processing the target words while filling the gaps of the text did not lead to more word knowledge than processing the target words as glosses, Keating (2008) found that learners processing the words during the fill-in task retained the same amount of productive word knowledge as the essay-writing group. That is, it seems possible that for different learners, the fill-in task resulted in the processing of words at different levels of involvement, leading to different patterns of retention.

Another aim of the current replication study was to develop further insights into the inconsistencies of these findings. Current results suggest that the fill-in task engaged students in processes that were not necessarily conducive to establishing form–meaning connections. The intermediate learners in this study were only able to choose and fill in the correct word meaning for about 65% of the target words. One possible explanation is that there may not have been sufficient textual clues for learners easily to choose the correct word meaning from the word list provided. Likewise, the five distracter words added to the list of 10 target words may have interfered with students' success in choosing the correct word for the gaps in the text. Even though the chosen distracters did not occur in the text, they were related to the topic. Alternatively, simply the number of words (15), which included a sample sentence, synonyms, and a translation, which learners had to choose from, may have been overwhelming. Since filling in the correct word meaning was moderately to strongly related to word learning, it becomes clear that choosing the correct word meaning triggered different word processing than the incorrect choices. It may have been that incorrect choices were based on guesses and a failure to validate the choice in the context. Even though an introspective analysis would be necessary to determine students' processing strategies during the fill-in task, it is safe to say that the fill-in task can be completed without engaging in evaluation processes predicted by Hulstijn and Laufer.

The additional analysis of text comprehension scores in the current replication study sheds more light onto the interaction between choosing and filling in words while reading a text for meaning and word learning. The current investigation revealed that learners who were prompted to fill gaps while reading comprehended the text less well than learners who had read the text enhanced with glosses. It seems that for these intermediate learners, filling in gaps may have interrupted the flow of text comprehension as compared to the gloss condition. Likewise, the inability to choose the correct word meaning easily from the list provided may have required too much attention, leaving fewer processing resources for text comprehension. That is, the two tasks, namely comprehending the text and filling in the gaps, may have resulted in a competition for attentional resources. Similarly, Rott (2007) had found that a more obtrusive task, such as recalling a word meaning during reading, negatively affected text comprehension. Interestingly, for students who were required to copy the target words into the text as part of the fill-in task, gaining productive word knowledge was related to text comprehension. Nevertheless, students who encountered the target words as glosses learned words independently of text comprehension.

The specific effect of the cognitive dimension of evaluation for lexical development was further assessed by comparing the receptive and productive word gain. This analysis sought to determine which type of word knowledge gain could be expected from tasks of varying degrees of evaluation. Whereas the gloss task that did not trigger the evaluation of the target word led to more receptive word knowledge retention, the fill-in task, which triggered evaluation of the word by comparing its meaning with that of 14 other words, led to about the same amount of receptive and productive word knowledge. The essay-writing task, in turn, which prompted evaluation through target word usage, resulted in more productive word learning. Since all three tasks varied only in the level of evaluation, the results suggest that the more learners engage in evaluating a word, the more likely they are to develop productive word knowledge.

These findings were based on the total of full as well as partial productive word knowledge. Partial word knowledge gain proved to be a significant factor in providing a more holistic picture of the effect of a lexical word intervention on overall word learning. Having already established a partial form–meaning connection or a partial memory trace of a word form will allow for filling in and restructuring information during subsequent encounters. Consequently, the availability of partial knowledge may free up processing resources necessary for developing advanced word aspects, such as collocational and syntactic word usage. In that way, tasks that result in partial word learning are essential to overall lexical development.

From a pedagogical perspective, the findings from this replication study suggest that the ILI may not successfully determine the effectiveness of all lexical interventions. Table 9.6 (overleaf) outlines variables the ILI cannot control and account for at this point. It may not be possible accurately to predict or control learners' processing strategies in more obtrusive interventions where the focus on words competes with completing the contextualized content-focused task, such as reading a text for meaning or writing an essay. Consequently, the effectiveness of lexical interventions should be assessed in the context of learners' performance on the content-focused task. Likewise, the involvement load construct does not make any predictions about the type and depth of word knowledge gain. Yet, for instructional purposes it would be essential to gain more details about word learning, such as receptive, productive, partial, and collocational word knowledge gain.

6 Limitations and future research

Whereas the current study was set up as an approximate replication of Hulstijn and Laufer's 2001 investigation, certain aspects could not be controlled. For example, the original study used a standardized reading passage that had been tested for its suitability for the student population. Even though the text used in the current study was considered suitable, it had not been tested before. That may have been the reason why learners were not able to fill in the correct word. In fact, one could argue that since learners were able correctly to fill the gap for only 65% of the words, the maximum number of learnable words was only 6.5

Table 9.6   Predictability issues for levels of involvement categorization

Dimension	Definition	ILI	Variables affecting predictability of ILI
Motivational: Need	Perceived need to comprehend or use an L2 word	Moderate (ILI 1): when imposed by an external agent, such as task or teacher	If no production is required, such as the availability of textual glosses, processing cannot be controlled.
		Strong (ILI 2): when imposed by the learner	(Learning tasks in this study did not involve the variable of strong motivation.)
Cognitive: Search	The attempt to find the meaning of an unknown L2 word for comprehension or production	(ILI 1)	(Learning tasks in this study did not involve the process of search.)
Evaluation	Comparing and/or combining the L2 word with other words	Moderate (ILI 1): when a differentiation between words or between different senses of a word has to be made	• The task of evaluation may compete with the main content task at hand (e.g., text comprehension). • The process of evaluation may compete for processing resources with the main content task at hand (e.g., text comprehension). • The number of words and the semantic closeness of words to be evaluated may impact success of the evaluation process. • Ease of evaluation may lead to a shallow level of processing and hamper word retention (Pulido, 2009). • The complex interaction between textual features (e.g., length of text, content familiarity, contextual word clues to evaluate fit of meaning) and reading ability may affect the evaluation process. • Evaluation may not lead to the correct word choice and lead to incorrect form–meaning connections.
		Strong (ILI 2): when a decision needs to be made on how to combine words with other words in contextual use	• The task of evaluation may compete with the main content task at hand (e.g., writing a coherent essay). • Morphosyntactic and collocationally correct use of the word cannot be controlled.

Note: definitions based on Laufer and Hulstijn, 2001: 14–15

instead of 10. Additionally, since the current study was also based on a different student population than the original study, explanations for the lack of word learning in the fill-in condition are limited to the current student population and are not generalizable. Therefore, future replication studies should compare word learning from multiple texts by the same student population. Likewise, future replication studies could determine whether a change in the set-up of the fill-in task would lead to the predicted degree of word learning. For example, if the word list were replaced with multiple-choice glosses in the L1, then choosing from a selection of possible meanings may be less intrusive, yet engage learners in evaluating the fit of the word.

Finally, since the current study showed that the fill-in word intervention task interfered with the content task, that is, text comprehension, it would be useful to determine whether the requirement to use certain words in an essay affects the writing process and the overall quality of the essay.

Acknowledgments

I would like to thank the late Johannes Eckerth for his ideas on the initial stages of this research, as well as the anonymous reviewers and Graeme Porte for their insightful comments on earlier versions of this manuscript.

References

Bahns, J. and Eldaw, M. (1993). Should we teach EFL students collocations?, *System*, **21**, 553–71.

Barcroft, J. (2009). Effects of synonym generation on incidental and intentional L2 vocabulary learning during reading, *TESOL Quarterly*, **43**, 79–103.

Barcroft, J. and Rott, S. (2010). Partial word form learning in the written mode in L2 German and Spanish, *Applied Linguistics*, **31**, 623–50.

Boogards, P. (2001). Lexical units and the learning of foreign language vocabulary, *Studies in Second Language Acquisition*, **23**, 321–43.

Brown, C. (1993). Factors affecting the acquisition of vocabulary: Frequency and saliency of words, in Huckin, T., Haynes, M. and Coady, J. (eds.), *Second Language Reading and Vocabulary Learning*, Norwood, NJ: Ablex, pp. 263–86.

Chun, D. M. and Plass, J. L. (1996). Effects of multimedia annotations on vocabulary acquisition, *The Modern Language Journal*, **80**, 183–98.

Cobb, T. (2003). Analysing late interlanguage with learner corpora: Quebec replications of three European studies, *Canadian Modern Language Review*, **59**, 393–423.

Cowie, A. P. and Howarth, P. (1996). Phraseological competence and written proficiency, in Blue, G. M. and Mitchell, R. (eds.), *Language and Education*, Clevedon: Multilingual Matters, pp. 80–93.

Davis, J. (1989). Facilitating effects of marginal glosses on foreign language reading, *The Modern Language Journal*, 73, 41–8.

Day, R., Omura, C. and Hiramatsu, M. (1991). Incidental EFL vocabulary learning and reading, *Reading in a Foreign Language*, 7, 541–51.

de la Fuente, M. J. (2002). Negotiation and oral acquisition of L2 vocabulary: The roles of input and output in the receptive and productive acquisition of words, *Studies in Second Language Acquisition*, 24, 81–112.

Ellis, R. and He, X. (1999). The roles of modified input and output in the incidental acquisition of word meanings, *Studies in Second Language Acquisition*, 21, 285–301.

Ellis, R., Tanaka, Y. and Yamazaki, A. (1994). Classroom interaction, comprehension, and the acquisition of L2 word meanings, *Language Learning*, 44, 449–91.

Folse, K. S. (2006). The effect of type of written exercise on L2 vocabulary retention, *TESOL Quarterly*, 40, 273–93.

Fraser, C. (1999). Lexical processing strategy use and vocabulary learning through reading, *Studies in Second Language Acquisition*, 2, 225–41.

Granger, S. (1998). Prefabricated patterns in advanced ESL writing: Collocations and lexical phrases, in Cowie, A. P. (ed.), *Phraseology: Theory Analysis and Applications*, Oxford: Oxford Clarendon Press, pp. 145–160.

Hazenberg, S. and Hulstijn, J. H. (1996). Defining a minimal receptive second-language vocabulary for non-native university students: An empirical investigation, *Applied Linguistics*, 17, 145–63.

Hill, M. and Laufer, B. (2003). Type of task, time-on-task and electronic dictionaries in incidental vocabulary acquisition, *International Journal of Applied Linguistics*, 41, 87–106.

Horst, M. (2005). Learning L2 vocabulary through extensive reading: A measurement study, *The Canadian Modern Language Review*, 61, 355–82.

Horst, M., Cobb, T. and Meara, P. (1998). Beyond a Clockwork Orange: Acquiring second language vocabulary through reading, *Reading in a Foreign Language*, 11, 207–23.

Horst, M., Cobb, T. and Nicolae, I. (2005). Expanding academic vocabulary with a collaborative on-line database, *Language Learning and Technology*, 9, 90–110.

Hulstijn, J. H. (1992). Retention of given and inferred word meanings: Experiments in incidental vocabulary learning, in Arnaud, P. J. L. and Bejoint, H. (eds.), *Vocabulary and Applied Linguistics*, London: Macmillan, pp. 113–25.

Hulstijn, J. H., Hollander, M. and Greidanus, T. (1996). Incidental vocabulary learning by advanced foreign language students: The influence of marginal glosses, dictionary use, and reoccurrence of unknown words, *The Modern Language Journal*, 80, 327–39.

Hulstijn, J. H. and Laufer, B. (2001). Some empirical evidence for the involvement load hypothesis in vocabulary acquisition, *Language Learning*, 51, 539–58.

Hulstijn, J. H. and Trompetter, T. (1998). Incidental learning of second language vocabulary in computer-assisted reading and writing tasks, in Albrechtsen, D., Henriksen, B., Poulsen, E. and Mees, I. M. (eds.), *Perspectives on Foreign and Second Language Pedagogy*, Odense: Odense University Press, pp. 191–200.

Jacobs, G. (1994). What lurks in the margin: Use of vocabulary glosses as a strategy in second language reading, *Issues in Applied Linguistics*, 5, 115–37.

Jacobs, G., Dufon, P. and Fong, C. (1994). L1 and L2 glosses in L2 reading passages: Their effectiveness for increasing comprehension and vocabulary knowledge, *Journal of Research in Reading*, 17, 19–28.

Joe, A. (1998). What effects do text-based tasks promoting generation have on incidental vocabulary acquisition?, *Applied Linguistics*, 19, 357–77.

Jones, L. and Plass, J. (2002). Supporting listening comprehension and vocabulary acquisition in French with multimedia annotations, *The Modern Language Journal*, 86, 546–61.

Keating, G. D. (2008). Task effectiveness and word learning in a second language: The involvement load hypothesis on trial, *Language Teaching Research*, 12, 365–86.

Kim, Y. (2008). The role of task-induced involvement and learner proficiency in L2 vocabulary acquisition, *Language Learning*, 58, 285–325.

Knight, S. (1994). Dictionary: The tool of last resort in foreign language reading? A new perspective, *The Modern Language Journal*, 78, 285–99.

Kost, C., Foss, P. and Lenzini, J. (1999). Textual and pictorial glosses: Effectiveness on incidental vocabulary growth when reading in a foreign language, *Foreign Language Annals*, 32, 89–113.

Krashen, S. (1989). We acquire vocabulary and spelling by reading: Additional evidence for the Input Hypothesis, *The Modern Language Journal*, 73, 450–64.

Laufer, B. (2003). Vocabulary acquisition in a second language: Do learners really acquire most vocabulary by reading? Some empirical evidence, *The Canadian Modern Language Review*, 59, 567–87.

Laufer, B. (2006). Comparing focus on form and focus on formS in second-language vocabulary learning, *The Canadian Modern Language Review*, 63, 149–66.

Laufer, B. and Goldstein, Z. (2004). Testing vocabulary knowledge: Size, strength, and computer adaptiveness, *Language Learning*, 54, 469–523.

Laufer, B. and Hulstijn, J. H. (2001). Incidental vocabulary acquisition in a second language: The construct of task-induced involvement, *Applied Linguistics*, 22, 1–26.

Lee, J. (1986). Background knowledge and L2 reading, *The Modern Language Journal*, 70, 350–54.

Long, M. and Robinson, P. (1998). Focus on form: Theory, research, and practice, in Doughty C. and Williams, J. (eds.), *Focus on Form in Classroom*

Second Language Acquisition, Cambridge: Cambridge University Press, pp. 15–63.

Luppescu, S. and Day, R. R. (1993). Reading, dictionaries and vocabulary learning, *Language Learning*, 43, 263–87.

Meara, P. (1996). The Vocabulary Knowledge Framework, Unpublished paper. Available online: www.lognostics.co.uk/vlibrary/meara1996c.pdf

Min, H.-T. (2008). EFL vocabulary acquisition and retention: Reading plus vocabulary enhancement activities and narrow reading, *Language Learning*, 58, 73–115.

Nation, P. (2001). *Learning Vocabulary in Another Language*, Cambridge: Cambridge University Press.

Nation, P. and Waring, R. (1997). Vocabulary size, text coverage, and word lists, in Schmitt, N. and McCarthy, M. (eds.), *Vocabulary: Description, Acquisition and Pedagogy*, Cambridge: Cambridge University Press, pp. 6–19.

Nesselhauf, N. (2003). The use of collocations by advanced learners of English and some implications for teaching, *Applied Linguistics*, 24, 223–42.

Pak, J. (1986). The Effect of Vocabulary Glossing on ESL Reading Comprehension. Unpublished manuscript, University of Hawai'i at Manoa.

Paribakht, T. S. and Wesche, M. (1996). Enhancing vocabulary acquisition through reading: A hierarchy of text-related exercise types, *The Canadian Modern Language Review*, 52, 250–73.

Peters, E., Hulstijn, J. H., Sercu, L. and Lutjeharms, M. (2009). Learning L2 German vocabulary through reading: The effect of three enhancement techniques compared, *Language Learning*, 39, 115–31.

Pigada, M. and Schmitt, N. (2006). Vocabulary acquisition from extensive reading: A case study, *Reading in a Foreign Language*, 18, 1–28.

Pulido, D. (2009). How involved are American L2 learners of Spanish in lexical input processing tasks during reading?, *Studies in Second Language Acquisition*, 31, 31–58.

Rott, S. (1999). The effect of exposure frequency on intermediate language learners' incidental vocabulary acquisition and retention through reading, *Studies in Second Language Acquisition*, 2, 589–620.

Rott, S. (2005). Processing glosses: A qualitative exploration of how form–meaning connections are established and strengthened, *Reading in a Foreign Language*, 17, 95–124.

Rott, S. (2007). The effect of frequency of input-enhancements on word learning and text comprehension, *Language Learning*, 57, 165–19.

Rott, S. and Williams, J. (2003). Making form–meaning connections while reading: A qualitative analysis of word processing, *Reading in a Foreign Language*, 15, 45–75.

Rott, S., Williams, J. and Cameron, R. (2002). The effect of multiple-choice L1 glosses and input–output cycles on lexical acquisition and retention, *Language Teaching Research*, 6, 183–222.

Schmidt, R. (2001). Attention, in Robinson, P. (ed.), *Cognition and Second Language Instruction*, Cambridge: Cambridge University Press, pp. 3–32.

Schmitt, N. and Carter, R. (2004). Formulaic sequences in action, in Schmitt, N. (ed.), *Formulaic Sequences*, Amsterdam: John Benjamins, pp. 1–22.

Smith, B. (2004). Computer-mediated negotiated interaction and lexical acquisition, *Studies in Second Language Acquisition*, **26**, 365–98.

VanPatten, B., Williams, J. and Rott, S. (2004). Form–meaning connections in second language acquisition, in VanPatten, B., Williams, J., Rott, S. and Overstreet, M. (eds.), *Form–Meaning Connections in Second Language Acquisition*, Mahwah, NJ: Lawrence Erlbaum Associates, pp. 1–28.

Walsh, M. (2009). Measuring involvement load "evaluation", *JALT 2008 Conference Proceedings*, Tokyo: JALT, pp. 1–16.

Waring, R. and Takaki, M. (2003). At what rate do learners learn and retain new vocabulary from reading a graded reader?, *Reading in a Foreign Language*, **15**, 130–63.

Watanabe, Y. (1997). Input, intake, and retention: Effects of increased processing on incidental learning of foreign language vocabulary, *Studies in Second Language Acquisition*, **19**, 287–308.

Webb, S. (2005). Receptive and productive vocabulary learning: The effects of reading and writing on word knowledge, *Studies in Second Language Acquisition*, **27**, 33–52.

Wesche, M. and Paribakht, T. S. (2000). Reading-based exercises in second language vocabulary learning: An introspective study, *The Modern Language Journal*, **84**, 196–213.

Yoshii, M. (2006). L1 and L2 glosses: Their effects on incidental vocabulary learning, *Language Learning and Technology*, **10**, 85–101.

Zahar, R., Cobb, T. and Spada, N. (2001). Acquiring vocabulary through reading: Effects of frequency and contextual richness, *The Canadian Modern Language Review*, **57**, 541–72.

Zaki, H. and Ellis, R. (1999). Learning vocabulary through interacting with a written text, in Ellis, R. (ed.), *Learning a Second Language Through Interaction*, Amsterdam: John Benjamins, pp. 153–69.

Zimmerman, C. (1997). Do reading and interactive vocabulary instruction make a difference? An empirical study, *TESOL Quarterly*, **31**, 121–40.

10   *Concluding remarks: The way forward*

Graeme Porte

In this final chapter I will review the key issues and address some of the challenges raised in the previous chapters and thereby suggest a number of ways in which the general paucity of replication research in applied linguistics might be addressed.

1 Graduate programs

In my Introduction I suggested that doing such research would seem to be generally regarded as a somewhat unglamorous undertaking and, consequently, one which was not actively encouraged in the community and particularly in university departments. A number of reasons for such perceptions were put forward there and in subsequent chapters by Mackey, Polio, Abbuhl, and Fitzpatrick, and we might now usefully make some initial suggestions for improving the situation in this area.

The practice and feedback reported on by Fitzpatrick in her university course have shown that the experience of completing a replication study can have beneficial effects, both in terms of its value as a teaching and learning instrument and in the outcomes of such practices through conference presentations and journal publications. Similarly, Abbuhl makes the specific recommendation that departments and faculty themselves might further encourage interest in such research by including replication studies among those suitable for theses and in "brown bag" sessions and poster exhibitions within the department facilities. What she refers to as "replication-related skills" (p. 137) can also be honed through closer attention to the reading of research, encouraging the critical faculties that foster the appreciation of such work and help students acquire the skills necessary to write up their own research (see also Brown, Chapter 7 this volume; Porte, 2010).

It is also clear from the experience reported on by Fitzpatrick that the undertaking of replication studies can have a useful washback effect on research practice. While being able to confirm or otherwise a target study's robustness or generalizability are good reasons for carrying out a replication study, we should not underestimate the value of doing such research as a teaching and learning tool. Thus, a researcher might be able to identify, through a conceptual replication, a better way of sampling data in a particular context. A further replication might then confirm or disconfirm this finding. Under the careful supervision of an experienced mentor, performing a replication study can become a useful introduction to the academic discourse for graduates. Because such studies must at least be as rigorous and detailed as the originals, these novice researchers are made aware at an early stage in their practice of the importance of following strict procedures in their experimental research.

Beyond the formal inclusion of replication research study on university courses, Mackey also remarked on the need for faculty to reassess the contribution of such research on staff portfolios. Promotion and tenure committees judge their candidates with respect to the perceived contribution of their work to the field. Just how such a "contribution" is to be judged has been a central issue throughout this book. Within the "pure" sciences, replication is recognized as the most common and traditionally most productive way of building on previous work and making that contribution. Just as traditionally, however, replication in our field has not been given the same status, and this may be partly a product of the current academic discourse and culture. Perhaps, as the *Language Teaching* Review Panel put it "everyone feels that they have to collect their own data rather than use another's" (2008: 13). A change of mindset is called for, hopefully triggered by some of the chapters in this book, in which replication research is seen as providing a valuable element in what I earlier referred to as "the self-correcting, cumulative cycle of acquiring empirical knowledge" (Introduction, this volume).

2 Availability of data

Mackey discussed the consequences of insufficiently detailed method descriptions in SLA papers, suggesting that a database of instruments might go some way to alleviating the problem of variability across operationalizations of concepts and coding systems. Abbuhl widened the idea of a collective database to help those interested in replicating a previous study. She noted that some researchers might be discouraged from undertaking replications because of the lack of information in published articles and the difficulty in accessing the kind and amount of data needed to consider embarking upon such a study.

One of the major obstructions to promoting more replication studies has always been the lack of detailed methodology and data sections in published papers, from which subsequent work might take its lead in the form of approximate or conceptual replication. The Web has now alleviated the problem of space, and journals such as *Language Teaching* and *Applied Linguistics* provide online supplements with data which can be freely obtained by subscribers interested in undertaking a replication of some sort. However, the wider availability of data in online depositories, in turn supplied by researchers perhaps as a condition of funding, would mean a number of the present obstacles to carrying out such research can be overcome.

Such a requirement for more detail in published papers may even have a beneficial effect on researchers' methods as the knowledge that this detail is likely to be scrutinized by colleagues may induce greater attention in the research process itself. Such data sets would ideally present all the information required to undertake a replication of the study. In respect to quantitative approaches this would include all the original data and details of subjects and procedures. As Abbuhl indicates, such data should have its personally identifying tags removed and a legal requirement " ... to credit the original researcher and not to use the data or materials in any way prohibited by law or standards of ethical conduct" (p. 146). Similarly, those interested in having a qualitative study replicated in some form would want to include information such as detailed descriptions of data-gathering through interviews, questionnaires, and think-aloud protocols as well as the digitized transcripts themselves. Such rich data are essential, as we have suggested in our brief discussions about replication in qualitative research, in any attempt to work with a qualitative study.

Of course, for such a data repository to function correctly and become a useful resource, it needs also to be sanctioned at an official level. Thus, graduate programs might also consider making such a contribution a certifiable requirement before thesis submission. This should, indeed, be regarded as part of a student's contribution to the field and can only enhance the potential impact of the work. The presence of this data in a central repository will most likely increase the chances of follow-up or replication studies being carried out. Journals whose subscribers can access such data online (see above) might wish to require authors to indicate clearly in their papers where the relevant detailed data can be found and any requested embargoes on that data (e.g., to guarantee the right of first publication to the original author).

3 Finding suitable studies for replication

A common call made throughout these chapters is that more replication studies should be undertaken; however, guidance is needed with regard to identifying studies which need or would benefit from replication. As I indicated in the Introduction, not each and every experimental study needs to be replicated, some are more "replicable" than others, and those that *are* vary in the ideal replication approach needed (i.e., approximate or conceptual). Mackey (p. 28ff.) suggested a number of aspects of a study that might identify it as a candidate for replication, including:

- The original study addresses an interesting and currently relevant research question.
- The study has continued relevance for the field but still remains to be satisfactorily investigated.
- The original study failed to control for a potentially significant variable.
- Different contexts or subjects might (or might not) be hypothesized to provide additional confirmatory evidence for the findings in the original study.
- Indications for replications are provided by the original study author in a "limitations" section.

Abbuhl (p. 143ff.) expanded on these suggestions and provided further advice to help researchers decide on possible candidate studies through critical reading of the original study, and Fitzpatrick described the selection process in practice as part of the Swansea postgraduate program.

It should also be made clear that, whereas this book has focused in the main on empirical studies concerned with L2 learning in the classroom, applied linguistics and SLA deal with other areas which are producing studies that doubtless would also reward replication. Fundamental questions relating to aspects such as the relevance of context on language learning, age-of-onset differences in ultimate attainment, and developmental sequences are equally important areas of research within which a number of key studies await further attention.

Nassaji also defended the idea of "internal replication," introducing the idea that the original researcher or member of a team of researchers might repeat their own experiment, through a resampling of the data. There is a continuing debate, however, as to whether a researcher closely involved in the original study should be directly involved with a subsequent replication of that study (i.e., other than as a consultant on aspects of the original study). Rosenthal, although admitting the possibility of such authorship, cautions that "a replication ... which obtains similar results is maximally convincing if it is maximally separated from the first experiment along such dimensions as time, physical distance, personal attributes of the experimenters, experimenters' expectancy, and experimenters' degree of personal contact with each other" (1990: 11). More recently, however, the *Language Teaching* Review Panel supports the idea since " ... the opportunity to replicate or improve on one's own study would encourage behavior that ... we want to ... [nurture]: researchers would not feel as much need to move too soon from one topic to another, but could learn from their experience or mistakes, and probably as much as, if not more than, an independent replicator could" (2008: 6).

4 The role of journals and professional associations

As Polio discovered in her research for this book, there appears to be a dearth of replication studies in the principal journals in the field. A number of reasons for this have been put forward in these pages, and in my Introduction I suggested editors may be wary of dedicating precious space to work which could be perceived as deriving from other research, rather than being "original." Furthermore, in an example of what appears to be typical practice in many journals, Goldacre (2011) has recently reported on the unwillingness of editors to accept papers which "merely" replicate the original study's findings, even though the replication responded to a stated need from the original study's author. Thus, whereas it may not be openly *dis*couraged in many journals, the path to publishing replication studies seems fraught with difficulties. These obstacles may be a product of current research agendas, the lack of exposure to such studies, or a failure to understand their potential contribution to current knowledge. However, it is also clear that there is a continuing need for many research outcomes to be queried and verified, and for the results of such work to be brought to the attention of researchers through wider dissemination. It is our belief that the field of applied linguistics will inevitably continue to evolve and, as it does so, and the database of research findings grows along with it, this need will become more and more pressing.

Those at the decision-making sharp end of the publication process in our field should formulate an agreed procedure regarding replication research. Apart from adopting a more openly receptive attitude, editors might take an active part in promoting such research by suggesting authors themselves call for replication of their papers where advisable, noting the kind of replication and changes of variable that might usefully be applied. By so doing, researchers are confirming the open-ended nature of the present research and participating in what I referred to in my Introduction as the "ongoing communication with fellow researchers" (p. 3). Similarly, editors could invite researchers to review delimited areas of the field and select studies that need or might reward replication. *Language Teaching* regularly features state-of-the-art critical reviews of recent research and, from 2011, submission guidelines include the request " ... wherever appropriate to include a reasoned assessment of key studies that would benefit from approximate or conceptual replication." Finally, some continuity can be encouraged between original studies and replicated ones by asking the author(s) of the original paper to add brief comments at the end of the published replication with their own reactions to what has emerged as a result of the replication of their work (see Chapter 8 by Eckerth).

To my knowledge, there are no print or online journals in the social sciences dedicated exclusively to publishing replication studies. As Mackey suggested in her "catch-22 of replication" scenario (p. 27), and as I have discussed elsewhere (Porte and Richards, 2012), it may well be the case that one reason why little replication work is being done is precisely because there is no obvious outlet for its dissemination. There is a case to be made for a dedicated journal which would help fill an enormous gap in the research literature and might through its own contents set out a replication research agenda.

Contributors to this book have noted how the perception of replication research in the community is not conducive to its wider dissemination. It may also be that journal reviewing panels serve as gatekeepers of the discipline and may themselves be unwittingly maintaining a posture which inhibits more frequent publication. The fact that many journals fail to mention replication studies in their submission guidelines needs to be rectified (see Polio, Chapter 2, this volume). As I indicated above, journal editors and reviewers need to ensure not only that more replication research is attracted for submission, but also that what *is* submitted is replicable in the first place by ensuring that sufficiently detailed data are made available in electronic form.

The opportunities to promote more replication research are not only limited to journals, however. In a question-and-answer paper on replication published in *Language Teaching*, some of the present contributors also sought to encourage more work by calling for:

> ... periodic 'Special Editions' for replication studies, possibly dealing with specific fields. There might also be 'replication strands' to the Special Interest Groups of various conferences. Indeed, it might be possible to have explicit 'replication' seminars, if not conferences. Web-based networks are also a way of establishing 'work-in-progress' sites where replication studies could be reported. Finally, funding agencies do not

give sufficient value to replication studies. It would be useful if policy statements from these funding sources were made in which the value and support offered for replication studies was made explicit.

(*Language Teaching* Review Panel, 2008: 13)

Despite over a decade having passed since Polio and Gass willed faculty to " ... assume the responsibility of encouraging graduate students to conduct replication studies" (1997: 505), there appear to be few who have taken up the call. However, the responsibility for encouraging replications must be spread wider to all those directly or indirectly involved with the everyday research affairs of the field. Not only scholars involved in mentoring researchers, but also professional associations must agree on replication research policy. If agreement can be reached within these associations or their research/special interest sections as to the need for such work within a particular set of research agendas – and ideally a series of key studies within each agenda identified as being in urgent need of such replication – we would have a sound foundation upon which to build greater awareness and interest into the field. Moreover, if we assume one of the functions of these groups is to update research skills in the profession, it may also be incumbent on them to provide clear guidance on how applied linguistics research is best conducted. Plonsky goes even further and suggests that many national and international professional associations have openly supported certain policy positions in the past but have been silent with regard to research methodology and that "a task force be put in place to construct methodological standards for L2 research" (Plonsky, 2011).

Our principle aims in this book were to call for a reassessment of the role of replication in applied linguistics research and encourage its undertaking and dissemination. Our principle conclusion is that its potential contribution to research in applied linguistics cannot be ignored. As a number of contributors have been at pains to point out, the accumulation of evidence from follow-up or one-shot studies (statistically significant or not, confirmed through power analysis and meta-analysis or not), only provides part of the information we need to construct knowledge. Follow-up studies from an original paper do not tell us the extent to which the original was sufficiently robust in the first place. Going on to base key pedagogical or policy decisions on the outcomes of a series of such unreplicated studies – where we might assume the presence of undetermined and/or unverified amounts of error – may well have proved counterproductive in some learning contexts in the past. Ignoring such implicit error or lack of verification is not without its consequences:

As we extend upwards the building that houses the sum of our expanding research knowledge we must, prior to beginning the construction of each additional floor, ensure the stability of the levels below. We must also regularly revisit the entire structure to satisfy ourselves of its overall integrity. Building on top of initial weaknesses or lacunae in our knowledge would forever leave that structure exposed to doubt and potential collapse.

(Porte and Richards, 2012)

We would not want the reader, however, to conclude that replication research will inevitably lead them to discover "the answer." The pursuit of knowledge is one which can only aspire to achieving ever greater insights into a particular phenomenon or observation, thereby adding to the body of available knowledge. Replicating a study may therefore help us to make more sense of things – to explain and predict – but at best it only takes us further along the way to finding that "answer." Thus, the aim of this (or any other) research is not to discover the "truth"; as a number of contributors have pointed out, scientific hypotheses, no matter how firmly established, are never "proved" right. Findings are essentially provisional. Furthermore, as revealed recently by Lehrer (2010) in a much-commented article on the uses of replication, the process is one which tends to be open-ended. It is not impossible for a finding to be replicated and discovered to be robust, only later to ascertain that, for example, increasing the size of the population observed or analyzing the data with emerging (new) technologies succeeds in reducing the effect observed and previously "confirmed."

It is our belief that replicating sound research is essential to the conduct of good science. It is also implicit in much of what has been written here that the underlying philosophies of what constitutes "sound," "acceptable," and "publishable" research need to be reassessed before any change will occur. We already work scientifically as "makers of knowledge," in the original Latin sense. Therefore, it would be unfortunate if we then went on to ignore, or even reject, the dual opportunity afforded us by replicating studies to seek confirmatory evidence for that knowledge, and to construct rather than merely accumulate that knowledge. For this to have a chance to happen, however, it is incumbent upon editors, doctoral students and their tutors, professional associations, and other researchers to show a greater willingness to consider the possible benefits that might accrue from embracing the entire gamut of methodological options in applied linguistics research.

References

Goldacre, B. (2011). Backwards step on looking into the future, *The Guardian*, Saturday, 23 April 2011.

Language Teaching Review Panel (2008). Replication studies in language learning and teaching: Questions and answers, *Language Teaching*, **41**, 1–14.

Lehrer, J. (2010). The truth wears off, *The New Yorker*, 13 December 2010.

Plonsky, L. (2011). Study Quality in SLA: A Cumulative and Developmental Assessment of Designs, Analyses, Reporting Practices, and Outcomes in Quantitative L2 Research. Unpublished doctoral dissertation, Michigan State University.

Polio, C., and Gass, S. (1997). Replication and reporting: A commentary, *Studies in Second Language Acquisition*, **19**, 499–508.

Porte, G. (2010). *Appraising Research in Second Language Learning: A Practical Approach to Critical Analysis of Quantitative Research* (2nd edn.), Amsterdam/Philadelphia: John Benjamins.

Porte, G. and Richards, K. (2012). Replication in quantitative and qualitative research, *Journal of Second Language Writing*, **21**, 3.

Rosenthal, R. (1990). Replication in behavioural research, *Journal of Social Behavior and Social Personality*, **5**, 4, 1–30.

Author index

Subject index